Max Keller

# FANTASTIC

# Max Keller

# FANTASTIC

## The Art and Design of Stage Lighting

Compiled with the
assistance of
Johannes Weiss

Prestel
Munich · London · New York

With a foreword by Dieter Dorn
and contributions
by Herbert Kapplmüller
and Manfred Wagner

Front cover, frontispiece: *Le Roi Arthus*
Bregenz Festival, 1996
Back cover (background photo and bottom left insert):
*Tristan und Isolde*
Set design by Jürgen Rose
Metropolitan Opera, New York, 1999

Photo credits see p. 239

Library of Congress Cataloging in
Publication Data is available

Die Deutsche Bibliothek – CIP-Einheitsaufnahme

Light fantastic: the art and design of stage lighting /
Max Keller. [Michael Robinson, trans.].
– Munich; London; New York: Prestel, 1999
(German edition: Faszination Licht)
ISBN 3-7913-2162-5

Prestel Verlag
Mandlstrasse 26 · 80802 Munich
Tel. (089) 381709-0, Fax (089) 381709-35;
16 West 22nd Street · New York, NY 10010
Tel. (212) 627-8199, Fax (212) 627-9866;
4 Bloomsbury Place · London WC1A 2QA
Tel. (0171) 3235004, Fax (0171) 6368004
E-mail: sales@prestel.de

Prestel books are available worldwide.
Please contact your nearest bookseller
or one of the above Prestel offices for
details concerning your local distributor.

Translated by Michael Robinson, London
Edited by Judith Gilbert, Munich
Editorial assistance: Danko Szabó, Munich

The publisher would like to thank
Prof. Julian Herrey, Berlin, and Elanor Higgins,
London, for technical consultation

Designed by: Cilly Klotz, Max Keller
and Johannes Weiss
Typeface: Weidemann Book and Meta Roman
Paper: 150 gm/s qm Galerie Art Silk
Lithography by ReproLine, Munich
Printed by Gerstmayer, Weingarten, Germany
Binding by Sigloch, Künzelsau, Germany

Printed in Germany on acid-free paper

ISBN 3-7913-2162-5

# Contents

   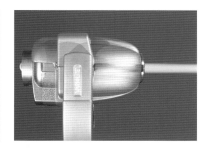

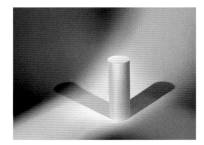

Physicists and physiologists define the phenomenon of light as a small sector of the scale of electro-magnetic oscillations that convey a sensation of brightness via the human eye. It affects our perceptions by triggering a large number of different stimuli. Light unscrambles chaos, takes the grey out of darkness.

Events on the stage reflect life, of which light is as much a part as its opposite, darkness. The space devised by directors and designers is first 'made' by the lighting designer in a quite fundamental way – light creates a new reality on stage. Thus the art of light is a constantly repeated act of creation.

It is impossible to work out what is at the heart of my work: that is the fascination of light, the 'light fantastic', to which this book is dedicated.

Max Keller

## Making Light – A Foreword

by Dieter Dorn

This is a book about light. It presents us with formulas, diagrams, technical descriptions, machines, lighting equipment, constructions and rigging plans. It also deals with theory and history, physics and chemistry. It is a compendium of everything we know about light and colour on the stage today – meticulously compiled, with a wealth of knowledge behind it. I have never come across a book like this before.

But what has all this really got to do with the art of theatre? How does it address the element that is at the heart of theatre, that makes it so powerful and effective: the emotion the actors unleash, for which audiences are prepared to buy seats night after night? Is *Light Fantastic* not taking us on a detour – past the theatre and straight into the technical studio, a threshold at which so many of the other arts are poised today?

A rhetorical question, of course. Certainly there are directors who occasionally yearn for the time when all they needed to do was light candles on the stage until it was bright enough. But if these directors were to go a bit further back in history, they would find themselves faced with daylight as the only source of stage illumination – and with the fact that the profession of director in the current sense had not yet been invented. Thus they gladly continue in the present, where the division of labour is clear and the theatre, like everything else, employs only specialists. Directors, after all, are specialists themselves.

So let's not be nostalgic or pessimistic when looking at what this book has to offer. On the contrary: I want to have the lot in my shows, HMIs and HQIs, sodium lamps and daylight flashes. What light can do on the stage today is fantastic, and it is tempting both to

play as well as to experiment with it more seriously.

The theatre is locked into a number of addictive processes, and working with light is one of these, entirely self-inflicted. The theatre is under just as much a spell as science. If something is available, then you want it. The bounds of the possible are always being extended, one broken barrier leads to the next one – the screw keeps turning whether you like it or not. And before you know where you are, something that used to be perfectly straightforward and could generally be done by hand becomes a difficult technical problem, needing a specialist to solve it. Now there are only electrically powered lines (all state of the art, of course) and no mechanical lines in the fly-tower, but there are certain subtle movements and transformations that are just not possible any more – without installing computer software that has not yet been developed. And if a machine gets stuck somewhere, there's nothing anyone can do; the performance is irredeemably dependent on the machine. If the man in the lighting booth has his work cut out watching the computer, he has no time to spare to look at the stage. But anyone who believes the numbers and icons on the display rather than what he sees with his own eyes – or could see if he would only look – is no use at all as far as art is concerned.

But here there is a problem, a paradox. We claim that the theatre is alive, we use the stage and the people on it as a defence against concentrated attacks by zombies from a ready-made world. We assert that the theatre is an artistic space, a free space, and probably a utopia as well. We describe our times, our world, make moves against it, devise counter-worlds on the stage, try to show that nothing is as it will remain,

1  Ernest Chausson
*Le Roi Arthus*
Director: Günter Krämer
Set Designer: Herbert Kapplmüller
Bregenz Festival, 1996

set artistic truth against apparent truth. And we do all this with precisely the resources (not only technical) that are part of the world in which we live. Our 'brave new world' gives us the means – and technical means in particular in this case – that help us to address it critically. So let's use them – what else is there for us to do in the end? Fighting the enemy with his own weapons may be a fine idea, but in doing so we run the risk of over-estimating ourselves.

In order to avoid falling victim to this danger, we must not deliver art into the arms of technology: Art must not become technology, technology must become art. Imagination can be properly developed in rehearsal only if the setting is precisely defined. It catches light from what is already there, even though it is well able to burn everything and replace it with something new. For this reason, and only for this reason, it is necessary to think some things out in advance. There have to be ideas and conceptions – and if they are any good, they affect the final result. But this method requires calculation not just from the artists, but also from technicians, particularly lighting technicians, who are largely responsible for 'creating' the space devised by the director and the designer. This lighting technology has to be part of the artistic process. It is not required simply to provide a service, to have what is presently available ready to be used on demand. In its way, and with its resources, it has to help to realize the artistic dream with technical imagination, to do things that have never been done before, constantly. Thus technical potential and conditions change in and through our work.

In everyday contexts, light serves to make existing things visible. On stage, however, it creates a new reality. 'Created' light helps us to thrust forward into spaces that establish and nurture their own reality, helps us to thrust forward into dimensions that are different from the ones we experience every day. Admittedly this only works if those who create this light – for me, Max Keller and his excellent team – are included in the conceptual and working process from the outset and are personally involved in it. Max Keller does become involved in it, and that is why light in our work is not just a technically definable element, but always goes beyond the bounds of what had previously been possible.

Just as we are always on the lookout for images that have never been seen in this way before, Max Keller constantly finds and invents new lighting. The light(n)ing that opened my production of Botho Strauss's play *The Park* is more than a magnificent technical innovation; it is a dramatic solution.

In our 1987 production of *Faust,* colours were changed by a continuous strip of gels stuck together in the right sequence and running mechanically on scrollers. Ten years later, for *Cymbeline,* we had an electronic device hanging there that could do all this and much more as well, with effects that could be called up in any sequence and in any conceivable hue – an apparatus that turned the whole stage into a coloured space – truly a stage-set-machine.

A great deal has emerged from demands made on technology by art. At last, a dimmable HMI! No more explosive noises when certain devices are switched on, a daylight flash – all these are the results of efforts of this kind. They then lived beyond their original function, the special effect that they were invented to create.

What is being asked for here is new. This can be seen from the fact that there is still no sensible name for this profession. We help ourselves out by crediting the person responsible for lighting along with direction, sets, costume, music and scripts. At the Münchner Kammerspiele, arguably the most prestigious repertory theatre in Munich, this has been Max Keller for the past twenty years. He has shown what light can do on the stage, implemented and developed the new things that can be found in this book – at this theatre throughout this period. He has gone a long way on his journey with art. I think that *Light Fantastic* could only have come out of this continuity, and only here. Looking at it in this light, I'd almost like to say that the Münchner Kammerspiele helped to write it.

When I first leafed through the manuscript I wondered, horrified and slightly jealous, whether this was not a magician taking all his dodges and tricks to market, so that anyone could copy them from now on. But make no mistake – reading Escoffier does not make one a master chef! In other words: Everything that lighting can do is in this book – but it yields up its true secrets only in the service of art. One needs to understand this to understand the book properly and to be able to use it – and thus be of use to the theatre. I hope for such readers, for the sake of the book and the theatre.

2 Beams of light with gobos bring light and life into the darkness

Light is existential for all of us. As well as its biological effects, it shows us reality in constantly changing ways, thus offering a number of visual impressions that affect our perception emotionally. Light is with us night and day and makes life possible. The colour of light is also very important for people as organisms. Colours motivate, enliven and worry us. They signal danger or sound the all-clear and control our subconscious.

It is not a lighting designer's job to shift the natural phenomenon of light into a closed space; he has to try to create an atmosphere related to the moment, using the technical resources of artificial lighting design.

A show at a theatre or other venue is an artistic event, whether it is a play, a concert, an opera or a ballet. Light is essential for the visual effect of any of these. Lighting that is suitable for the performers and the setting has to be created artificially. But a light composition can never be as effective as natural

lighting effects, whose complexity cannot be imitated. The success of the visual effect also depends on the individual's emotional state. Fortunately there is no generally valid reaction to lighting effects. Light, like music, is a particularly subjective sphere. Sensuous perception of light is seldom a conscious process. Perhaps it is precisely because its emotional effect is unconscious that it affects our sensibilities so incisively. A particular lighting design will always be subject to critical assessment, just like sets, costumes and direction. The visual presentation of an event is intended to support what is happening on stage and influence it emotionally. But if lighting equipment is perfectly handled, light can become an independent entity and takes on a different expressive form. It is only when the lighting, direction and set start to work together that the concept of the whole production becomes clear.

Designing light is a profession, and information should be available about this very specific and little known job and the experiences it offers. It is hardly possible to prevent much of what is written from being rapidly overtaken by technical innovations. But despite all these further developments, the general principles of stage lighting will still apply. Technical instructions are to be seen as subject to change and never as binding.

The activity of 'making light' is not restricted to a single aim, but on closer consideration includes three linked factors:

• general techniques
• specialized knowledge
• creativity

The art of lighting design is bound by optical laws laid down by nature. There are physical laws restricting the possibilities of technical imitation, which means that creative work is needed to develop a harmonious overall concept for a performance. Various aspects have to be considered when devising a lighting design.

The visible result depends first and foremost on the kind of lanterns used. The most important factor is not how many of them there are, but how,

where and when they are brought into the lighting sequence. A complete lighting state is usually made up from many individual light sources. The first priority is to arrange and grade them. Devices from the range offered by the lighting industry that will best achieve the overall concept are selected for sound dramatic reasons.

Several fundamentally different criteria have to be considered when choosing a particular quality of light. Determining a quality is not enough to provide a technical lighting concept, which consists above all of contrasts between various kinds of light and colour combinations. For example, bright, clear, open surface lighting can be seen as a contrast to subtly adjusted mood lighting. Or a rousing, highly contrasting, rhythmically underpinned lighting movement can be set against a still, monochrome soft lighting state. Are shadow effects intended as part of the concept? Is suggestive lighting necessary for this? Is it appropriate to use highly coloured light, rather than weaker or even pastel tints? Should lighting sources with different colour temperatures be mixed? Do additional effects help or hinder the desired interpretation? To what extent should a theatre's lighting crew understand the analytical preparations?

The daily routine of a theatre certainly does not give every lighting expert time to take all this into consideration in his work. But it is important that he should know that his activities are decisively influenced by such questions. Even simple, straightforward lighting fulfils a theatrical function. What is crucial for the lighting concept devised with the director and the set designer is not the sum of lanterns and lighting changes used but the system and logic according to which they are used.

Subsidized repertory theatre, as practised by most German-speaking theatres, makes particularly heavy demands on the lighting department because of its special staffing structure. In the Anglo-Saxon theatre world, where artistic lighting design developed to a large extent, lighting tasks are divided into two completely separate sets of skills. One part of the

profession is responsible for technical and the other for artistic matters. This situation should not and cannot be copied. But technical requirements must not carry more weight than artistic ones; they should support the art of theatre through their special interpretation. Thus a lighting expert has to be able to handle a dense and varied series of tasks; technical, organizational and artistic matters have to be harmonized. This often leads to misunderstandings about the challenges of such important work. It is therefore necessary to make a

few remarks about lighting as generally practised in German-speaking theatre.

The head of lighting is usually responsible for personnel management, day-to-day organization and purchasing materials – but mainly for artistic lighting design, even though training and examinations do not usually equip him for this. Far too little attention is paid to the fact that his actual principal activity – conceiving and designing lighting for stage, shows, film and television – makes a substantial contribution to a good overall result.

Generally, however, another kind of thinking is starting to prevail in the theatre, now that lighting design has become an accepted art, as is also the case in architecture, advertising and animation. Guiding and reinforcing feelings and situations with light have adapted to current visual habits and ways of looking at things. Heads of lighting departments are still not in the best possible position to be able to follow these progressive changes with appropriate training. But those responsible for specialist training are now

making an effort to move with the times, which has led to courses for lighting designers and the new career description called specialist in events technology.

The lighting designer cannot evaluate his work and his art alone, however. No one should want to determine himself how his efforts are judged – recognition and acceptance must come from the people with whom one works. Those responsible for a lighting department will realize that it is to their advantage not just to work by the book, but to place themselves as mediators between art and technology. Any argument against this disintegrates if the work is done with commitment; the only measure is the quality of the demonstrable result.

The colourful effect of light is so powerful and can be applied in so many ways. This makes the profession of lighting designer a fulfilling one. Creating space for visual effects and trying to convey ideas visually should be a lighting expert's first concern. Creative work and commitment mean constantly developing new variants. Just as Adolphe Appia and Mariano Fortuny cleared all the clutter off stage sets and Loïe Fuller added an avant-garde note to the theatre at the turn of the century with her dance impressions, modern technology should be used to implement ideas selectively but generously – combined with subtly chosen light and colour. The many types of lanterns and the introduction of dichroic colours into the repertoire of technical possibilities can inspire progressive work which may lead in completely different visual directions. Making light artificially is by no means an exclusively technical profession. It should be a mixture of the tried and tested as well as the new – in a way that produces art.

The spectrum of 'light' offers so many creative possibilities. This infinitely varied, exciting and apparently endless range helps every specialist to grasp the full extent of this medium's fascination and to use impressions, feelings and ambience to point the way forward for the theatrical arts. But we should always bear in mind a quotation by Jean Cocteau: 'The sum of all the lanterns should never be greater than the light shining from the actors' hearts.'

3 Philippe Boesmans
*Reigen*
Director: Luc Bondy
Set Designer: Erich Wonder
Théâtre Royale de la Monnaie
Brussels, 1993

4 Walter de Maria installed his earth sculpture
*The Lightning Field* in South Mexico in 1977.
Four hundred stainless steel masts, tapering to
a point, have been let into the ground in a rectangle
over an area of one kilometre by one mile, at a
distance of 76.05 m from each other (16 masts wide
and 25 masts long). The points of the masts are all
at the same level, 6.25 m above ground level.
Atmospheric discharges into the metal poles enter
into a dialogue with the forces of nature to produce
an ever-changing sequence of angry lightning patterns

10 'And now it must be remembered that the chandeliers are to be set as close to the scene as possible; but in such a way that they are not in a position to block the view of machines that are lowered from the sky in the interludes, if such are given. If this is the case, they must be placed towards the side walls, so that the centre can be left free and empty. Further it should be considered that very few, indeed no lights should be set in the middle of the room, so that the houses maybe most clearly visible.' From: Nicola Sabbatini, *Pratica di fabricar scene e macchine ne' teatri*, Ravenna 1638

11 'Let A be the vessel through which the torch BC is passed, which must be sufficiently long that the part B sticks out at the top and part C remains beneath the vessel. When the time comes to use it, one person must hold part C in his hands, after the torch has been lit at B. If the intention is to allow the flames to blaze out immediately, then the vessel should be rapidly raised up in the air, and immediately the resin will be sprinkled out through the holes pierced in the paper C. It is necessary that care be taken during these actions, as bad accidents often occur. Actions of this kind should not be undertaken by clumsy or stupid people.' From: Nicola Sabbatini, *Pratica di fabricar scene e macchine ne' teatri*, Ravenna 1638

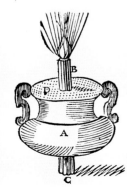

smoke and smell that this produced were very irritating, but the real problem was how to black out the stage. All this was discussed by the architect Nicola Sabbatini (1574–1654) in his book on theatre techniques (*Pratica di fabricar scene e macchine ne' teatri*), in which he postulated various mechanical blackout methods. One of these involved lowering sheet-metal tubes slowly over the flame. A later one placed the light-source in the centre of a half-cylinder, which could be turned to reduce the intensity of light in one direction. Sabbatini also described how and in what order the various lights on the stage could be lit at the beginning of a performance. He suggested an iron wire with wicks attached to it, which led around the chandelier and then into the wings so that it could be lit more or less invisibly. But this process went wrong very easily. The wicks went out or fell on to the actors or the stage. Thus Sabbatini recommended that an adequate supply of tubs and buckets should be kept in readiness in the wings and even between the borders in case of emergency. Entirely aware of the fire risk, he also described how the whole stage set could be ignited using pieces of cloth soaked in alcohol.

Practical considerations of this kind smoothed the way for the first use of dramatic theatrical lighting. For example, Leoni de' Sommi (1527–1592) felt that cheerful light was more suitable for comedy, while a darkened auditorium was more likely to put the audience into the appropriate frame of mind for the changing moods of a tragedy. At the same time, Angelo Ingegneri remarked that a stage seemed brighter and drew more attention to itself if the auditorium was in darkness. For this reason the lights were put out in the Italian theatre before the performance began, even at that time. This separation of stage and auditorium, the division between the two that we take for granted, became the key feature of the Baroque theatre.

The theatrical situation was different in England. When the young Shakespeare came to London in 1590 there were already three great theatres that had become accepted features of life in the city. Despite abundant source material, it is unfortunately not possible to reconstruct Elizabethan theatres precisely. There was no uniform type for exterior and interior in the early stages. They were partially roofed round or polygonal wooden structures, with galleries with benches running all the way

round. The pit – standing room only – was located in the middle, with the raised, roofed playing area thrusting into it. Shakespeare's stage, or the dominant theatre type of the period, can be more easily reconstructed from the plays. The stage furnishings were not restricted to elements mentioned in the plays, however. There were also doors and various mobile setting pieces, and even then they were not able to do without lifting devices and trapdoors. Most of the performances were during the day, so stage lighting was not needed. The torches, candles and other lights that were used were usually for dramatic purposes. The various times of day had to be created in the spectators' minds; if an actor came on to the stage with a torch, it was night. Lighting did not become essential till later,

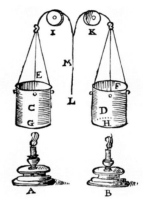

12 'Let the two lights that have to be dimmed be A and B, and the cylinders C, D with the air holes in the middle of the upper part at E, F, and open at the bottom at G, H. The threads that hold the cylinders run over the pulleys I, K in such a way that they are vertically above the lights A, B, and that the said threads are joined only at one end L. If the lights are to be dimmed, then allow the end of the thread L to rise upwards, so that the cylinders C, D cover the lights A, B. To uncover them again one will pull the said thread from M to L, where it first was, so that at the same moment the said lights are again uncovered. The same has to be done with all the others, so that as many threads as is at all possible come together in one single threadend. In this way it will succeed as described.' From: Nicola Sabbatini, *Pratica di fabricar scene e macchine ne' teatri*, Ravenna 1638

when plays were performed almost exclusively indoors. Thus the stage tended to be pragmatic – a few candles, torches, simple footlights or a chandelier had to suffice. So the English theatre of the day, with a very few exceptions, was not influenced by contemporary developments in Italy.

Inigo Jones (1573–1652) was perhaps the most famous English theatre architect. He introduced Palladian architecture to England, but he was also responsible for taking over ancient stage forms, including its periact technique and lighting methods, following the Italian model. He set up the theatre in Whitehall palace, and perspective stages with allegorical and mythological motifs were erected under his direction. He opted for the lighting technique that had now been perfected in Italy, which used coloured glass to create various lighting moods or even different times of day.

In Germany, Italian stage and lighting techniques were adopted and developed by Joseph Furttenbach (1591–1667). Even though he clung on to the periact system, which had become antiquated in the meantime, Furttenbach was a pioneer in German stage lighting. His numerous writings confirm this. For example, he recommended a large number of concealed oil lamps in the wings and was the first to suggest a light above the stage in the borders, which was reflected downwards by mirrors. Further, he advocated continuous footlights with reflectors, so that the audience were not dazzled. He used a similar technique for lighting backcloths. To save money at matinées, the stage was to be lit by appropriately designed windows. The fundamentals of this lighting approach were retained until the second half of the 18th century.

In 17th-century Paris, ballrooms that could serve as temporary theatres were made available for the various strolling troupes; some of them were later converted into permanent theatres. Even such famous theatres as the Comédie Française and Molière's Illustre-Théâtre came about in this way. Except for court events, the furnishings were relatively simple at first. Some of the theatres had windows, so that elaborate lighting was not needed in daylight, if this coincided with the performance. At first they restricted themselves to such modest resources as candles, lanterns and torches. Soon the chandeliers on the stage and in the auditorium became essential lighting devices. In the Hôtel de Bourgogne there were six large chandeliers in front of the proscenium arch above the forestage, six more behind it and three on each side by the wings. Thus the auditorium was brightly lit as well. In the Palais-Royal, the two round lanterns at the very front were drawn upwards through round apertures in the

13 Oil lamp with screw holder

14 Candleholder with Flender gold reflector. Both illustrations from: Joseph Furttenbach, *Mannhafter Kunst-Spiegel*, Augsburg 1663

ceiling at the beginning of the overture, and at the same time 50 sheet metal oil lamps, each with five flames, lit up on the lower edge of the stage. Unlike the Italian theatre, the auditorium was always very brightly lit, and this changed gradually only in the mid 18th century. For a long time theatrical performances that were part of festivities lasting several days at Versailles during the reign of Louis XIV remained unsurpassed. These concluded in an impressive firework display as a tribute to the king. Louis XIV had entertained his guests with a breathtaking firework display when celebrating his accession. A platform occupying the whole of the Marble Courtyard was built for the performance of Lully's opera *Alceste* (ill. 15). Countless lights were lined up on the roofs and cornices, in windows and on the parapets of balconies, bathing the entire courtyard in blazing light. In this case, the usual Baroque stage effects were sacrificed to impressive lighting. Five enormous on-stage chandeliers

were the principal component of a production of Molière's *Le malade imaginaire*. But the court and the nobility were not just spectators, they were also part of the production as a whole, which was intended as a demonstration of power and Baroque self-assertion. This was why the auditorium was still lit in the 19th century in many places. Spectators did not sit on fixed seating of the kind with which we are familiar. The audience usually stood, and at court performances the ruler sat in the middle of the room as a continuation of the axis of the central perspective – also an expression of absolutist thinking. Firework technology and stage effects of all kinds became a fundamental element of the performances. In 1688, 24,000 lights were used to illuminate the park of Versailles alone, presumably all wax candles, the usual source of royal lighting and an extremely expensive one.

The first opera houses established a new theatrical form throughout Eur-

ope: the stage with scenery. The Baroque theatre of illusion, developed by GIOVANNI BATTISTA ALEOTTI (1546–1636), came into being, with all its countless possibilities for transformation. Elaborate mechanisms made it possible to change all the wing flats and borders, including the backcloth. Cleverly devised constructions lifted sets or performers. Lighting effects were increasingly perfected, and highly impressive ways of using fire, smoke and lightning flashes were found. Flying equipment made spectacular entrances from above possible. The techniques using transparent scenery must have been particularly impressive; the whole stage was lit by thousands of lamps fitted invisibly behind transparent scenery. When the royal opera house opened in Berlin in 1742, the lighting depended on 1,300 flames, which could be divided into 11 different groups. Even though they were very expensive, candles were preferred to other light sources as they provided

*Premiere Journée.*
Alceste, Tragedie en musique, ornée d'entrées de Ballet, representée à Versailles dans la cour de marbre du Chasteau éclairé depuis le haut jusquen bas d'vne jnfinité de lumieres.

*Dies primus.*
Alcestis Tragœdia, perpetuo cantu et variis Saltationibus decorata, in marmoreo Palatij Versaliarum cauædio, vndequaque facibus accensis illuminati, acta.

le Pautre Sculps. 1676.

time. This situation did not improve until the early 19th century. The rigid symmetrical arrangement of the stage began to break down, and the previous stress on central perspective was gradually replaced by the wonderful innovation of diagonal perspective. The stage set no longer continued the axis of the auditorium to infinity. The set was placed so that spectators looked at the stage along a diagonal, with the depth distributed on either side. Wings and backdrop were no longer simply set up one behind the other, they were interlinked to an extent and became involved with each other. There was an ever-increasing demand for lighting that followed nature, just as stage painting now did. FRANCESCO ALGAROTTI (1712–1764) said in 1750: 'If one were to learn the art of light distribution correctly, in other words if one directed particularly strong beams of light at certain parts of the stage and left other parts in darkness – would that not be a successful transfer on to the stage of the strong

16  Design by Marcantonio Chiriani for the opera *Nerone fatto Cesare* by Giacomo Antonio Perti, Teatro Malvezzi, Bologna, 1695

15  Ill. left:
Festival performance of the opera *Alceste* by Lully and Quinault in the Marble Courtyard in Versailles, to launch the court festivities arranged there by Louis XIV in July and August 1674. Copperplate engraving by Le Pautre, 1676

more light than oil lamps, which also gave out an overpowering, fatty smell. The items used to light an opera performance in Stuttgart in 1779 were noted with meticulous precision: 170 wax lights, 1,176 tallow candles, 430 pounds of olive oil, 1 pound wax tapers (for lighting the candles), 3 pounds of vegetable brimstone (for lightning) and 200 pitch rings for pitch torches. But this also involved large numbers of staff. So-called lamp cleaners were constantly needed to trim wicks or replace candles, even during the performance. This work faded out as oil lamps and then, increasingly, gas lamps started to be used in the theatre.

Magnificent theatricality was to be seen outside the theatre in those days as well: in the Baroque churches. The most impressive example of this is the high altar of the monastery church of Weltenburg. Double columns are arranged like staggered wings, and St George appears in the dark architectural frame illuminated sculpturally like a *deus ex machina* from an invisible window. *Trompe l'oeil* architectural painting on the back wall continues the space at the rear. But the Baroque proscenium theatre was more like a frame of light in which the performers were illuminated from below, from the front of the stage, from the wings at the side and from the borders above. The light shining from the edges faded towards the centre, and so the place that

17  A stagehand trimming the footlight wicks during a performance of *Jeppe vom Berge* by Ludwig Holberg, Grönnegade-Theatre, Copenhagen, early 18th century. Reconstructed drawing by R. Christiansen, 19th century, from the theatre museum in the Christiansen Palace, Copenhagen

should have been brightest was in half-shadow. Thus the only effectively lit position was downstage by the footlights, where the performer was closest to the source; the majority of the action had to take place in this very small area. Another disadvantage was that the light came unnaturally from below, so the performers' legs were more brightly lit than their faces, which were prone to look hideously distorted. Any attempts to create effective front or border lighting by using reflectors failed because the light sources were too weak at the

and lively "clair-obscur" we have seen in Rembrandt's painting? It would perhaps even be possible to produce on the stage the delightful relations of light and shade that we find in the pictures of Titian and Giorgione' (ill. 19).

Painters rather than architects were increasingly responsible for stage sets. The aesthetic sensibility of the age looked for sophisticated lighting moods such as twilight and darkness. Important and innovative research was devoted to the reflector and its shape. Simple, flat reflectors were replaced

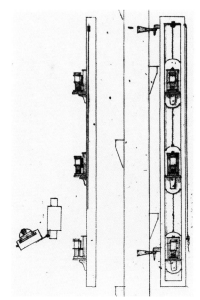

18 Wing post with swivelling lamp board, Italy, 18th century. University of Cologne Institute of Theatre Studies, Niessen Collection

by concave ones. ANTOINE-LAURENT LAVOISIER (1743–1794) recommended various reflectors, so-called *réverbères* in the auditorium and *réverbères paraboliques* between the wings for the stage; these were adjustable in terms of both the direction and the intensity of the light (ill. 20). Soon these simple spotlights were also mounted on revolving stands on both sides of the stage and downstage, so that this

19 Design by Andrea Urbani for the opera *La diavolessa* by Baldassare Galuppi, Teatro di San Samuele, Venice, 1755

lighting could be used to produce something like the old masters' chiaroscuro, because the footlights, which seriously impaired lighting effects, were no longer essential.

This reflector technology and an oil lamp developed by the physicist AIMÉ ARGAND (1755–1803) in 1780 pushed developments forward. An improved oxygen supply meant that this lamp not only provided brighter light, but that it was smokeless as well, and an adjustable wick allowed brightness to be regulated to a certain extent. A disadvantage was that the glass cylinders tended to shatter, unfortunately sometimes during the performance, forcing the audience to leave their seats as quickly as possible. This remained the brightest light source, and when used in conjunction with reflectors it could produce both top and front lighting. Mood lighting was possible for the first time; the red of the sunset no longer had to be painted, sunlight did not come from below any more, and performers could be lit to correspond with the light as painted on the wing flats. The desire for a theatre of illusion with bright lighting that caught the moods of natural light was finally fulfilled as technology was industrialized in the 19th century. Gaslight was followed by all the varieties and gradual developments of electrical lighting, and the theatre could now deliver everything

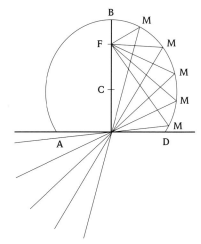

20 Reflector for indirect auditorium lighting. Antoine-Laurent Lavoisier, 1781

that had been anticipated theoretically from the outset.

In America, strict Puritanism, combined with hard pioneering work, had prevented an independent theatrical scene from emerging. An American theatre run along British lines was introduced as a result of touring companies. Philadelphia followed temporary venues in warehouses with its first dedicated theatre in 1766, and New York did the same a year later. But the 19th century was half over before Europe's technical lighting achievements began to be used in America.

The introduction of electric light then led to the total disappearance of illusionistically painted light. Architectural elements were built in three dimensions, and the appropriate light could be supplied, along with its accompanying shadows. Painted light – accepted as natural for centuries – had to give way to real light. Representing it was no longer a task for painting, but was logically handed over to lighting.

21–24 Ill. pp. 21–23:
W.A. Mozart, *Lucio Silla*
Director: Peter Mussbach
Set Designer: Roberto Longo
Salzburg Festival, 1993

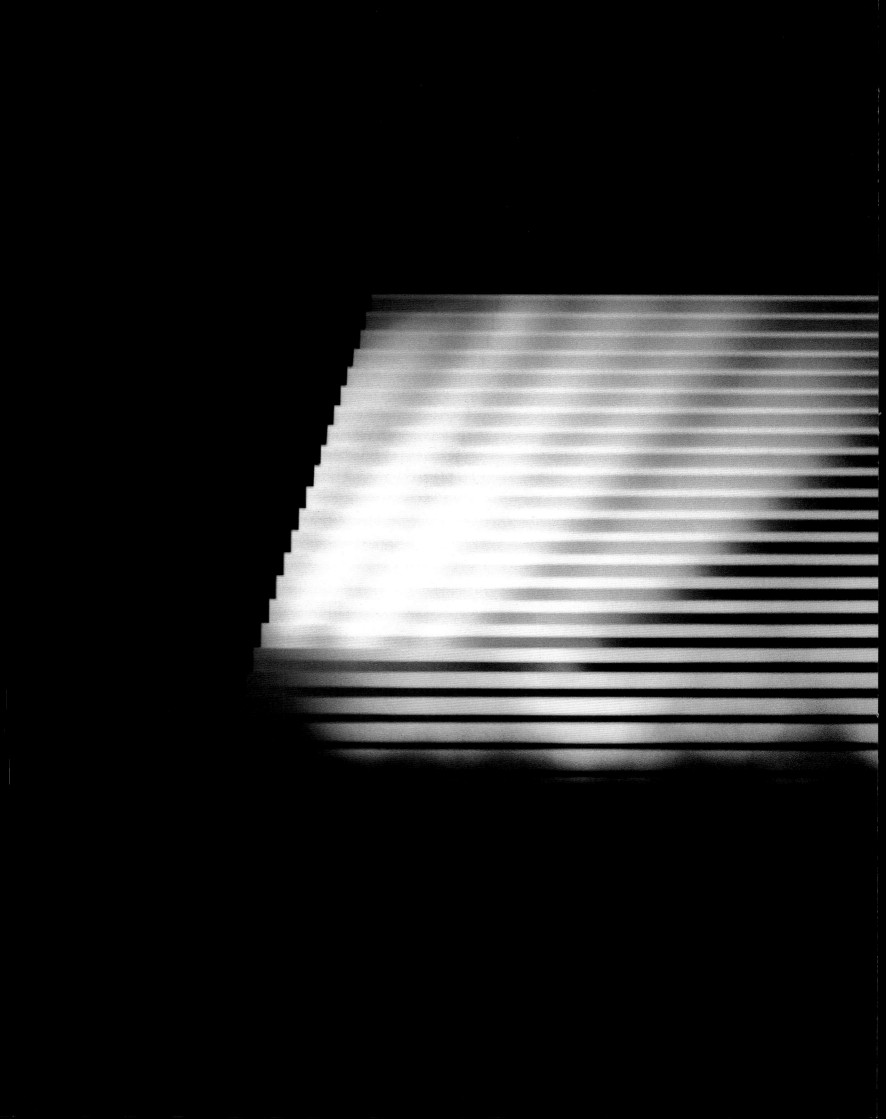

# Light and Colour

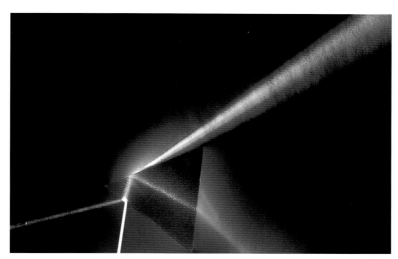

26 Light refracted by a prism

## SEEING

The eye is able to register:

- differences in brightness
- colour differences
- shapes
- movements
- distances

Lighting is intended to make it easier for the eye to fulfil these functions, or even to make it possible in the first place. A certain minimum illumination is needed for seeing, perceiving and recognizing; perception is an individual process, invoking a sensation, triggered by the psychological and physical effect

of the interaction of the five points mentioned above.

## LIGHT

Light is a form of radiated energy. Light spreads from a source in waves, evenly, in all directions. The waves differ in length and frequency, and these two factors produce the speed. The wavelength of visible light extends from approx. 380 nm for the blue band to 720 nm for the red band (nm = nanometre = one millionth of a millimetre). The eye's sensitivity is low at the beginning and end of the scale, extending only from 400 nm to 700 nm.

Rays from the invisible bands can be transformed into visible light with the help of various minerals.

## THE SPECTRUM OF LIGHT

Light with different wavelengths appears to the eye as different colours. The composition of white light can be made visible by its spectrum (see Newton and Goethe). The colours are at their most intense at:

Violet  = 440 nm
Blue   = 480 nm
Green  = 520 nm
Yellow = 570 nm
Red    = 650 nm

The following elementary colours can be seen in the spectrum: violet – cyan – green – yellow – orange. The physiological context makes it impossible for the sixth elementary colour (magenta) to appear.

The colours of the rainbow appear in a similar way to the spectrum. Sunlight is refracted in countless water-droplets suspended in the air, and the radiated energy is dispersed according to wavelength. As light is refracted twice within a water droplet, two rainbows are produced, a strongly and a weakly coloured one, placed opposite the sun. Different degrees of refraction occur in diamonds, cut glass and mirrors. When

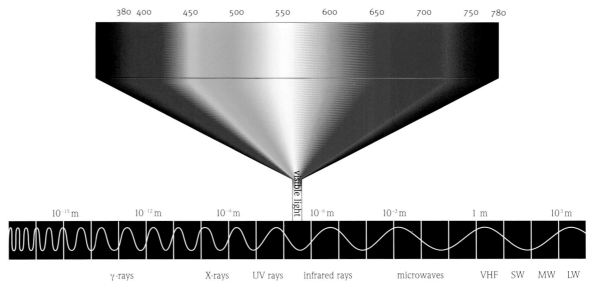

27  Light waves – the colour spectrum of visible light

white light is refracted in a prism the rays are diverted from their axis and dispersed in various directions. The violet rays with short wavelengths are diverted the most strongly, the red ones with long wavelengths the least.

## COLOUR

Colour is the result of a physiological process generally triggered by a physical stimulus (colour stimulus). There are three types of photoreceptor cells in the retina of the human eye that are sensitive to rays in different wavebands. These are called 'cones'. Alongside the 'cones' are other receptor cells, the 'rods', that are responsible for sensitivity to brightness.

Data from the various photoreceptor cells is transmitted via the nerves to the brain, where they trigger the appropri-

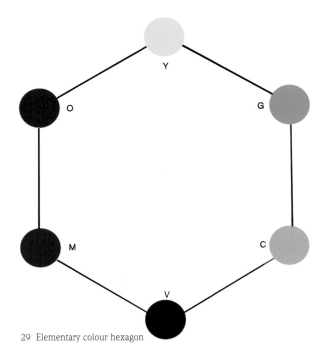

29  Elementary colour hexagon

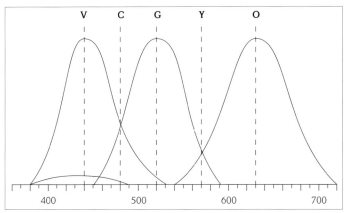

28  Response curves for the three receptor cones

ate sensory reaction. The three 'cone types' have overlapping receptor fields, and therefore they cover a whole band of the spectrum rather than just a certain wavelength. We call these ranges primary colours. Their wavelengths are approximately:

Violet blue  =  448 nm
Green        =  518 nm
Orange red   =  617 nm

## ELEMENTARY COLOURS

The eight elementary colours correspond to the three receptor types (primary colours). Ill. 31 shows their composition. The elementary colours black and white are called 'achromatic' and the others are the 'chromatic' colours. The following abbreviations will be used from now on:

White        =  W
Orange red   =  O
Black        =  B
Cyan         =  C
Violet blue  =  V

Yellow   =  Y
Green    =  G
Magenta  =  M

## MIXED COLOURS

Mixed colours are produced when subsets of colours come together. Each nuance of colour consists of a chromatic and an achromatic value. The chromatic value is made up of chromatic elementary colours and the achromatic value can be composed of chromatic or achromatic elementary colours.

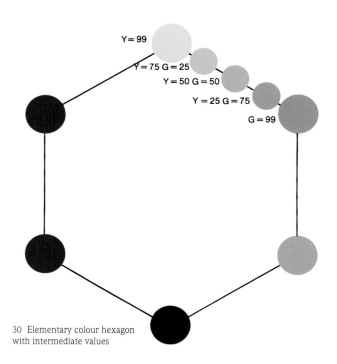

30  Elementary colour hexagon with intermediate values

Light and Colour

## PRIMARY COLOUR INDEX

The primary colour indexing system is used to identify individual colour tints. It identifies the potential of the three primary colours. The greatest possible colour perception is identified as '99'. It is possible to make all gradations between 00 and 99. If we work on the basis that 99 is the extreme primary colour, the eight elementary colours come out as shown in the table. The maximum values of a colour are set at 99 rather than 100% – the 1% difference is insignificant. The colour composition of individual colours can be fixed precisely with the help of this system.

## DISTINGUISHING CHARACTERISTICS

Each colour has four distinguishing characteristics: chromatic type, achromatic type, colour degree, brightness. A colour hue can be defined if at least three of these characteristics are present and identifiable.

• CHROMATIC TYPE
About 200 colour tints can be distinguished. The chromatic type gives information about the specifications of the colour type.
• ACHROMATIC TYPE
About 50 achromatic types can be distinguished. Achromatic types are white, all the greyscales and black.
• COLOUR DEGREE
The colour degree gives the extent of the colour. The greater the colour degree, the more intense the colour.
• BRIGHTNESS
The brightness scale is represented by the value that equates a colour perception with a certain perception of the achromatic types.

## COLOUR PERCEPTION

The chromatic type, achromatic type, colour degree and brightness of a colour hue lead to a certain perception of colour. Unlike the ear, the eye is integrative. For example, if the ear is trained, it can distinguish the upper harmonics of a sound. But the eye is not able to recognize the individual components of a beam of light. Given the same brightness and the same chromatic type, the eye is able to distinguish about 120 different tints.

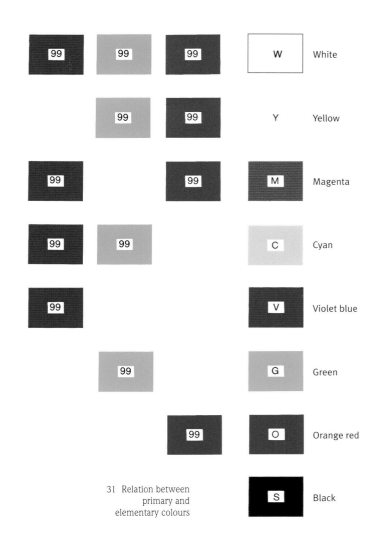

31  Relation between
primary and
elementary colours

White — W
Yellow — Y
Magenta — M
Cyan — C
Violet blue — V
Green — G
Orange red — O
Black — S

## COLOUR TEMPERATURE

The theory of colour temperature is based on the fact that there is a fixed relationship between the temperature of an incandescent body and the colour of the light that it emits. This 'light colour' is defined as colour temperature.

The colour temperature of non-incandescent light sources such as clear blue sky, for example, is not real, as the sky does not glow at a temperature of approx. 25,000°C above absolute zero, which its colour temperature would suggest. The colour temperature of a light source is determined by comparing the colour of the light that it emits with that emitted by a comparative radiator. The comparative body absorbs any outside radiation that strikes it and is called a 'black body' – also known as a Planck radiator. It is heated until it shows the same colour as the light source. This temperature is called 'colour temperature', and is measured in Kelvin degrees. The Kelvin scale is equivalent to the Celsius scale. The only difference is that the Kelvin scale starts at absolute zero, −273°C. The

first dull gleam from incandescent bodies starts at about 800 K. Daily occurrences such as fire and incandescence show us that a body that is beginning to glow changes colour and starts to take on an orange hue, which is in the long-wave visible band. Thus low colour temperatures relate to red light and high colour temperatures to bluish-white light. In colour temperatures between 7,000 and 10,000 K, the short-wave rays are dominant. The light-colour, which has developed from orange via yellow to white, now shifts to violet.

Measuring devices are available for assessing colour temperature, but the resulting values are not necessarily precise. However, such devices provide helpful information and reference aid.

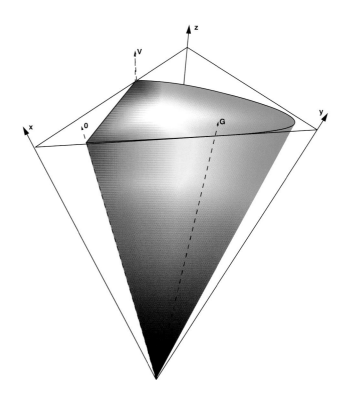

32 Primary values z, x, y, starting from the black point to full colour saturation, with vector lines

## THE CIE SYSTEM

The CIE system (CIE = Commission Internationale de l'Éclairage) was recommended by the International Lighting Commission in 1931 and has become very important for science. Although it deviates somewhat from theories about lighting techniques, we will still take a look at it, as it is particularly helpful in understanding the links between colour temperature, colour rendering and light sources. It is based on additive colour mixing. The additive primary colours are represented not by spectral bands, but by monochrome rays. They are called 'primary values' or 'normal values'. The three primary values increase from the black point (also called zero point) until the colour is saturated. The saturation point is the limiting point for this colour field. Monochrome rays reach their full colour saturation – their absolute degree of colour – at these saturation points:

z = violet blue saturation point
= 435.8 nm
y = green saturation point
= 546 nm
x = orange red saturation point
= 700 nm

Ill. 32 shows the colour progress of the three primary values from zero to colour saturation and the colour progress of the colour field. The precise locus on the spectrum colour line – that is the colour borderline – is fixed by determining the values x, y, z. The vectors surrounding the complete colour field in their outermost position are necessary for fixing the precise values. Ill. 34 shows the border area of the colour field in ill. 33. As a rule, 'z' is not given. The achromatic degree white lies in the middle area – at x = 0.33 and y = 0.33. The division of the co-ordinates is graded between 0 and 1 and fixed by the following definition:

Orange red + green + violet blue = 1
= achromatic white

The further the colour locus of a light or body colour is from the achromatic point on the colour table, the higher its colour degree. This way of looking at colour is very useful in determining the degree of colour and makes the colour temperature theory particularly plausible. As we have already established in the section on colour temperature, the low temperatures are in the red band, and the colour locus approaches the achromatic point as the temperature rises. Now it makes sense to explore the colour field and understand the necessary markings.

As has already been mentioned, the Planck radiator is the starting point for colour temperature measurement. Its different colours produce a curve, the so-called Planck curve, at different temperatures. The precise colour locus of a light or body colour in the field of the curve is determined with the aid of Judd's scale. The curve is divided into two phases: up to a temperature

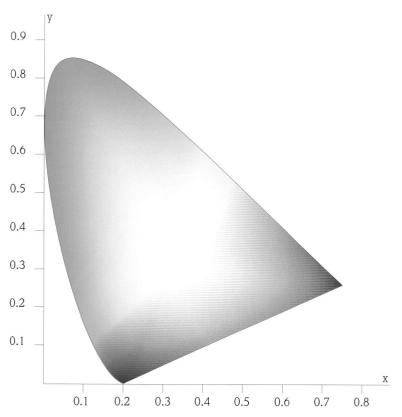

33 CIE colour field – the standard colour table

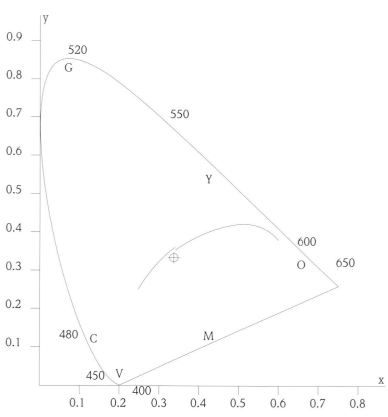

34 Standard colour field with Planck curve and achromatic point white

Light and Colour

39 Following double page:
*Lucio Silla*
Salzburg Festival, 1993

of 5,000 K the Planck radiator provides the related illuminant; upwards of 5,000 K, the ray distribution of natural light is to be used as related light.

## COLOUR RENDERING INDEX, STANDARD LIGHT TYPE

To determine the colour-reproduction index ($R_a$), the locus in the colour field must first be determined. Light sources are divided into illuminants (light types) according to their measured colour temperature. Selected spectrum divisions are defined as standard light types.

Standard light type A   = 2,856 K
the level of a light-bulb

Standard light type C   = 6,774 K
daylight level

Standard light type D65 = 6,504 K

Colour rendering qualities are evaluated according to the standard lighting type used. For example, standard light type D65 is used for the practical requirements of daylight lighting, which can be effectively simulated with a xenon lamp.

Eight or fourteen test colours are used to define the general colour rendering index. Standard light types and the light source to be defined are compared and fixed as a colour shift. The highest value that can be achieved is 100, representing the best possible colour rendering. The lower the figure the lower the quality of the colour rendering. For practical lighting the colour rendering qualities of light sources are divided into the following levels:

| Level | $R_a$ bands | Requirements | Use |
|---|---|---|---|
| 1A | $R_a$ 90–100 | Very high | Colour sampling |
| 1B | $R_a$ 80–89 | | Home, office |
| 2A | $R_a$ 70–79 | High | Industries that work with colour |
| 2B | $R_a$ 60–69 | | |
| 3 | $R_a$ 40–59 | Medium | Industry |
| 4 | $R_a$ 20–39 | Low | Industry |

## COLOUR RENDERING

Generally, anyone observing an object expects the colours to be reproduced as exactly as possible. This depends on the spectrum of the light source lighting an object, for example, ordinary daylight or an artificial light source with a daylight spectrum or light-bulb quality.

As we know, every light source has an individual mixture of spectral bands. Body colours constantly change their appearance because of light. Only the radiated energy contained in light can be reflected by the object. If the light does not contain any radiation that can be reflected by the object, then it appears achromatic or dark. An experiment shows this effect (ill. 35–38).

## LIGHT COLOUR

Light colour is defined by colour temperature and is divided into three groups:

| Colour rendering $R_a$ | Closest colour temperature | Light colours |
|---|---|---|
| Level 3 | Under 3,300 K | Warm white (ww) |
| Level 2 | 3,300–5,000 K | Neutral white (nw) |
| Level 1 | Over 5,000 K | Daylight white (dw) |

35  Coloured objects illuminated with white light

36  Objects illuminated with yellow light

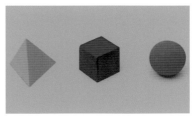

37  Objects illuminated with blue light

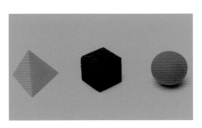

38  Objects illuminated with green light

## COLOUR MIXING

This is an important subject for lighting specialists, as a great deal can be expressed in stage lighting through the use of colour.

All kinds of colours – painted, projected, as colour prints – are based on three principle colour-mixing laws:

- additive colour mixing
- subtractive colour mixing
- integrated mixing (pigments)

Colour mixes are not demonstrated with a printed product here, but 'lit' instead, in other words, shown under the conditions we find in the theatre. Three projectors are used for additive mixing, one for subtractive mixing.

### Additive colour mixing

(Additive = putting individual colours together to produce the achromatic colour white)
- ADDITIVE PRIMARY COLOURS
Violet blue, green, orange red, black

- BASE COLOUR
Achromatic colour black
- SECONDARY COLOURS
Yellow, magenta, cyan, white

When two additive primary colours that are to be projected are mixed, the colour mix produced is a subtractive primary colour. If all three additive primary colours are projected at the same time, white light is produced. The secondary colours in the additive mix are identical with the primary

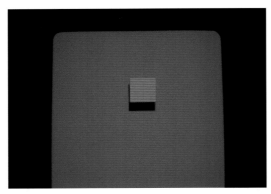

40 White cube surface – orange red light = orange red surface

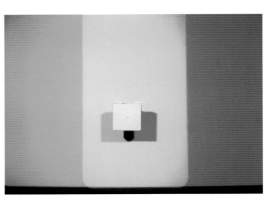

41 White cube surface – violet blue and green light = cyan surface

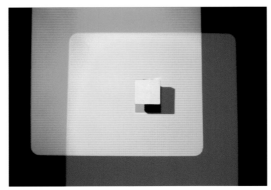

42 White cube surface – orange red and green light = yellow surface

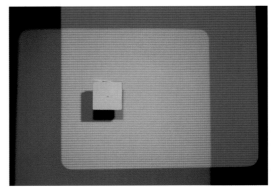

43 White cube surface – orange red and violet blue light = magenta surface

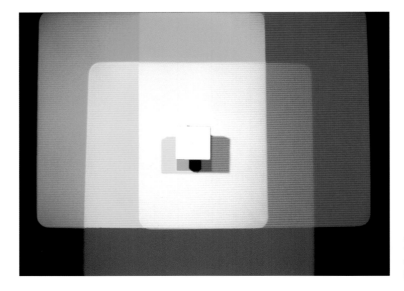

44 Additive colour mixing:
white cube surface,
orange red light, violet blue light and green light = white surface

colours in the subtractive mix. When mixing additive colours it is essential to work with at least two different light sources, as the use of one only would lead to mutual absorption, producing the achromatic colour black. The ideal colours for an additive colour mix are:

Violet blue  = 448 nm
Green       = 518 nm
Orange red  = 617 nm

As the illuminated examples here clearly illustrate, adding to the three chromatic additive colours results in

the creation of three new chromatic primary colours:

Violet blue  + orange red = magenta
Green        + violet blue = cyan
Orange red   + green       = yellow

### Subtractive colour mixing
(Subtractive = filtering out spectral bands, modulating primary colours with overlaid filters)

• SUBTRACTIVE ELEMENTARY COLOURS
Cyan, yellow, magenta, white
• BASE COLOUR
Achromatic white

• SECONDARY COLOURS
Violet blue, green, orange red, black

Filters in the subtractive primary colours let about two thirds of the spectrum through. Thus two cone types are addressed (see p. 26, ill. 28). This means a filter for one subtractive primary colour is transparent for two other primary colours.

Results of a subtractive mix:

Cyan     + magenta = violet blue
Yellow   + cyan     = green
Magenta  + yellow   = orange red

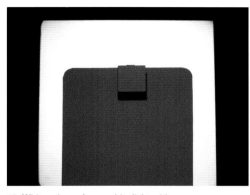

45  White cube surface – white light with magenta filter = magenta surface

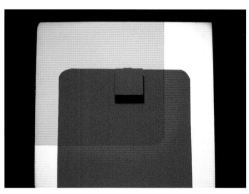

46  White cube surface – white light with magenta and yellow filter = orange red surface

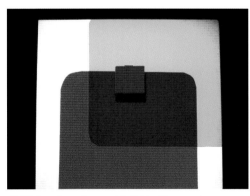

47  White cube surface – white light with magenta and cyan filter = violet blue surface

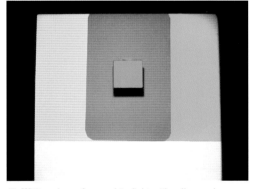

48  White cube surface – white light with yellow and cyan filter = green surface

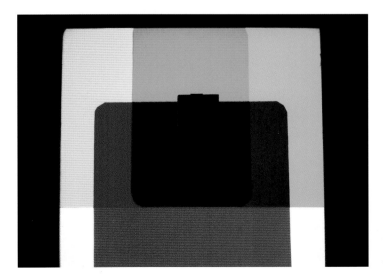

49  Subtractive colour mixing: white cube surface – white light with magenta, cyan and yellow filter = black surface

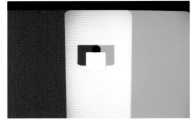

50  White cube surface, orange red and cyan light = white surface

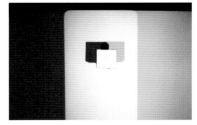

51  White cube surface – violet blue and yellow light = white surface

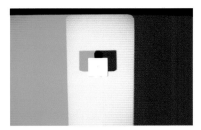

52  White cube surface – green and magenta light = white surface

53  Beams of coloured light cutting through the darkness. Additive colour mixing takes place in the air at their intersection point. Complementary colours combine to produce white light

## Complementary colours

Thus approximately equal proportions of violet, green and orange, used additively, produce white light. But the same result can be produced by combining an elementary colour with a secondary colour made up of the sum of the two other elementary colours. Two coloured lights of this kind, produced by the addition of white light, are complementary colours. Additive colour mixing experiments can be set up using various colour discs. For effective use in the theatre it is not essential to fulfil the absolute, basic physical requirements of spectrum composition, as the colour violet in particular is very dark and lets through very little visually effective light. Of course, colour mixtures with the given ideal values result in the cleanest mixtures and are absolutely essential for demonstration purposes in particular.

LEE commercial filters were used for the illustrations of colour mixtures:

| | |
|---|---|
| Violet blue | No. 132 |
| Cyan | No. 115 |
| Green | No. 124 |
| Yellow | No. 101 |
| Orange red | No. 164 |
| Magenta | No. 113 |

## Integrated colour mixing

Integrated colour mixing is a system based on subtractive colour mixing. Here we are not dealing with applying layers of colour one on top of the other, but with mixing elementary colours to create a new hue. This mixture can be used to cover a layer of colour underneath it. All eight elementary colours are used to produce this mixture. Thus an integrated colour mixture can be made up of both chromatic and achromatic elements. It is clear where it will be useful: as a system for mixing covering colours that are to be applied to a base surface.

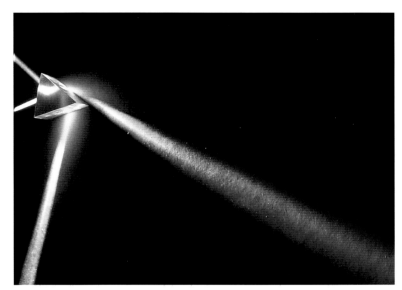

54 A beam of white light, as seen by Newton through a prism

## COLOUR THEORY

### Isaac Newton 1643 – 1727

Isaac Newton developed the first physical theory of colour. After splitting white daylight into the colours of the rainbow with a prism, he identified a total of seven colours. He used these to construct a chromatic circle in which he linked short-wave violet with long-wave red in a continuous sequence. If the number and valuation of the colours are not taken into account, then this circular arrangement is still valid in the colour theory of painting today, because it also gave rise to the idea of complementary colours. But the three colours that could be most clearly distinguished in the prism were red, green and violet – for Newton, the primary colours of physics.

### Johann Wolfgang von Goethe 1749 – 1832

Goethe criticized Newton's theories throughout his life, sometimes in a highly polemic fashion. This may seem nonsensical to us today, especially as Newton's scientific insights do not conflict with an aesthetic approach.

Newton used a prism to break down a thin beam of white light into the three primary colours mentioned above, but Goethe observed a black strip against a white background and saw the colours yellow – purple – blue, the so-called peripheral spectrums. From this

he developed a circular diagram in which the primary colours purple – blue – yellow alternate with the three secondary colours orange – violet – green. This chromatic circle was quick to show the complementary colours that Goethe interpreted as harmonious. He was never prepared to accept the physical theory that white light is the sum of coloured lights. Goethe thought that colours were produced on bright-dark borders by the interplay of light and darkness. This went back to the Greek natural philosophers, who classified all colours between white and

black. In his *Farbenlehre* (Theory of Colours) Goethe stated: 'The edges show colours because light and shade meet each other there; and so colour is produced at the same time by light and that which is opposed to it.' On closer consideration, however, his investigation of the peripheral spectrums does not mean that Newton's theories are incorrect.

Goethe's basic assumption is that there is a distinction between 'light and non-light'. For light he chose the colour yellow, and the colour blue, which is close to darkness, stands for non-light. These two colours produce the new colour green, as the sum of the harmonization of the colour poles. But the two colours yellow and blue, when shifted towards light or darkness, lead to tints with a suggestion of red. 'Elementary colour theory need concern itself only with these three colours: yellow – blue – purple; or six colours: yellow – yellow-red – purple – red-blue – blue – green, which can also be enclosed in a circle.' Despite all

55 Goethe observed a black strip against a white background, which led to the three basic colours in his theory

physical misinterpretations, the chromatic circle has held its own in artistic theories because of its regularity. In addition, yellow, purple and blue anticipate the three primary colours of modern colour printing. According to this, the chromatic circle constructed from the peripheral spectrums looks as shown in ill. 56.

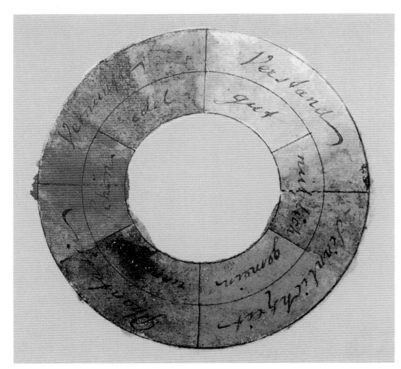

56 Chromatic circle with colour interpretations by Goethe

For Goethe, colour is 'specific, characteristic, significant at all times'. Generally speaking, the colours fall on to two sides. They represent a contrast that is called polarity and can be defined in terms of plus and minus:

| + | − |
|---|---|
| **Yellow** | **Blue** |
| Impact | Deprivation |
| Light | Shade |
| Bright | Dark |
| Strength | Weakness |
| Warmth | Coldness |
| Closeness | Distance |
| Repulsion | Attraction |
| Related to acids | Related to alkalis |

### Arthur Schopenhauer 1788 – 1860

The philosopher Arthur Schopenhauer's particular achievement in terms of colour theory is that he brought the complementary colours and their specific brightnesses together. His theory is based on activity levels within the retina: from full activity (light and white) to inactivity (darkness and black). Chromatic colours are activated only within certain ranges of this scale.

57 Schopenhauer's scale showing the receptivity of the retina

| Black | Violet | Blue | Green | | Red | Orange | Yellow | White |
|---|---|---|---|---|---|---|---|---|
| 0 | 1/4 | 1/3 | 1/2 | | 1/2 | 2/3 | 3/4 | 1 |

Black and white are not colours, as they have no connection. 'True colour theory always deals with pairs, and the purity of a particular colour depends on the harmony of the implied ratio. Colour always appears as a quality, since it is the qualitative bisection of retina activity.'

Schopenhauer goes on to say: 'If the retina is forced to divide its activity by an external stimulus, the other half automatically follows the half activated by the stimulus, as the retina has the natural instinct to develop the full range of its activity.' This link makes the contrast that Goethe had already described easier to understand, the so-called after-image, whereby every colour invokes its complementary counter-colour. Schopenhauer describes a practice-related phenomenon as follows: 'It is only through my theory that we can understand why artificial lighting with a bright flame is more tiring to the eye than daylight. The flame bathes everything in reddish-yellow light (and hence the blue shadow as well). Consequently, for as long as we are seeing by artificial light, only ²/₃ of the retina's activity is stimulated, yet it has to bear the whole effort of seeing, while almost ¹/₃ is idle.'

### Phillip Otto Runge 1777 – 1810

Runge was the first painter to value colour theory highly. His theory is based on notional ideal colours, which he compares with related material colours that cannot be presented so clearly. Thus the colours in the colour sphere he developed are also to be seen as ideal, just as the colour sphere itself is not a product of art, but a mathematical calculation based on philosophical considerations.

Runge was not just trying to establish a psychologically justified system for ordering colour, nor to produce a practically applicable colour table. For him, the globe character of his colour sphere indicated a world view. Starting with Goethe's chromatic circle, which forms the equator, Runge added the two poles: 'white' at the top and 'black' at the bottom. When creating the sphere he was able to represent the mixture of the chromatic colours with black and white, but not the change of intensity by lightening and darkening that is different for our perception, because that would have needed a fourth dimension. Hence he assumed that colour by its very nature occurs in double form, transparent and opaque. If we now accept a chromatic sphere

58 Runge's chromatic sphere and section through the plane of the equator with greyscales

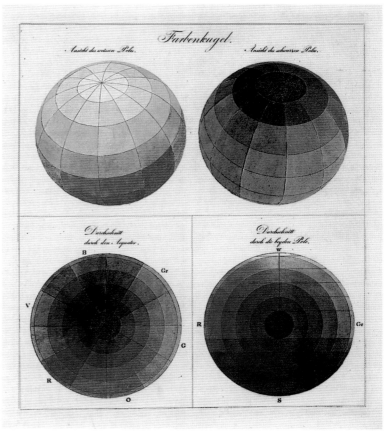

with transparent colours, then we see that the poles coincide with the centre point and the whole form dissolves. Thus the representation of the chromatic sphere is restricted to opaque colours, and the transparent colours can exist only in our imagination. This phenomenon, described by Schopenhauer as the 'duality of colour' also formed the basis for criticism of Goethe's colour theory, as this distinction was missing there. Nevertheless Schopenhauer's colour theory, which was developed at the same time as Goethe's, contains essential principles that he defined in almost the same terms as Goethe and that have retained their validity to the present day.

### Eugène Delacroix 1798–1863

Unlike Runge, Delacroix was a painter who used colour theory mainly as an artistic and technical aid. He felt that an artist who was genuinely concerned with colour should not just use the colours that the layman sees in reality, but should be capable of enhancing the expressiveness of certain coloured effects and of using quite different colours from those that are visible in the final effect. He said that grey was the death of painting, and that colours should express passion, creativity and imagination.

The starting point for these practical considerations was the colour triangle that he used, which contained red, yellow and blue as primary colours and orange, green and violet as secondary colours. He also made practical use of the colours' complementary relationship to each other; for example, strongly lit, intensely coloured bodies developed shadow in complementary colours. This enabled Delacroix to include all the shadow effects that had previously been painted grey or brown in the colour scheme.

Goethe had already mentioned the complementary contrast, but no one made this phenomenon the basis of his painting as Delacroix did. His work as a colourist followed a highly abstract method. Before starting on major commissions he spent weeks combining colours with similar tonal values on his palette. He made meticulous notes of their intended use for reflection, shadows, light, desired emotional effect and other important factors.

The drops of water on a woman's body in the 1822 picture *Virgil and Dante* are a particularly clear example of his work with complementary colours. These exclusively complementary colours give an impression of glittering wetness and disappear if the picture is viewed from a short distance away. However, Delacroix's colour triangle did not include black, white or brown, which is a colour that is important to many painters because of its warmth. Previously, white had been used for lightening and black for representing shadows, and so these two now acquired a new significance as colours in their own right. White retained its role as a lightener, but black was omitted in shadows. Black contributed to the palette only as a colour in its own right, tinted with other colours. This black enriched with other colours found a new importance for Manet and the Impressionists. Brown was increasingly abandoned by Delacroix in favour of a general enhancement of colour.

### Vasily Kandinsky 1866–1944

Colour and form theory played an important part in Kandinsky's long and very productive career as an artist and theoretician. He did not see colour in isolation but went further to develop a language of form and colour. There is an inevitable relationship between form and colour, as it is only form that makes it possible to represent colour by placing restrictions upon it. Kandinsky divided colours into the categories warm/cold and light/dark. Warmth and coldness of colour generally mean an inclination towards yellow and blue respectively; lightness or darkness of colour to white or black. But for him yellow and blue marked the greatest contrast, which can be seen most clearly from the spatial effect of colours. A yellow circle seems larger than a blue one of the same size. Yellow is eccentric, in contrast with concentric blue. This effect is greater if the difference between light and dark is considered as well, that is, the effect of yellow is enhanced by the addition of white, and that of blue by the addition of black. If green is produced by mixing yellow and blue, the forces contained in yellow and blue are cancelled out, producing 'complete motionlessness and peace.' He described this green as being 'like a fat, very healthy, very still cow, capable only of chewing the cud and looking at the world with stupid dull eyes.' Adding yellow brings green back to life again, youthful and joyful, but if the green moves in the direction of blue it becomes serious and reflective. Thus it is activated, but it moves in two divergent directions.

Green stands in contrast with red, which also has no spatial existence but does have a strong active glow within it. They both have the same internal movement of red; but yellow makes orange strive to come closer to the viewer, whereas blue makes violet move away from the viewer.

The interplay of form and colour is shown most clearly by the combination of colour and angle. The acute angle is the warmest, thus yellow; the obtuse angle is the coldest, thus blue; in between is the right angle, to which the static red is assigned. As the typical angles can develop further into geometrical shapes, the relationships between line, shape and colour are self-evident. Kandinsky put forward the following schematic assignation:

| | | |
|---|---|---|
| Acute angle | – triangle – | yellow |
| Right angle | – square – | red |
| Obtuse angle | – circle – | blue |

These assertions, Kandinsky explained, were the result of empirical and psychological insights and were not based on absolute science.

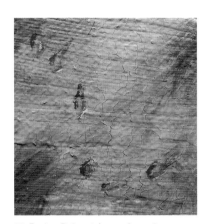

59 Eugène Delacroix's use of complementary colours

60 Vasily Kandinsky: the three primary colours, allocated to the three basic shapes, 1923

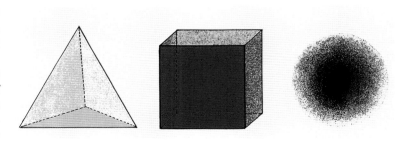

### Johannes Itten 1888–1967

Fixing six primary colours precisely, and establishing the way in which colours contrast with each other was a fundamental component of Itten's theoretical work. A note in the diary covering his later years gives a clear idea of his thinking: 'Just as a word acquires its unambiguous meaning only in context with others, individual colours acquire their unambiguous meaning and precise sense only in the context of other colours.' He defined yellow, red and blue as colours 'of the first order.' He declared the colours obtained by mixing these, orange, green and violet, to be colours 'of the second order.' Itten lists the following seven colour contrasts:

• The COLOUR-AS-SUCH CONTRAST is the simplest. At least three adjacent colours are needed to produce it. The strongest contrast is yellow–red–blue, declining as the colours move further away from each other.

• The LIGHT-DARK CONTRAST is based on the brightness value of two different colours, the strongest being between black and white.

• The COLD-WARM CONTRAST relates to colour temperature. For example, orange is a warm colour, blue a cold one. However, it is also produced between orange and magenta.

• The COMPLEMENTARY CONTRAST occurs between two coloured lights that produce white light when combined.

• SIMULTANEOUS CONTRAST refers to the phenomenon whereby the eye simultaneously and independently produces the complementary colour, even when it is not present. The simultaneously produced complementary colour occurs as a colour sensation in the eye and does not exist in reality (cf. the successive contrast that Schopenhauer describes).

• The QUALITY CONTRAST refers to the difference between two colours with differing degrees of purity; that is, the prismatic colours as colours with the highest saturation in contrast with grey, gloomy colours.

• The QUANTITY CONTRAST refers to the relationship of size and the relative luminance of two areas. For example, a yellow area has the same quantity as a violet area that is three times larger.

## EFFECT OF COLOURS

The use of colours, whether painted, as material or in the form of light, makes a definite statement. As we know, colour is created by light. Thus everything that we see stems from the interplay of chromatic colours. The achromatic colours white and black do not occur in the spectrum and thus exist only as surface colours, and they produce the strongest and most radical contrast. Interplay results in a large number of intermediate colours within the chromatic colours. All these intermediate tints, including the six primary colours, affect us psychologically: coldness, warmth, joy, sorrow, beauty, ugliness, hardness and tenderness.

This insight has various applications today. For example, the advertising and packaging industries exploit the psychological effect of colour and apply it to very precise ends. Of course, this way of conveying feeling also applies to the theatre. The interplay of colour on stage and in costumes is largely based on this principle, although many decisions about colour are certainly made on an emotional basis. Here individual evaluation of moods, situational and symbolic associations and personal relations to colour are important factors. I have restricted myself to yellow, orange, magenta, violet, cyan and green in my survey of the essential primary colours and have classified intermediate tints with the colour closest to them. The two achromatic colours black and white are also included.

### Warm colours

Warm colours are those that contain the colour yellow. They are classified as warm because of associations with sun and fire:

Yellow-orange – red – yellow-green

### Cold colours

Cold colours contain the colour blue. They produce a mental connection with ice-blue mountain lakes and the bluish colour of steel:

Green-blue – blue – violet

The colour green is mediatory. It can be both a cold and a warm colour, but in general it tends towards cold.

### Highly saturated colours

Colours that are not mixed with black, grey or white, in other words with a high chromatic level, create power-ful, aggressive impressions, indicate force and might, and invoke strong moods.

### Pale tints, pastel colours

Colours with a great deal of white or grey mixed into them are particularly suited to making delicate, cultivated effects and to conveying a refined, subdued atmosphere.

## OPPOSITIONAL COLOUR CONCEPTS

| Negative | Positive |
|---|---|
| Cold | Warm |
| Dark | Light |
| Shady | Sunny |
| Transparent | Opaque |
| Soothing | Exciting |

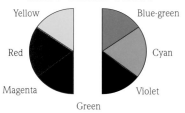

61  Chromatic circle divided into active – inactive – passive

| Thin | Thick |
|---|---|
| Distant | Near |
| Hard | Soft |
| Light | Heavy |
| Moist | Dry |

### Black and white

Colour effects in black and white are simple but harsh in appearance. These epitomes of elementary colour show unambiguously that light and shade form the basis of lighting technique. This phenomenon is visible and reflected as a clear formation, austere and definite.

## COLOURED SHADOWS

When we talk about shadows, we think of an object that is getting in the way of light. A shadow appears on the side of the object that is not facing the light, and a shadow is cast on the surrounding area. Generally, shadow is understood to be the colour black, as shadow is non-light. Experiments and colour theory show that this is not the case. According to Goethe, two conditions

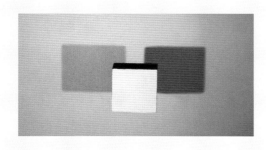 

62 Two projectors lighting a white cube against a wall crosswise, the left-hand projector with yellow, the right-hand with violet blue. The mixed colour on the surface of the cube appears as white. The coloured shadows cast on the wall adopt their complementary colour in each case

63 Experiment set up as in ill. 62. Left-hand projector with cyan, right-hand projector with orange red

pertain to coloured shadow. First, the effective light should colour the white surface in some way; second, a counter-light should illuminate the shadow cast to some degree. (See also Schopenhauer and Delacroix for related theories.)

Coloured shadows are the result of a simultaneous contrast. The shadow in a complementary colour follows the colour of the lead light.

Yellow light = violet blue shadow
Orange light = blue shadow
Green light = red shadow

According to Itten, every coloured light produces a shadow in the complemen-

tary colour in daylight. If this experiment is taken further, it shows that by using two light sources of different colours the two shadows will add up to a third colour at the point of intersection. This is additive colour mixing. This phenomenon can be proved only in absolute darkness.

## AERIAL AND COLOUR PERSPECTIVE

In the early 15th century, many artists developed aerial perspective from coloured visual experience. The further away they are, all colours appear more

bluish and are increasingly diffuse in the direction of the horizon. This is based on the same phenomenon that makes the sky seem blue. Little particles in the atmosphere, no larger than a tenth of the wavelength, and air molecules disperse the sunlight, making it considerably stronger at the violet end of the spectrum. Thus in a clear atmosphere the sky seems blue, often even dark blue. Then if there are larger particles in the air the effect described is not so powerful; the sky becomes greyish and whiter. At sunrise or sunset the short-wave violet rays of the sun are even absorbed by the atmosphere, increasingly as the sun gets lower. This is

64 Practical application of colour perspective:
Botho Strauss, *Ithaca*
Director: Dieter Dorn
Set Designer: Jürgen Rose
Münchner Kammerspiele, 1996

65 Practical application of aerial
and colour perspective:
*Reigen*
Théâtre Royale de la Monnaie
Brussels, 1993

especially evident in the warm red light of a sunset or sunrise. In daylight the blue light of the atmosphere works like a filter, so that objects seem to be more blue the further away from us they are. If the light is not so clear it has the effect of a grey veil. Early Dutch painting in particular made great play with this phenomenon in creating the illusion of deep skies and infinite distances.

## COLOUR CHARACTER

Greater investigations into colour character can be found in specialist literature. I have chosen and assembled the ideas that are most important to me subjectively. (The table on pp. 42/43 draws on sources including: Heimendahl, *Licht und Farbe;* Frieling, *Gesetz der Farbe;* the following is quoted in translation from Küthe/Venn, *Marketing mit Farben.*)

### Red

Red is not subordinate to any other colour. It is so dominant that it immediately takes over from other colours and stimulates the eye to the greatest extent. When set among other colours it looks as though it is much closer to our eye than the others, such as green or even blue, for example. Red expresses living power and energy. It symbolizes love and addresses the greatest range of human feelings. Heavy, dark red stands for dignity and burning seriousness. Cardinal red is the colour of toppling, of overthrow. The brighter the red becomes, excitement increasingly retreats in favour of warmth and joy. In the light hues in particular (pink), red is light-hearted, joyful and young.

### Blue

Blue is the colour of sky. The deeper the blue, the more metaphysical it becomes: blue-black has the note of overwhelming cosmic mourning. Blue is and always will be an enigmatic colour for us. It always seems distant and may be soothing, but still it radiates seriousness, cold and yearning, with an undertone of sadness. Blue makes a hole in the picture – says the painter – and this means that blue always seems to be drawing back. Ultramarine is also cool but has an agreeable, calming, peaceful effect, because it behaves passively. Blue-green fuses blue's reticence and yearning with the peace and freshness of green. Blue-green induces yearning but is soothing at the same time.

### Green

Green, particularly the fresh green that is often called 'young' green, expresses spring and youth. Darker green loses this symbolic quality. Green is also the symbol of a full and healthy life. However, while orange expresses higher spiritual life, green stands for vegetative, full bodily life. Green is the most peaceful of all colours and can thus even out differences. Green attracts the eye, satisfies and invigorates it. If green is mixed with yellow, it becomes more youthful, more lively and more active. When mixed with brown it strikes a different note, becoming heavier and more serious.

### Violet

Violet is the most remarkable of all the colours. It is neither cold nor warm. Yet it has something mystical about it, something that can be depressing for some people and trigger a sense of malaise. Violet appeals to those who tend to be deep and mystical, sometimes even a little odd. A particular shade of violet can make a profound impact on people, even move them. Violet has an almost numbing effect on the very sensuous, and such individuals tend to avoid it. A violet in which blue is predominant is further enhanced in its tendency to the ethereal, to striving upwards (ultramarine). Red-violet, in which the red strikes only a gentle note, becomes more delicate the more it is lightened. It then exudes a refined, delicate, 'feminine' aura. But dark violet-red is more dignified and becomes episcopal purple. Lighter shades of violet (lilac) combined with white and lemon-yellow can create a very intense and feminine effect.

### Yellow

Yellow has a very stimulating effect, but without causing the kind of excitement we associate with red. Pure yellow is the brightest colour in the chromatic circle and symbolizes fertility, blessing, abundance, and – if raised to the plane of gold – it expresses power, glory and majesty. The brighter yellow is, the more it moves into the foreground. Yellow has a dominant effect. If it is divided, it increases in power. However, it loses its cheerfulness or majesty if it becomes darker. The brighter yellow gets, the more it is refined, becoming less weighty, more delicate and more noble, and then optically more reticent.

### Magenta

Magenta is the colour of the unnatural and thus also of the supernatural and transcendental. We see not only the superficial but also the broader context. We try to find out what lies beneath the surface and how everything fits together. Here we are dealing with order

and justice, with matters of principle. Magenta can indicate abnormality but also an awareness of the special, or it can even suggest undue claims to power.

### Brown

Brown is the earthiest, densest and most real of all the colours. Brown cannot be called noble and refined, but it is powerful, expressing health and solidity, earthiness. This very typical quality is changed when brown is mixed with other colours. When mixed with red or violet it gives the impression of sunshine on earth. This violet-brown then has a very attractive power, moving into the realms of magic and mystery.

### Gold

As such, gold tends to be toneless and thus soulless, but its density and magnificent radiance give it a festive, majestic quality. Like the sun, gold expresses the highest life force, in spiritual terms. It also expresses power and dignity; the richer and more powerful the age, the more gold was used in the furnishings (coronation churches, throne rooms, chambers in royal residences).

### Silver

Like gold, silver is toneless and soulless, but its radiance is quite different from gold. Like grey, it is assigned to coloured objects but lessens their joyful quality. Silver is not as enticing as gold; it does not dazzle the eye but attracts

it gently. It is said that silver is 'the light among the metals', and for this reason many people feel that it is nobler than gold. Gold radiates warmth, but silver always seems cool.

### Black

Black equals absolute darkness, embodied as material. Black is serious, negative and dark, and suggests mourning. It is closed and sublime. Set against white it produces absolute contrast.

### White

White is beyond good and evil. White is also not a colour in the sense of chromatic quality. It is the strongest counterpole to black. The unconditional nature of this contrast is easy to understand. While black expresses mourning, white is associated with gaiety. For us white symbolizes innocence and purity. If something essentially simple but powerful and significant has to be expressed, this is best realized by the contrast between black and white.

### Grey

Grey is the essence of gloom. It could be seen as symbolizing indecision. Grey is indifferent, toneless, it neither warms nor cools. It is a background or secondary colour. Grey can balance and neutralize and thus plays an important part in moderating unduly great colour contrasts or bringing colour contrasts together harmoniously. Grey is like the pause in music.

66  Luigi Pirandello
*I giganti della montagna*
Director: Ernst Wendt
Set Designer: Johannes Schütz
Münchner Kammerspiele, 1980

| COLOUR PERCEPTION | White | Yellow | Orange | Red | Purple |
|---|---|---|---|---|---|
| **Meaning** | Openness, boundlessness, spirit | Light expansion, excessive increase, frivolity | Light intensity, joy, relaxation, passion, overthrow, revolution | Light intensity, power, immediacy, directness, life, blood | Sovereignty, dignity, might |
| Psychological plane | Peaceful, good, perfect, innocent, positive, simple, purity | Summer, excess (gold), intuition, making contact, comfort, inspiration, madness | Festivity – Joy, warmth, brilliance, wealth, fertility | Vigour, blood, activity, aggression, archetypal, paternal, intellectual, enlivening | Exceptional qualities, religion, spirituality, luxury |
| Physiological plane | Savoury, mild, clean, pure, free | Light, clean, poisonous, bitter, internal | Fresh, healthy, vitamins | Warmth, dryness, heat | Ornament, calories |
| Ear, hearing symbols | | Piercing, major key | Loud, major key | Loud, trumpet | Powerful, solemn |
| Smell, taste | Savoury-sweet, creamy | Sour | Substantial | Sweet, strong | Overpoweringly sweet |
| Metaphorical plane (symbolic) | Eternity, beginning, piety, faith, truthfulness, precision | Mendacity, jealousy, envy, miserliness, joy, honour, rapture, exclusion, Eastern spirituality | Enjoyment, distractedness, relief | *Joie de vivre*, desire, sexuality, eroticism, imagination | Ancient power, colour of church dignitaries, kings and emperors |
| Past ways of making colours | Chalk, calcium sulphate, natural gypsum, yellowish clay, ground bones, lead carbonate | Ochre, lead compounds, arsenic yellow, Indian yellow (Monghir Piurie), saffron | Crocus, saffron, mixed colour | Blood, rubia tinctorum (madder), kermes (berry), lousewort, alum | Sea slugs, with great effort, and with the utmost secrecy |
| **Advertising** | | | | | |
| General associations | Starkest contrast with black | Light, clear, free, lively | Hearty, happy, glowing, cheerful | Active, exciting, challenging, masterful, happy | Times, association, advertising |
| Sensory-related associations | Purity, freshness, innocence | Very light, smooth, clean | Warm, close, glinting, dry, crumbly, saturated | Hot, loud, full, strong, sweet, firm, sharp | |

| Violet | Blue | Green | Brown | Grey | Black |
|---|---|---|---|---|---|
| Tension, reluctance, repentance, magic, excitement, modernity | Constancy, seriousness, order, reason, faithfulness | Hope, contentment, *joie de vivre*, esteem, environment, sacred colour of Islam | Earthy, calming, impure, powerful | Shadow, overcoming, coolness | Taciturnity, mourning, fear, darkness |
| Emancipation, vanity, artificial, unobjective, high demands, originality | Distance, silence, infinity, philosophy, cold, water | Naturalness, liveliness, excitement, peace, dampness, archetypal, feminine | Unerotic, comfortable, hidden | Age, homeliness, conformity | End, emptiness, death, magic, elegance, humility |
| Extravagance | Old, cool, damp, external | Tangy, fresh, sour, bitter, nourishment, chlorophyll (leaf-green) | Crisp, aromatic | Neutrality | |
| Sad, deep, minor key | Soft | Muted (if dull), shrill (if gentle) | Dark, minor | Pause in music | Confined, angular, hard, inscrutable |
| Heavy-sweet | Odourless | Sour-juicy | Musty, stale, fried, chocolate, cocoa | Mouldy, ashy | Spoilt, inedible, liquorice |
| Piety, repentance, faith, imagination | Sympathy, longing, harmony, spontaneity, friendliness | Hope, relaxation, confidence, tolerance, security, life, love (courtly love) | Laziness, immoderation, probity, earthy | Pensiveness, punctuality, insensitivity, equanimity, modesty | Magic, mourning, egoism, guilt, power, oppression, distress |
| Mixed colour | Lapis lazuli, azure, indigo (plant), woad (plant) | Verdigris, malachite (basic copper carbonate), emerald, leaves, aldehyde green, Paris green | Mixed colour | | Chinese ink, charcoal, soot, tar, mixture of woad and soot |
| | | | | | |
| Dignified, gloomy, dubious, unhappy | Secure, peaceful, distant, spacious | Calming, casual, passive, peaceful, budding, refreshing | Earthy | Boring | Starkest contrast with white |
| Putrid-sweet, narcotic fragrance | Cool, wet, soft, strong, large | Juicy, damp, sour, poisonous, young, full | Chocolate, cakes and pastries | Neutral | Monopolizing, rich in contrast |

67–80 Previous and following pages:

William Shakespeare, *Cymbeline*, director and set designer: Dieter Dorn, Münchner Kammerspiele, 1998.
Location is defined on the horizon with powerful colours and their planes of perception in this production.
With a few exceptions the playing area is lit evenly and calmly.
The colours are allotted as follows:

■ Yellow = king
☐ Dark blue = night
☐ Strong blue = Italy
■ Grey = witch
▨ Green = nature
☐ Red = war

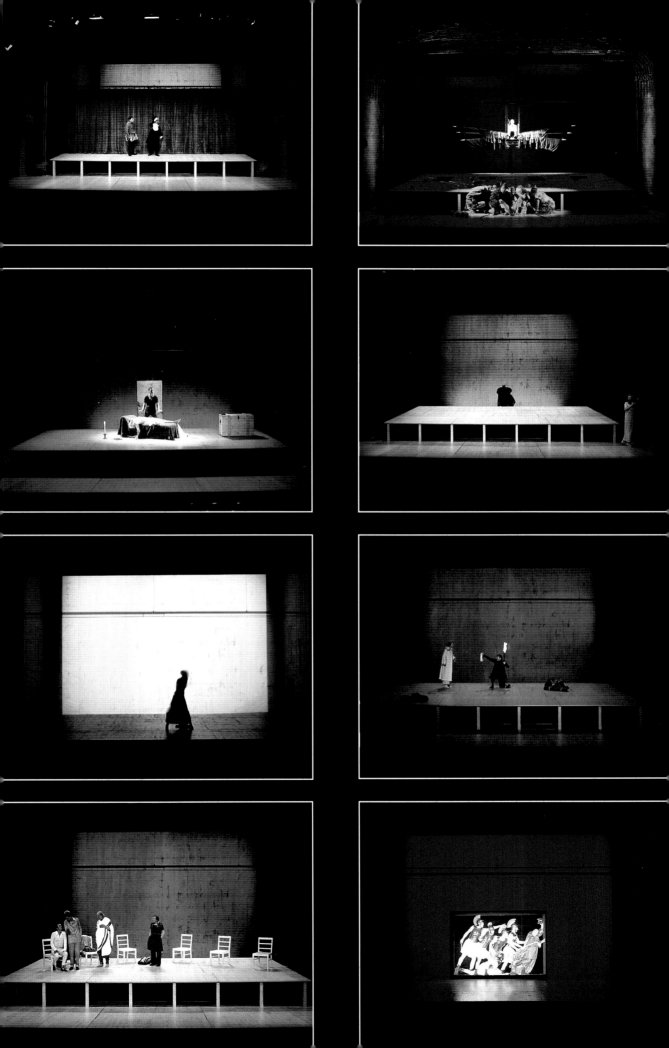

81  School of Rembrandt, *A Man Seated Reading at a Table in a Lofty Room*, no date, The National Gallery, London

## LIGHT IN PAINTING

Any visual experience is dependent on light, which does not merely enable us to see but also conveys atmosphere and drama. The effect of light can be very clearly demonstrated with the aid of some examples from painting. The intention here is not to transfer paintings on to the stage, but the examples selected can show us the possibilities that arise when working with light.

The story of light in painting is also a story of shadow, and it is not always true that we see more in light than in darkness. Artists have been addressing this central theme since the early 15th century. The following examples demonstrate how painters from different periods handled light and, especially, how they showed people in the right light.

GEORGES DE LA TOUR (1593–1652), a brilliant loner, occupies a particular place in the history of painted light. Coming to terms with light and darkness is a central theme of his work. As in the works of Edward Hopper, produced three hundred years later, night has become the refuge of the unfortunate in the painting *St Sebastian Tended by St Irene* (ill. 82). The flaming torch above the martyr's head – almost like a halo – symbolizes that life is not yet extinguished, while also serving to illuminate the event. It is the only device determining the pictorial composition, lending the image forcefulness and simplicity with its steady glow. Its light is cast calmly and evenly over all the figures and objects and in this way emphasizes their sharp, precise forms. The torch ligh extends throughout the entire composition as reflected light, holding together the depicted event. But this reflected light has the effect of having independent light sources and weakens the luminosity of

Handling Light and Colour

the original light source. There are no disturbances or distractions caused by light falling on the scene from the side or from outside. Neither a room nor a particular atmosphere are established; instead, the peace and seclusion of the situation are emphasized.

The painting from the SCHOOL OF REMBRANDT (ill. 81) forms a marked contrast with this. A clear shaft of daylight shines into the room, that is, into

Thus the veiling shadow here is just as important as the illuminating light. The strong contrast of light and shadow gives the room an impressive sense of depth, but the colouring of the light is restricted to shades of brown.

HONORÉ DAUMIER (1808–1879), who worked mainly as an illustrator and caricaturist, was influenced by this brown-based chiaroscuro painting. Tragedy and fate can be sensed in the

spectators' faces in an almost demonic, morbid fashion.

The theatre is also central to the work of the French Impressionist EDGAR DEGAS (1834–1917), though he was even more interested in the world of the concert café and the ballet, and the glamorous, magical artificial light of the metropolitan world. Unlike other painters who use the theatre in their work, Degas simply seemed to be looking for a pretext to paint light – and theatrical light in particular. Most Impressionists painted their pictures on the spot, but Degas also based his on sketches he made in his studio, which distanced his work from theatrical reality. Thus his later pictures have something visionary about them, the ballerinas have a ghostly quality, and the unreal theatrical lighting acquires an ever greater measure of independence. In our example, *Dancers at the Old Opera House* (ill. 84), the situation and the space are clearly defined by theatrically specific light from gas-powered footlights. The whole image has the effect of a snapshot. The picture captures the momentary quality in the light of the clothes and the people; the shimmer in the pieces of clothing conveys the movement of the fabrics. It is just a fleeting glimpse from the wings, without a great deal of sentimentality.

The Berlin painter LESSER URY (1861–1931) went even further in depicting artificial light and thus entered into the 20th century. What moved him most was the hectic hustle and bustle of a big city at night (ill. 86). Flickering car headlights and street lamps, reflected on the rain-wet streets, or illuminated street cafés at night were his preferred subjects. As Degas had started to do, Ury painted his visual experiences of a major modern city at the beginning of a technical age, with all its kaleidoscopic interplay of colours and light. He composed his images with lively brush strokes and powerful colours, abandoning detail in favour of atmosphere. People disappear into the darkness and can be made out at best as minimal reflections. The light forces out the individual in favour of the omnipresence of atmosphere, and thus it is not surprising that people increasingly disappear from Lesser Ury's pictures with the passage of years.

Night and day were also the subjects of work by GIORGIO DE CHIRICO (1888–1978), but he disturbed his viewers and made them feel uneasy by breaking from conventional depictions of times of day. A clock, for instance,

82 Georges de La Tour, *St Sebastian Tended by St Irene*, c. 1649, Musée du Louvre, Paris

the picture. Light handled in this way, and this kind of contrast between light and dark, was to have a great influence on stage lighting in the late 18th century. At first glance this is an empty room with nothing actually happening in it. The dramatic incidence of light from the outside suggests seclusion, but we suddenly discover a person – a man reading underneath the window. With the exception of some reflected light he is presented as a silhouette, which is a striking example of the fact that one does not have to be in the light to draw attention. Not lighting a character can often have great dramatic significance.

light in all his drawings. He often turned to the theatre and especially its lighting for the small number of paintings he produced. *The Drama* (ill. 83) shows the people involved lit by a harsh spotlight. A figure of a desperate woman in a gleaming white robe making dramatic gestures forms the centre of the picture. Although she is lit from the wings, she seems to be the actual light source in the picture, in turn illuminating the orchestra and the spectators, all the way to the back row. This removes the division between stage and auditorium, and the on-stage action is reflected in the

83 Honoré Daumier,
*The Drama*, *c.* 1860
Neue Pinakothek, Munich

It is an empty, metaphysical space without people, containing only light and objects that cast shadows. Time stands still. The horse stops one step away from the abyss. Here nobody has a chance – except on a plinth, as part of a world that does not count the hours. The statue is waiting to be redeemed from motionlessness.

The premise is completely different in the work of the American realist EDWARD HOPPER (1882–1967). Whether as daylight or artificial light, light is depicted accurately, with its own particular quality. Colour temperature and the angle of incidence establish the precise time of day, as do the reflected lights and the illuminated surfaces and structures.

Hopper adopted an idea from European Mannerism in his night pieces; the night becomes a place of refuge for the unfortunate and the abandoned. His figures are also left alone in the daytime. Light does not dissolve forms, as it does with the Impressionists – it defines them more precisely and emphasizes them at the same time. Thus the isolation of the woman in *Morning Sun* (ill. 87) is emphasized and becomes the actual subject of the picture. This statuesque loneliness and the tragedy associated with it become particularly clear in conjunction with the soulless, alienating architecture.

All these pictures show how differently light can define a situation and how the right light can, in fact, bring action into a picture. These are examples of the immense range of expressive possibilities that light has to offer. Lighting designers should look at the way in which painters use light and similarly develop a concept of their own that is precisely suited to the space and the situation.

shows midday, while low light suggests the evening sun. In his pictures, the shadows are often more powerful and seem more real than the objects that are casting them. De Chirico also played with various light sources in the painting *The Rose Tower* (ill. 85), using them like theatre spotlights. The spaces in his pictures recall the central perspective of a Renaissance stage. The pull exerted by the perspective makes us long for distance. The architecture is transformed into decoration, as though the façades and arcades have been pushed onto the stage like flats in a set in order to make us feel cramped.

84 Edgar Degas,
*Dancers at the Old Opera House*,
*c.* 1877, National Gallery of Art,
Washington D.C.

Handling Light and Colour

85  Giorgio de Chirico, *The Rose Tower*, 1913, Peggy Guggenheim Collection, Venice

86  Lesser Ury, *The Elevated Railway Station at Bülowstrasse*, 1922, private collection

## COLOUR IMPRESSIONISTS

We have now met some of the most important colour theorists. Their ideas stimulated other artists and thinkers to express their views of this field as well. Three very different personalities who, in addition to their other areas of research also addressed the subject of colour, show what range of possibilities can there are for responding to and explaining colour.

### Henri Michaux, painter and writer, 1899 – 1984

Henri Michaux's life was devoted to writing, painting and travel. These pursuits were mutually influential. It is not possible to determine whether his writing inspired his pictures or his pictures his writing. In any case his many endeavours shaped his imaginative thinking. He also saw the interplay between his creative activities as an exciting journey into imagination and inspiration.

Henri Michaux started as a writer. In 1925 he went to an exhibition including work by Paul Klee, Giorgio de Chirico and Max Ernst. Their Surrealist pictorial world of colour and form opened a new window on art for him. He did not just look at these pictures, he experienced them. Even though he had had no artistic training, one thing was clear: from then on he would try to combine his writing with painting. The conflict between these two very different expressive forms excited his passions. He tried to forge his creative adventures into a unity, to create a link with the inner world he wanted to make visible. In 1937 and 1938 he painted with dense colours on a black ground. He called the black paint his crystal ball, from which figures, heads and landscapes grew like apparitions. It is certainly possible to draw a parallel here with Rudolf Steiner's blackboard drawings. Michaux's published pictures with texts had the same subject, and he too worked on the basis that motifs in the pictures related to the texts.

Somewhat later, Michaux took to working with transparent watercolours. A profound private twist of fate caused him to produce several hundred drawings in a few weeks. Some of them contain essential moments of visionary Expressionism. He wrote fewer and fewer texts and devoted himself mainly to painting. He experienced Paul Klee's pictures in a personal and unique way: '... a line dreams, never till then had anyone let a line dream.'

Experimenting with hallucinogens – especially mescaline – altered his sensibility and his consciousness and is the explanation behind many of his drawings and paintings. The forms of painterly presentation and the expressive force of the words he wrote acquired a different quality. His mescaline drawings have a very specific morphology and influenced his artistic work into his late period.

There are many ways in which consciousness can be altered. Experience of this kind opens up the path to a person's inner self: the everyday covering is stripped off and the subconscious lends a new dimension to the imagination. Colours and their forms are perceived differently, and this can range from meticulous detail to generous, soaring euphoric visions. For most people this kind of journey into the subconscious is entirely harmless, so long as it is undertaken in a spirit of orderly interest. A person under the influence of mescaline behaves very calmly and is interested in the spectrum of his own experience, whereas a person under the influence of alcohol can often become loud and aggressive.

In this creative period Michaux found writing restrictive, but drawing and painting liberating. In an homage to Giorgio de Chirico, Michaux wrote:

The opiate that stops the pain in the entrails / also stops time / makes the hours longer / builds the tower / and calls back the centuries that have passed / hands the city to the temples and the gods.

## Magic

Many people try to strive toward spiritual creations by using the fakir method. This is an error.

Everyone must find his own way. If I want to make a live frog appear (a dead frog is easy), then I do not do any violence to myself. I simply turn to painting a picture in my mind. I sketch the banks of a stream, choosing my greens very carefully, and then I wait for the stream. After a time I hold a stick down over the bank; if it gets wet, I am relieved, I only need to keep on being patient for a short time and soon the frogs will appear, jumping and diving.

If the stick does not start to get wet, then you have to give it up. /
Then I make the night, a very warm night, and when I /
walk through the countryside with a lantern it is rarely very long before they start to croak. /
It has nothing to do with this, but I have to say it, it is going to happen to me, it is very close: I'm going blind.

### Rudolf Steiner, founder of anthroposophy, 1861–1925

Rudolf Steiner, the founder of anthroposophy, his universal spiritual philosophy of people and the world, had a profound effect on many aspects of life in the first quarter of the 20th century. His teaching and world view meant changes of direction in medicine, science, society, economics and education. This was not an alternative, but intended to extend and complement existing sciences. His ideas on education (Waldorf schools), medicine, agriculture (biological and dynamic) and in the social field are once more gaining increased attention and recognition today. He also pointed to new ways forward in the realm of art. He was creatively active himself and stimulated artists in their own work, both in his courses and by his own example.

Steiner held over 5,000 lectures, which he often accompanied with blackboard drawings. These drawings do not look antiquated today – his painting and drawing techniques were well ahead of his time. These fascinating and sensuous images, which certainly served to inspire later artists, remained largely unavailable to the public for over 70 years. As their themes were closely linked with his lectures, it is almost impossible to analyse them in their own right. Steiner would draw during his lectures, working in coloured chalk on black paper that was fastened to the blackboard. There are over 1,000 of these drawings, each measuring 1 x 1.5 m. They are now published in a 28-volume complete edition.

Steiner's lectures also contain interesting points about the various qualities and properties of colours. Thus he distinguishes four 'picture colours' and three 'glowing colours'. The picture colours are black, green, peach-blossom and white; black stands for the spiritual image of death (of minerals), green presents the dead image of life (the vegetable kingdom), peach-blossom (flesh-colour) the living image of the soul (animal kingdom), and white is the

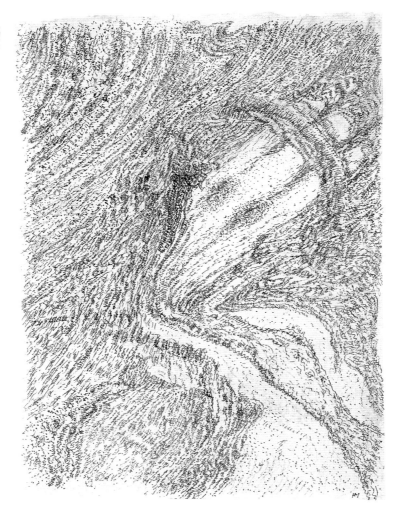

88  Henri Michaux, *Untitled.* From the series of mescaline drawings, 1969

'External warmth, the warmth we feel when we touch things, the external warmth carried in the air – if this is to be absorbed by the human organism, it must be transformed in such a way that the actual warmth itself in the human being, if I may express myself like this, is to be found on another plane from the one outside. If I define the level of warmth that outer warmth has in this way, then, when it is absorbed by us, it must be inwardly somewhat transformed so that the organism intervenes everywhere where we are not, in the outer warmth. The organism must intervene in even the tiniest quantum of warmth. Now, imagine I am going to walk through the cold, and because the cold is too great, or because the cold is flickering in moving air or in a draught, I am not capable of transforming the world's warmth into my own warmth as quickly as would be necessary. And this puts me at risk of being warmed by the warmth of the world like a piece of wood or even like a stone, things that are warmed from the outside. This should not be. I may not be exposed to the danger of allowing external warmth to flow into me merely as if I were an object. I must always be in a position to be able to seize the warmth immediately from places on my skin and to make it my own. If I am not able to do that, then a cold will set in. That is the inner process of a cold. A cold is poisoning by external warmth, when the organism has not taken possession of it.'
Translated from: Rudolf Steiner, *Der Mensch als Zusammenklang des schaffenden, bildenden und gestaltenden Weltenwortes. Zwölf Vorträge* (GA 230). Eleventh lecture, 10 November 1923, Dornach/Switzerland 1993[7]

spiritual image of the mind (human kingdom).

The colours yellow, blue and red he sees as glowing colours, as something shines within them: yellow ('the glow of the mind'), shines outwards from the centre, making itself brighter, unable to tolerate any limitation. In contrast with this, blue ('the glow of the spirit') requires the strongest saturation on the outside, and wants to make itself brighter towards the inside. Red ('the glow of the living') occupies the space evenly, 'it wants neither to shine nor to block itself, it does not want to run away, it asserts itself' (see Rudolf Steiner, *Das Wesen der Farben*, GA 291, Dornach 1991).

Steiner's concept of eurhythmics is an entirely new art of movement, which he continued to develop from its early stage in 1912 until the end of his life. Eurhythmics is an anthroposophical art of movement and a form of therapy in which the spoken word, vocal and instrumental music can be translated into expressive movement. There are numerous institutions that teach it today, and guest performances by artists attract public interest all over the world. Eurhythmics tries to express everything that language, poetry or music contain in the form of laws, motion and sound through the instrument of the human body. Steiner called this new art form a continuation of Goethe's view of metamorphosis (transformation of forms) in the field of

human movement. Thus he calls sound eurhythmics, which takes the form of a recitation, a 'visible language,' and eurhythmics designed as a piece of music is known as 'visible song.'

Steiner developed an entirely new approach to the art of lighting for presenting eurhythmics on the stage in the years after 1920: light-eurhythmics. The eurhythmically enacted poems and pieces of music were to be accompanied by changing coloured lighting. But the light was not projected onto the stage in concentrated form, using spotlights, the usual practice in theatres. Instead it was designed to fill the whole stage with its colours as evenly as possible, thus creating a light-space that can enclose the sequences of movement. In order to achieve the required objective of soft, diffuse, but extremely intensive lighting for the whole space, a new kind of lighting rig had to be devised for the stage in the first Goetheanum theatre in Dornach near Basle. This was a difficult task given the technical facilities of the day, as it was not possible to use normal stage lighting equipment. Steiner commissioned a young colleague who was well versed in electrical questions to solve this problem. His name was Ehrenfried Pfeiffer, and he later went on to become the first lighting director for the Goetheanum. Pfeiffer developed the whole rig to suit Steiner's purposes. To produce an even effect that was as close as possible to daylight, spotlights with

convex rather than concave reflectors were built. They were also covered with a layer of white chalk to achieve the maximum possible diffusion. The light sources were mounted at a height of six metres on both sides of the stage, and the footlights were also extended across the full width of the stage. Thus it is easy to calculate how many lanterns were needed to equip the main stage of the Goetheanum in Dornach (stage dimensions: inner frame width 24 m, depth 17.5 m, height 22 m).

In order to achieve the desired intensity and variety of effects created by mixing colours, six colours were available both from above and from downstage: white, red, yellow, blue, green and violet. In this way an infinite number of hues and nuances could be produced according to the colour mix and the brightness. Steiner was interested not only in the effect of the space filled with coloured light, but also with the performers' clothes and veils, and the way in which, to the spectator, their colours could be made to change, stand out or almost disappear. In this case, Goethe's colour theory was applied in the theatre.

How was this coloured lighting used for eurhythmic performances? Steiner himself did not lay down any rules but always designed according to his immediate artistic instincts. There are lighting notes for over 400 poems and numerous pieces of music, written

'For someone who looks at it with imagination, the whole rainbow shows an outpouring of the spiritual, a disappearance of the spiritual. In fact it shows something that is like a spiritual roller, quite wonderfully. And at the same time one notes in these spiritual essences that, by emerging from there, they are emerging with great fear, and when they go in there they are going in with quite unconquerable courage. If one looks for a red-yellow colour, then fear pours out, and if one looks for a blue-violet colour then one begins to feel: there, everything is alive, like courage. It is already possible to say, if one approaches the sages of the 11th, 12th, 13th centuries, then one must understand such things. Not even those who come later can understand them any more, they cannot understand Albertus Magnus, when they read him with the knowledge of today. They have to read him with a kind of knowledge that is aware that such spiritual matters were still a reality for him; only then will one understand how he uses words, how he expresses himself.' Translated from: Rudolf Steiner, *Mysterienstätten des Mittelalters. Zehn Vorträge* (GA 233a). First lecture, 4 January 1924, Dornach/Switzerland 1991[5]

down by Steiner himself or by Ehrenfried Pfeiffer. Steiner often noted them along with the colours of the performers' clothes and veils. Thus for Goethe's poem *Gefunden* (Found) he gave the following instructions:

'Ich ging im Walde
so für mich hin,
und nichts zu suchen,          white above
das war mein Sinn.          blue below
(I walked in the wood
just for my own sake,
my intention was
to look for nothing.)

Im Schatten sah ich
ein Blümchen stehn,
wie Sterne leuchtend,          add red
wie Äuglein schön.          above
(I saw a little flower
standing in the shade
shining like stars,
beautiful as little eyes.)

Ich wollt es brechen,
da sagt es fein:
Soll ich zum Welken          add blue
gebrochen sein?          below
(I wanted to pick it,
it said gently:

Am I to be picked
in order to wither?)

Ich grub's mit allen
den Würzlein aus,
zum Garten trug ich's          white below,
am hübschen Haus.          red above
(I dug it up
with all its little roots.,
I carried it to the garden
by the pretty house)

Und pflanzt es wieder
am stillen Ort;
nun schweigt es immer          add red
und blüht so fort.          below
(And planted it again
in that quiet place;
now it is always silent
And carries on flowering like that.)

Costumes:
I blue veil, yellow dress
II green veil, red dress.'

The poem was enacted by two performers. Usually one lighting state was retained for a full stanza, while colour changes within a stanza were the exception. Mixing notes were often given for the lighting as well, for example:

'bright light = bottom half and top full moderate white below = the colour at the top is dominant and the white below simply a counterpoint, without destroying the colour above.'

When accompanying music, lighting changes according to the characteristics of the piece. As a rule, the intention was to keep the light as calm as possible, but with changes from one colour to another happening quickly. This demanded a great deal of artistic empathy from the person responsible for lighting. Steiner wanted to use lighting to add a further artistic element to his works based on movement by using his coloured lighting effects. The colours were intended to reveal the basic psychological mood of a poem or piece of music. Thus moods of joy, cheerfulness, activity, or major keys are more suited to reds, yellows, whites; mourning, melancholy or minor keys more to the darker colours. Steiner firmly rejected colour symbolism, or even naturalistic colour rendering, of the kind that might emerge within the content of a text (blue sea = blue) as inartistic.

The following statement, taken from Steiner's lectures, shows how he felt

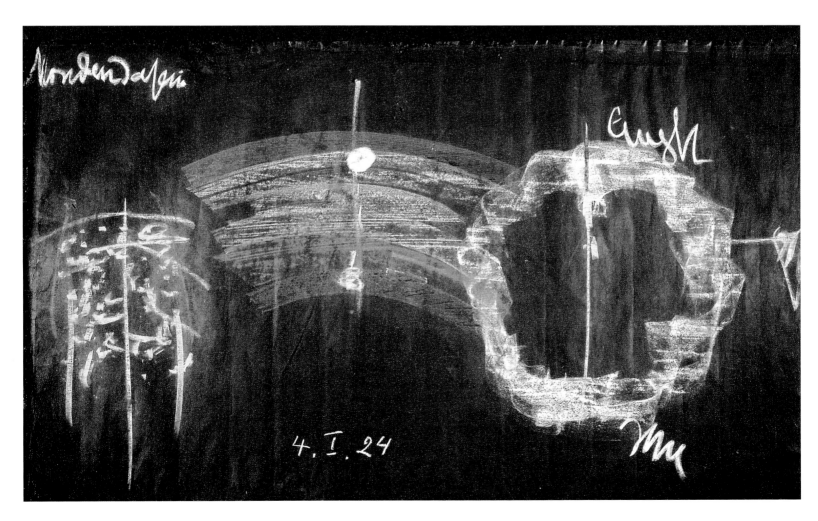

audiences should understand coloured lighting in eurhythmic performances:

Those revered spectators who have frequently seen our eurhythmic performances here will have noticed that recently we have tried to add lighting effects to the stage picture created by the movements and momentum of individuals or groups of people. This lighting is not to be related naturalistically to individual gestures; just as music and melody have to be sought out in the sequence of the individual notes, the same should be apparent here in eurhythmics in the sequence of the lighting effects, which is what we are seeking to achieve. The lively eurhythmic image is placed within suitable lighting sequences, which now become a kind of lighting eurhythmics in their own right.

## Ludwig Wittgenstein, philosopher, 1889–1951

Wittgenstein often said himself that the point of his writings was not that they should simply be understood. No, someone else should reconstruct what he had read at a later date and then be pleased that he, Ludwig Wittgenstein, had already formulated it.

Wittgenstein's career falls into very different periods and offers a number of explanations as to why his philosophical observations are stated incomprehensibly and, in part, polemically.

His training – he studied mechanical engineering and mathematics – should certainly be seen as the basis of his later thought processes when interpreting his philosophical works. He wrote his most important work, the logical and philosophical treatise *Tractatus Logico-Philosophicus,* at an early age. Most of his intellectual work was produced in England, where he also worked as a professor of philosophy. Wittgenstein was restless and often very discontented with himself; he worked as a primary school teacher for a time and also as an architect and amateur sculptor. He volunteered for war service in 1914; in the Second World War he was a lab assistant in the medical service. He often visited Norway and his home town of Vienna, as well as the United States. He continued to work on his various writings throughout his travels.

In 1930 Bertrand Russell noted that Wittgenstein maintained that a colour that is blue could also be red or green. Russell found it wrong to assert that it is one of these colours, and that it

would be nonsense to assert that it is loud or shrill, as Wittgenstein did. Wittgenstein called a series of possibilities of this kind a 'space'. Thus, Russell continued, there is a 'space' for colours and a 'space' for sounds. There are various relationships between the colours, and they represent the geometry of this 'space'.

Wittgenstein worked as an architect in Vienna from 1926 to 1928. It seems most unusual for a philosopher to have wanted to involve himself in such a technical craft. He set himself the highest standards in this new work as well, working just as painstakingly as he did in research in his own profession. The house in Kundmanngasse (Palais Wittgenstein) in Vienna was built to sketches by Paul Engelmann, combining Wittgenstein's philosophical thinking with architecture.

It was based on a neo-classical building shape, divided into encapsulated cubes of different sizes and constructed largely of stone, metal and glass. The spaces were generously proportioned, and the windows were arranged to admit the maximum of light into the unassertive rooms, which were furnished in a sensitive but Spartan fashion. Space was distributed, and floor and wall areas divided in a spirit of proportional harmony. The transparent spaces had light and colour as the key features of their decor, and Wittgenstein was also involved elsewhere with designing all the details of the fittings such as radiators, and handles for doors and windows.

His basic craft training was most useful to him in this creative context, and so was his view of the world, which had been perfected within itself and which made an unmistakable impact on his geometrical forms. He designed the electrical system himself and he reduced the light fittings to holders with one bulb. His construction designs, using screwed light-section steel for the doors and windows, required new and laborious structural variants.

Wittgenstein's philosophical insights were often formed on a mathematical basis. His *Bemerkungen über Farbe* (Remarks on Colour), one of his last pieces of writing, was published in the year he died. It is written in very simple, very clear language, and yet it is still extremely difficult to find an overall pattern of meaning. To the unprepared reader, his words seem to exist in isolation, and he often attaches questions addressed to himself to his statements. Wittgenstein's remarks on

colour and light are detached from reality and have nothing to do with our scientific insights. He tried to go his own way. A remark made about his most important work, the aforementioned *Tractatus Logico-Philosophicus,* also applies to his philosophical interpretation of colour. 'This book will perhaps only be understood by someone who has himself once had the thoughts expressed in it – or similar thoughts.'

The following is translated from Wittgenstein's *Bemerkungen über Farbe:*

26. It is suspicious that some people think they can discern three primary colours, and some four. Some insist that green is an intermediate colour between blue and yellow, but I, for example, feel that this is wrong, quite apart from any experience I have had.

Blue and yellow, like red and green, appear to me as contrasts – but that may simply be because I am used to seeing them as opposite points on the chromatic circle.

Why is the question about the number of pure colours important to me (psychologically, so to speak)?
27. I seem to see *one* thing that is important logically: If we call green an intermediate colour between blue and yellow, then it must also be possible to say, for example, what an only slightly bluish yellow is called or a blue that is only slightly yellow. These expressions mean absolutely nothing to me, but might they not mean something to someone else?

So if someone were to describe the colour of a wall to me as reddish yellow, I could understand that in such a way that I would be able to pick out one that was approximately right from a number of samples. But if someone described a colour to be a somewhat bluish yellow, I could not show him a sample in that way. Here we tend to say that we can imagine a colour in one case but not in the other. This is a misleading expression, however, because in this case it is not necessary to think of an image emerging before the inner eye.
28. As there is such a thing as perfect pitch, and such a thing as people who do not have it, it would also be possible to think that there is a whole range of different susceptibilities to seeing colours.

For example, compare the concept of deep colour with warm colour. Should everyone be familiar with

Handling Light and Colour

warm and cold colours? Unless you simply teach them to call a particular disjunction of colours the one or the other.

For example, would it not be possible for a painter to have absolutely no concept of four pure colours, indeed to find it ridiculous to talk about such things?

34. Things can be red-hot and white-hot, but what would brown-hot or grey-hot look like? Why can these not be seen as a weaker degree of being white-hot?

35. It is said that light is colourless. If so, then in the sense that numbers are colourless.

42. We talk about dark red light, but not about black-red light.

65. Brown light. What if someone were to suggest a brown traffic light?

76. Runge says that there are transparent and opaque colours. But this is not taken as a reason for painting a piece of green glass in a picture in a different green from a piece of green cloth.

90. I doubt that Goethe's remarks about the characters of colours could be useful for a painter. Hardly for a house-painter.

152. Would it not be possible for gloss black and matt black to have different colour names?

234. Semi-darkness could be painted in semi-darkness. And the 'right lighting' for a scene could be semi-darkness (stage painting).

91 Ludwig Wittgenstein, hall on the first floor of the Palais Wittgenstein, Vienna 1929. With 200 W bulb and silk shade as ceiling illumination

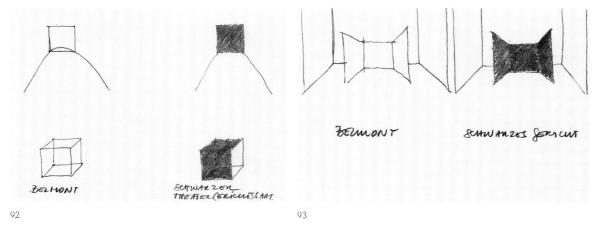

92

93

# I WALK WITH MY LANTERN . . .

by Herbert Kapplmüller

*He who knows white,*
*but survives in black,*
*is the world's measure*
*                    Lao Tse*

The end has come for Belmont, Portia's homogeneous, closed, bright and immaterial world, a white cube 4 x 4 x 4 m, in Shakespeare's *Merchant of Venice*. Bassanio has chosen the right casket, and Portia goes to Venice as a theatrical judge who is all too obsessed with words. Two stagehands with buckets of paint and large brushes transform the white space into a black

space – PAUSE – a courtroom in Venice (ill. 92, 93).

This theatrical sequence reminds me of the dull and yet lightly swishing sound made by drawing velvet curtains, the rattle as roller blinds are closed, the click as Venetian blinds are flicked shut, and the banging of window shutters closing in bright middle-class homes throughout the 19th century. It is reminiscent of the parallels between windows and lamps; back then, one suddenly regarded the natural daylight entering the room through the window as aggressively

white, like a naked electric light bulb (ill. 94–96).

Attempts were made to moderate artificial light by using white muslin and gauze, and to diffuse the cold austerity of daylight by diffusing it into the room. Windows and lamps were covered up. Lampshades, intended to mitigate the increasing intensity of artificial light, and curtains, intended to mitigate the increasingly perceived aggressiveness of natural light, became thicker and darker at the same time.

The black court on stage and the completely darkened middle-class room remind us of the problems encountered by the citizens of Schilda, who fell over each other in the windowless town hall and gave themselves bloody noses:

When the work was finished / the Lales wanted to go into their town hall / and dedicate the same in the honour of all Stultorum / and then subsequently in the name of all fools to try / what it would be like to have their first council meeting in there: but when they all went in with all due deference / ecce vide look peer see gawp squint Velte videte / it was utterly and completely dark there / so that they could scarcely hear one another. About which thing they were not a little afraid / and they could not wonder enough / what the cause might be / whether perhaps something had been missed out in the building / so that the light was thrown down and stopped.

Who knows / whether the light and the day could not be carried in a sack / just as water is carried in a bucket. None of us has ever tried to do it: that is why something is missing / and so we will stand by that. If it succeeds / then we will have all of the credit / and will reap great praise as inventors of this art. But if it does not work / then it will be quite serviceable and convenient for our plans of foolery.

This counsel pleased all the Lales to such an extent / that they decided / to follow it with all due haste. And so for this reason after midday / as the sun was shining at its best / they all came to follow their oath for the new town hall / each with a vessel / so that as they thought they could capture the day and carry it in. And others also brought with them / picks shovels / hoes / forks and other things / because they were anxious / that no mistakes should be made. So as soon as the bells had

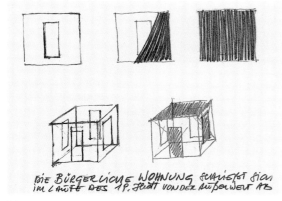

94

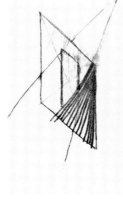

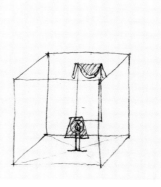

95

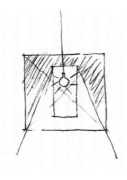

96

chimed one / then one of them is said to have seen his miracle / as they all started to work. Many of them had long sacks / and let the sun shine in to them down to the bottom / then quickly fastened them up / and ran into the building with them / to shake out the day. And they convinced themselves / that the sacks were heavier to carry / than before when they had been empty. And others did just the same / with other covered vessels / like pots / kettles / tubs / and that kind of thing. One of them loaded the day into a basket with a pitchfork / the other with a shovel; others dug it out of the earth. One Lale in particular should not be forgotten / who thought he could catch the day with a mouse-trap / and thus take it by force and bring it into the house. To cut a long story short: everyone did / as his foolish head suggested and put it to him.

And such things they did then the whole thing through / because the sun had shone / with such zeal and earnestness / that they all became weary / and collapsed and succumbed with the heat. But their work achieved so little / as before the enormous giants / who piled up great mountains / in the hope of storming the heavens. And so finally they said: and now it would have been a fine art / if we had been successful.

Translated from: *Lale· und Schiltbürgerbuch*, 1597/98 (ill. 97)

Is this the same darkness that blind Josette is trying to come to terms with in *Des aveugles* by Hervé Guibert?

When Josette was ten years old her mother shut her up in a room full of obstacles, as part of her education. Josette immediately sensed the smell of a man in the room, and she started to question and threaten him. But there was no man in the room, and she thought of a snake, she saw snakes in rather the same way that sighted people imagine prehistoric animals, she did not want to challenge it, she just didn't want to be stung or bitten, she wanted to make herself as small as possible. She had not moved since coming into the brightly lit room. She wanted to feel her way along the nearest wall and thus make her way around the unfamiliar room. She wanted to cry, to make her mother feel sorry for her.

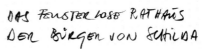

97

She crouched down on the floor, urine accumulated in her bladder, she held it back and stood up again. She stretched out both hands and threw herself forwards, but she immediately stumbled because one of the prism-shaped obstacles that her mother had set up for her was only hip-high. She was immediately aware of the edge and felt down one of the sides to find an opening, but the first surface ran into another one that was equally closed. It did not occur to her that this was a hollow object, but thought of a machine with a hidden trigger mechanism, and she went round the pyramid three times before discovering that she could turn it round by gripping one of its edges between her thighs, and she found herself touching a square surface. That would be something I could drum on, she said to herself, but this is not the right moment to do it. She carried on exploring and took good care not to move in a straight line, she moved around all over the place and drew back every time she got close to a wall again. In this way she failed to notice any of the jelly-like creatures that her mother had stuck on the walls. Her right foot, which she always moved forward first, hit a sphere, which rolled away. I would have done better to stay with my mountain, she thought to herself, and went on, but her foot didn't find the sphere again. She went down on all fours to feel for it, she imagined that she was in an anthill or a sewerage system and fell asleep. When she woke up, she was hugging the sphere to her stomach, then she rocked herself on it, and pulled herself forwards with both hands to make it roll underneath her. I am a shell, she said to the sphere, and you are my tortoise, poor tortoise. She

kept the sphere with her. After she had worked her way around the room in all directions she realized that she had not come across the pyramid again, and that at the same time – she felt it quite clearly – a new object had eluded her. She put her sphere down on the floor, perhaps they are all magnetic, she said to herself, but the sphere did not move. She made a quick calculation in her head and came to the conclusion that the object that she had not yet touched must be three steps to her left and three steps behind her. It was a cube, and she sat down on it. The pyramid was now within her reach, she pushed in its bottom and put it on her head like a hat, then she picked up the sphere in her hands again and waited. She'll come back and fetch me, that idiot, she said to herself. Her mother was waiting behind the door, she had a bag of cotton wool and a bottle of tincture of arnica ready for the bruises, but Josette had not bumped herself once. You'll deal with life all right, said her mother, who had taken such trouble making the three wretched cardboardshapes. (ill. 97)

Translated from: Hervé Guibert, *Des aveugles*, Gallimard 1985

And I am sitting under a heavily covered table in incomprehensible darkness. The power of imagination is greatly enhanced in this silence and darkness. The senses of hearing, taste, smell and touch become much more sensitive. The attempt to create this lost world of daylight in the mind's eye reminds me of the old stage designing method of using white drawing on a black ground (ill. 98).

But now and again a slight draught stirs the cloth on the table, so that thin, horizontal cracks of light open up,

98

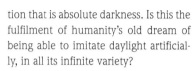

99

surrounding me in a square and thus mapping out the dimensions of the different spaces. (ill. 99).

Here, I am reminded of Louis Kahn's note. He set himself the task of drawing a picture in which light was visible, but then realized that where there was black, there was no light. And the more he put his pen to paper, the more strokes he made, the more he came to understand where the light was not – that is, where he had drawn black strokes. Only then did the picture become brilliant, illuminated, to him.

I am pleased with the light-filled bag in my hand, which is glowing red. It is a portable lamp, a mobile spotlight, in the black stage model box. I am dreaming about Lucio Fontana's neon installations, Picasso's light drawings and about UV light and UV colour in the black theatre. Suddenly the Bremen City Minstrels' cat leaps at the face of the spy sent by the robbers who have been frightened away and scratches it when the man comes too near. He mis-

the light coming in through the tent entrance is dazzling, and the dagger in the Philistine's hand in Rembrandt's *Blinding of Samson* from the Städelsches Kunstinstitut in Frankfurt thrusts into Samson's pain-wracked face (ill. 100).

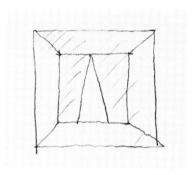

100

tion that is absolute darkness. Is this the fulfilment of humanity's old dream of being able to imitate daylight artificially, in all its infinite variety?

The theatre went for a long time without light coming from above, light endowing everything with brightness and form. Baroque stage lighting, which was above all lighting based on the central perspective, was discredited even in the 18th century. Bourgeois realism, with its ancestry in 17th-century Dutch painting, demanded concrete handling of light in the manner of chiaroscuro painting. Theatre lighting was not yet capable of imitating the said Rembrandt picture, those relationships between light and shade on the stage. Stage lighting as developed in the Baroque theatre, with fundamental tenets that survived into the 19th century, was arranged with rigid symmetry and operated at very low light levels. It was thus capable only of creating a frame of light. This frame was formed from three lighting positions: side lighting, located in the proscenium frame and in the wings – one wing lit the other wing; the footlights, which lit the performers from the front and from below; border lighting, which was mounted on the proscenium frame and among the borders – one border lit the next border. Thus the centre of the stage remained largely unlit. E.T.A. Hoffmann had been quick to remark sarcastically that the actors lit from below would distort into repulsive grimacing masks.

Technicians and theatre people continued to try to achieve something that was still technically impossible – to replace lighting from the footlights below with lighting from above. Antoine-Laurent Lavoisier (who developed the theory of combustion in 1770) already had ideas on this subject: 'The various day-

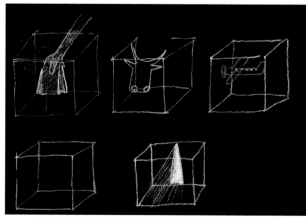

101

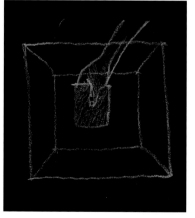

102

takes its glowing eyes for pieces of coal in the dark (ill. 101, 102).

A beam of light penetrates through the central slit in the model curtain, thus lighting up the whole model. So

A beam of light tears me away from the darkness under the table. The sun is present in my stage model in such a way that it dissolves any visible quality and creates a bright space without loca-

Handling Light and Colour

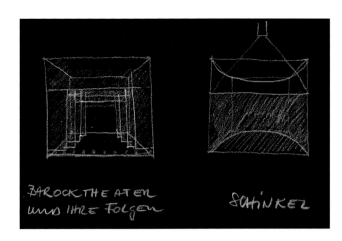

BAROCKTHEATER UND IHRE FOLGEN    SCHINKEL

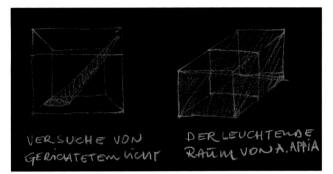

VERSUCHE VON GERICHTETEM LICHT    DER LEUCHTENDE RAUM VON A. APPIA

103 (above), 104

light moods can be conveyed faithfully: bright sunlight, the dark lighting of a thunderstorm, sunrise or sunset, night, a full moon etc. All this can be achieved very straightforwardly with the aid of parabolic, or even simple, spherical reflectors, mounted in the stage arch over the forestage.'

This new lighting marked the end of stage painting as the old way of creating an illusion (painted skies on canvas). It was replaced by architecture, whose three dimensions responded to the natural effect of electric spotlights (ill. 103).

Adolphe Appia called real light, as opposed to painted light, living light. He made stage lighting into his very own design device. Appia created a real space for his performance and activated this with light. In this way he made a clear and logical distinction between general lighting and accentuating light. Action on the stage was determined by the creative force of light, and the part that it played in the design: for example, it could establish the time of day, by using steep or shallow incident light, by representing the moon, torches or things of that kind.

Edward Gordon Craig also designed a lighting rig – the first lighting bridge. He suggested using the spotlight in every way, in every direction, to fade in and out, to disperse or focus light, to colour the stage. The flux of light was

for him a part of the stage design itself, to highlight individual features of the actors against the darkness.

Appia felt that the only logical conclusion for productions using these new possibilities appropriately was three-dimensional staging with flexible lighting design. Lighting that made a contribution to design based on Appia's principles was first used in Hellerau near Dresden. He installed spotlights in the ceiling of the auditorium that were visible only when in use, as well as a gigantic shading system that was effectively inverted, that is, light fell on it from the outside. A contemporary of Appia's wrote: 'The auditorium in Hellerau was a glowing space, rather than a space that had been lit. Today, light from overcast skies outside no longer comes in the shape of cones, which for centuries the Catholic heaven caused to shine mildly through the blue between the parting clouds; instead we have a vertical, two-dimensional movement that is of course invisible' (ill. 104).

First-class dioptric colours:

The space that we consider empty would inevitably have the quality of transparency as far as we are concerned. Now if that space fills up in such a way that our eye is not aware of what is filling it, this produces a material, more or less physical, transparent medium that can be like air or gas, liquid or also solid.

Pure translucent opacity is derived from the transparent. It can thus present itself to us in what I see to be a threefold fashion. Complete opacity is white, the most indifferent, lightest, first non-transparent filler for a space.

Transparency itself, seen empirically, is already the first degree of opacity. Further degrees of opacity, up to non-transparent white, are infinite.

Translated from: Johann Wolfgang von Goethe, *Farbenlehre*, 1810

This glowing, immaterial and shadow-free space was first realized on a proscenium stage by Max Keller at the Münchner Kammerspiele. He makes it absolutely clear to the audience that when the curtain goes up they see an image and experience the space only by means of directed and moving light and the actors' actions (ill. 105).

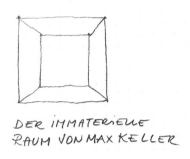

DER IMMATERIELLE RAUM VON MAX KELLER

105

Images have not been structured illusionistically since the days of Cézanne and Cubism. Not a depiction of reality, but the image as image, as its own reality, as the thing itself. Cubism invented the fourth dimension in the image. Juxtaposing three-dimensional simultaneity in two dimensions makes visible the time that one needs, for example, to see every surface of a cube when walking round it, or a face

106

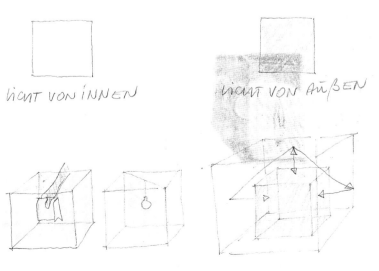

LICHT VON INNEN          LICHT VON AUßEN

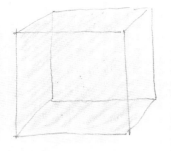

KuWait NACH DEM GOLF KRIEG

KuWAit VORm GOLF KRIEG

107

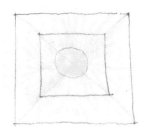

SONNENFINSTERNIS 1842

108

109–111 Ill. right:
*Le Roi Arthus*
Bregenz Festival, 1996

head on and in profile (multiplane). This is the basis on which we work today. Have we theatre people and our audiences ever thought of and looked at things as a logical conclusion of this?

Hans Sedlmayr, the renowned Austrian art historian, saw this supposedly Promethean theft like this:

Light has been eliminated by colour since Cézanne. All the dignity, power and force of light, which used to be independent of colour and had precedence over it, have been transferred to colour. These qualities have effectively been given substance here on earth, but at the same time have ignited to create terrible apocalyptic eruptions of colour. Now colour becomes the surrogate of light, indeed of inner light.

Translated from: Hans Sedlmayr, *Der Tod des Lichts*, 1964

Ever since I installed a stage-lighting power station under my desk, I have been sitting in my lantern – happy in the light-filled bag – BLACK – astonished about the wonderful light coming from the outside, perfect inside, and evenly lit (ill. 106).

During the eclipse of the sun on 8 July 1842, and in the daytime sky of Kuwait, darkened by clouds of smoke, cubes were transformed in the same way, but on a gigantic scale. The bright, daylight exterior (white cube) became the largest gigantic interior (black cube), illuminating it is as bright as day by the burning torches of the oil-fields (ill. 107, 108).

Adalbert Stifter wrote on the same theme of that eclipse:

Finally the effects became visible on earth as well, and increasingly, the narrower the glowing sickle in the heavens became; the river did not shimmer any more, but became a taffeta-grey band, dull shadows lay all around, the swallows became uneasy, the beautiful, gentle glow of the sky was extinguished, as though it was being dulled by a breath, a cool breeze began to blow, so that we could feel it, an indescribably strange but leaden light brooded over the meadows, there was no movement more in the play of light over the woods, and peace lay upon them, not the peace of slumber, but that of impotence – an ever greater pallor

poured over the countryside, which stiffened more and more – the shadows of our forms lay empty and meaningless against the walls, faces became ashen – this gradual dying was distressing, amidst the earlier freshness of the morning. All at once the afterworld had disappeared and this one back again, a single drop of light squeezed out at the upper edge light white-hot molten metal, and we had our own world back – it thrust out, this drop, as though the sun itself was extraordinarily pleased that it had won, a sunbeam immediately shone down, a second found itself room – but before we had time to shout: 'Ah!' at the first flash of the first atom, the masked world had disappeared and ours was back again.

'When the lamp is shattered
The light in the dust lies dead'
*Percy Bysshe Shelley*

Herbert Kapplmüller
Designer and director, holds the chair
of stage and costume design at the
Mozarteum University, Salzburg

Handling Light and Colour

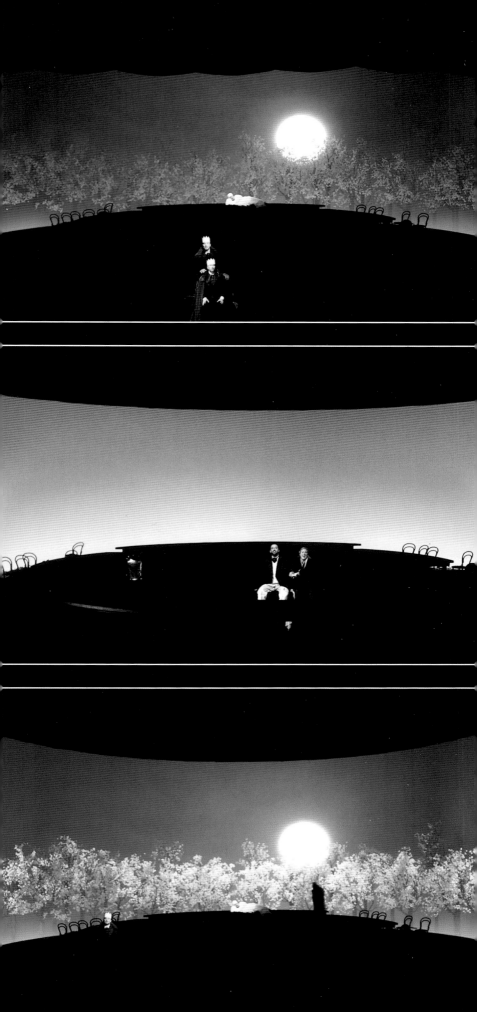

112/113 Ill. top:
Carl Sternheim, *The Snob*, director: Hans-Reinhard Müller, set designer: Jürgen Rose, Münchner Kammerspiele, 1983

114–116 Ill. bottom:
J.W. v. Goethe, *Torquato Tasso*, director: Ernst Wendt, set designer: Johannes Schütz, Münchner Kammerspiele, 1981

Anything affecting the direction, concentration or dispersion of light in the theatre is determined by the physical laws of optics. It is therefore necessary to know how these laws relate to the devices used in stage lighting. It is not just the familiar lens, but above all the combinations of lenses and also the reflector that help to realize all the various possibilities.

### Basic concepts

• OPTICAL AXIS: Line connecting the centres of curvature of all the reflecting and refracting surfaces of a centred system; centre lines for lens combinations; constructional axis for reflectors.

• FOCAL POINT: Point on the optical axis at which incident rays parallel with the optical axis converge after refraction or reflection.

• FOCAL LENGTH: Distance from a lens or a lens system to the focal point of the refracted rays.

Light is a form of energy that can be transmitted without a solid medium. An *optical medium* is matter through which light passes and with which it interacts. *Optical density* causes a change of speed within a medium. The *refractive index* (n) identifies this extremely important material quality. This is the ratio of the speed of light in a vacuum to that in the medium concerned. Refraction is dependent upon the medium itself, the wavelength of the light, the temperature and, especially in gaseous and liquid media, the pressure.

When beams of light pass from one medium into another, they change their direction according to the refractive index of that medium. They are refracted from their original direction towards the optical axis or away from it. Dispersal of beams of light within a medium is always linear. If two media with different refractive indexes are traversed, the medium with the higher refractive index has a *higher optical density* and the medium with the lower refractive index a *lower optical density*. A material is known as a homogenous medium if the direction of all the light passing through it remains the same.

The following are refractive indices for some important substances, disregarding special pressures or temperatures:

| | |
|---|---|
| Air: | n = 1.00 |
| Water: | n = 1.33 |
| Glass: | n = 1.45–1.8 |
| Diamond: | n = 2.42 |

When the beams refracted by an optical medium converge, this point is known as the *focal point*. This term is also used for the convergent beams created by a concave reflector. The distance between a refracting or reflecting medium and the focal point is known as the *focal length*.

## REFLECTION – SPHERICAL REFLECTORS

### Reflection
A beam of light is reflected if it does not penetrate a medium, but is deflected

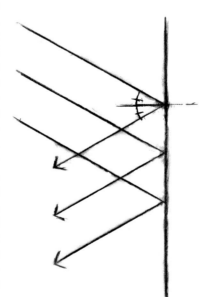

118 Reflection from a plane surface

wholly or partly by its surface. The incident and the reflected beam have a common angle to the axis of incidence: angle of incidence = angle of reflection. If the angle of incidence is 0°, the light will be reflected back in the original direction.

### Reflection from a curved surface
The law of reflection applies to all reflectors, whether they concentrate (concave surface) or disperse (convex).

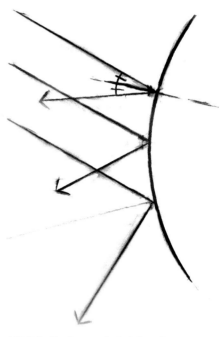

119 Reflection from a spherical dispersion surface (convex reflector)

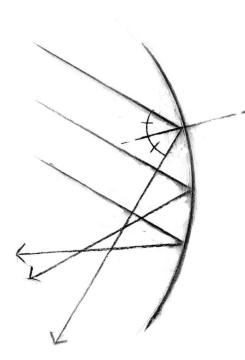

120 Reflection from a spherical converging surface (concave reflector)

117 Light refraction by a plano-convex cylinder lens. The light beams originate from an argon-ion laser, which emits beams with two wavelengths – in the green and blue ranges. The beam is split up into four partial light beams and falls from above on a diagonally placed plano-convex cylinder lens. Reflection loss in the beams reflected to the left can be seen very clearly, as can the focused beam of light that has passed. The colour defect in the lens can also be precisely observed, as the blue beams are more strongly refracted than the green ones

### Image produced from a curved surface

Ill. 121 shows how an image of an object is produced. This effect is not used very often in the theatre, but it is shown here because spherical reflectors are used in spotlight and projection technology.

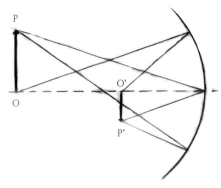

121  Image resulting from curved surface

### Spherical reflectors

A spherical reflector reflects the light from a bulb back in the direction of the light source, in order to exploit this light that is reflected back. In this case the light source has to be placed at the focal point of the reflector, with the reflected inverted image of the lamp filament placed beside the original light source filament.

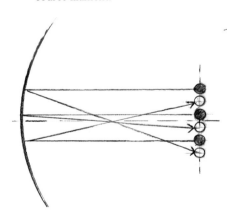

122  Lamp filament image in a spherical reflector

## ASPHERICAL, SYMMETRICAL REFLECTORS

### Ellipsoidal reflectors

Ellipsoidal reflectors are aspherical with a rotational axis of symmetry. They have two focal points. One contains the light source, the other is used as a focal point for projection purposes. In spotlight technology this reflector is used as a focusing system for profile spotlights; it is an outstanding albeit not inexpensive basis for a spotlight.

### Parabolic reflectors

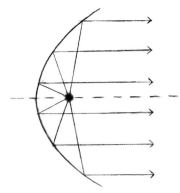

123  Beam path of a parabolic reflector

Parabolic reflectors are aspherical, symmetrical reflectors with one focal point. If the light source is at the focal point of the reflector, the light emitted by the reflector is parallel with the axis. The smaller the light source and the larger the focal length of the reflector, the narrower the light beam. Ideal light sources are xenon lamps or low voltage lamps.

### Trough reflectors

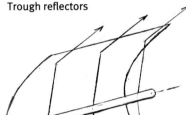

124  Beam path of a symmetrical trough reflector

Trough reflectors are used for linear filament lamps. Here, the cross-section of the reflector is usually parabolic or ellipsoidal, and trough-shaped. Light dispersion can be affected only orthogonally to the axis of the lamp – in the case of a parabolic cross-section as a band-shaped reflection of light.

## ASYMMETRICAL TROUGH REFLECTORS

An aspherical, asymmetrical trough reflector does not disperse light evenly in the two horizontal beam directions, but unevenly, weighted towards one of the two sides.

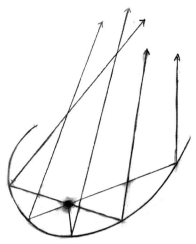

125  Beam path of an asymmetrical trough reflector

## REFLECTOR MATERIALS

Most of the reflector systems generally used today are made of aluminium. The reflectors have highly polished or rough matt surfaces, depending on the purpose for which they are to be used. When a high degree of precision is needed, or critical demands are made on the spotlight's thermal characteristics and efficiency, spherical silvered glass or metal oxide vaporized reflectors – also known as infrared or cold reflectors – may be used.

For these, a reflective coating is condensed on a glass surface. This coating consists of a large number of interference layers that are permeable to infrared rays. This means that the heat radiation can be directed backwards, and the heat transmitted by the beam of light is reduced by about 75%.

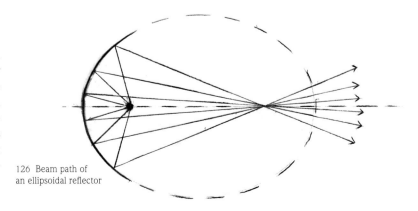

126  Beam path of an ellipsoidal reflector

## LENSES

### What is a lens?

As well as refelectors and other reflective surfaces, glass optical lenses are
used for concentrating and dispersing
beams of light. A lens is a glass or plastic object with spherical surfaces. Light
is refracted only on the periphery of the
lens, caused by the change of medium.
Two categories of optical lens forms can
be distinguished:

129   Colour defect in a plano-convex lens

127   Converging lenses – positive lenses
Reduced vergence

Plano-convex       Biconvex       Concavo-convex
                                  (positive meniscus)

128   Diverging lenses – negative lenses
Enlarged vergence

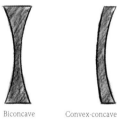

Plano-concave      Biconcave      Convex-concave
                                  (negative meniscus)

### Converging lenses = convex lenses

A convex lens reduces the vergence
(aperture angle) of the beam. Identifying characteristic: The converging lens
is thicker at the centre than at the
periphery.

### Diverging lenses = concave lenses

A concave lens enlarges the vergence.
The thickness at the centre is less than
at the periphery.

### Positive meniscus = concavo-convex lens

This type is used above all in projection technology, when an optical system
requires a shortened focal length. Fresnel lenses are often produced in this
form.

### Chromatic aberration in lenses

The physical properties of light cause
different waves to be unequally refracted by optical lenses. Shorter wave
blue rays are more strongly refracted
than the longer wave red ones. This 'secondary spectrum' has a reddish outer
edge. This phenomenon is particularly
evident with simple lens spotlights.

### Loss by reflection and absorption by a lens

Loss by absorption occurs when light
passes through a medium. Part of it is
reflected when it enters and leaves the
medium. Loss by reflection is determined by the refractive index of the
glass (see ill. on page 66).

### Fresnel lens

This convex lens was developed
around 1800 by the French physicist
Augustin Fresnel and used for theatrical
spotlights from about 1930. The Fresnel lens is made up of concentric rings
with a common focal point. The radius
of curvature of each ring allows the
light to be refracted to the common
focal point. This has the advantage that
the thickness of the lens is negligible.
It is thus possible to produce thinner
lenses, which is particularly important

when manufacturing large-diameter
lenses. This also has the positive effect
of reducing heat absorption. Unlike a
plano-convex lens, the thickness of a
Fresnel lens is independent of diameter
and focal length. Fresnel lenses are
moulded from borosilicate glass that is
not affected by temperature change.
The surfaces are uneven and not transparent in order to prevent a projection
of the individual skipped rings. For this
reason a beam from a Fresnel spot
seems very diffuse. This refraction process also makes the chromatic aberration of the lens no longer perceptible.
The angle of aperture can be up to
60° of the median dispersion. These
lenses are available hardened and un-
hardened. It is also possible to apply a
heat-resistant coating to the back of
the lens, which increases the durability
of the colour gels.

## BEAM VERGENCE

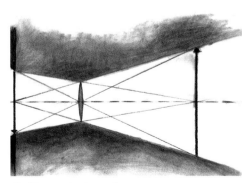

131   Vergence in a beam of rays

Imaging uses only a limited portion of
the rays of light. This is caused by the
mechanical apertures such as the iris
diaphragm, the lens system, the reflect-
or etc. The resulting rays are called a
beam. The size of this beam is determined by the angle of spread, or the
vergence. If the beam spreads out from
an object point and the angle increases,
this is known as a divergent ray. If the
beam becomes narrower, it is convergent. Thus the vergence of rays in a
beam determines the nature of the
image.

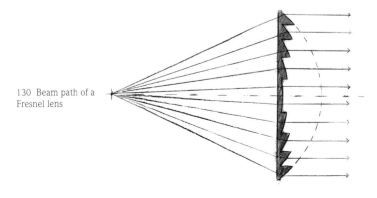

130   Beam path of a
Fresnel lens

## OPTICAL IMAGING

Positive, convex lenses are the most common in spotlight technology. In order, for example, to produce an optical image with a biconvex lens, three possible configurations are important. (ill. 136–138).

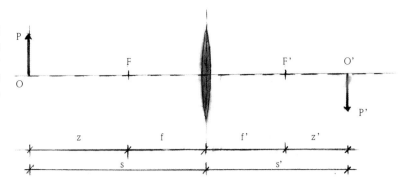

135 **OPTICAL VALUES**

O  = axial object point
O' = axial image point
P  = extra-axial object point
P' = extra-axial image point
y  = object size (P1–P2)
y' = image size (P'1–P'2)
F  = object focal point
F' = image focal point
f  = object focal length
f' = image focal length
s  = distance: object point – lens
s' = distance: image point – lens

z  = distance: object point – object focal point
z' = distance: image point – image focal point
n  = air refraction index
n' = medium refraction index
r  = lens radius of curvature
d  = lens diameter
e  = lens thickness

## SETTING UP
## A LENS IN
## THE LIGHT RAY PATH

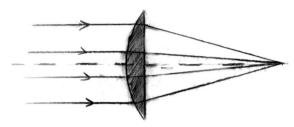

132 Object distance = ∞, image distance = f

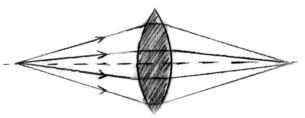

133 Object distance = image distance, regardless of f

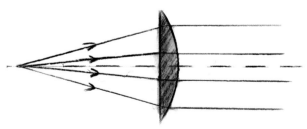

134 Object distance = f, image distance = ∞

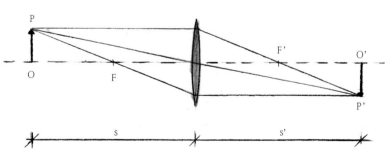

136 Optical reduction: If the distance s is larger than s', the projected image is smaller than the object. The image is real, inverted; s > 2f

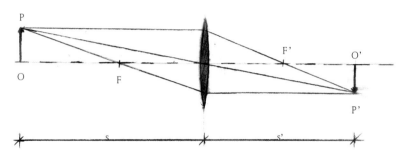

137 Optical image 1:1: If the distance of the axial object and the image points s = s' and f = f', then the image ratio is 1:1. The image is real, inverted; s = 2f

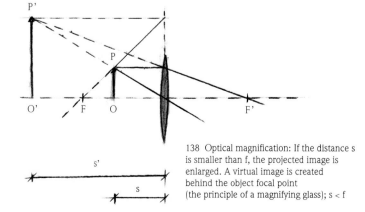

138 Optical magnification: If the distance s is smaller than f, the projected image is enlarged. A virtual image is created behind the object focal point (the principle of a magnifying glass); s < f

## Calculating focal length

When calculating the focal length (f) of a plano-convex lens, the diameter of the lens (d) and the thickness of the lens (e) have to be found.

$$r = \frac{d^2}{8e} + \frac{e}{2} \quad ; \quad \frac{1}{f} = \frac{n'-n}{r} \quad ; \quad f = \frac{r}{n'-n}$$

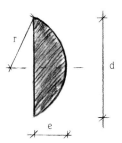

139 Plano-convex lens with calculation values for determining focal length

It is also possible to find the focal length of a convex lens or objective by a quick practical method. We know that the focal length of a convex lens of constant diameter decreases with increasing lens curvature. If we hold a convex lens or lens system opposite the trade mark on a light bulb, it is possible to produce a sharp image of this mark on the surface illuminated. The distance between this surface and the object is the focal length.

## Objectives

Projector objectives are similar in design to photographic objectives. Because of the relationship between the lighting system and the objective lens, large apertures are preferred. A projector objective works in precisely the opposite way to a photographic objective. A compact optical lens system's function is to create a beam according to the desired image distance size. Long projection distances need a long focal length, and short ones need a wide-angle objective.

The aperture of a lens is based on the ratio of the lens diameter to the focal length. The greater this ratio, the brighter the images produced by the objective.

## Variable focus lenses

Variable focus or zoom lenses are systems with a focal length that can be changed. The system changes its focal length by moving individual lens components without changing the plane of the image. The change in the focal length makes it possible to enlarge or reduce the projected image. The image is less bright than that produced by a normal objective, as the additional lenses also absorb light.

## Slide projectors

The slide projector is used to produce static images. Its optical configuration is independent of the size of the image to be projected. Light coming from the light source is focused by the lamp optical system, the condenser lens. The directed beam of light illuminates the slide evenly and converges to the projection lens. This produces the desired image size according to the focal length selected. The condenser lens collects the rays, that is, the beam from the lamp determines the angle of aperture. A simple condenser for an aperture angle of 30 to 40° consists of two plano-convex lenses. For a greater angle, a third lens in the form of a positive meniscus lens is added. A spherical reflector additionally utilizes the light from the projector lamp that is emitted towards the back. As there is a considerable thermal load on the condenser lenses, heat-proof glass is often used to absorb heat. The former optical cooling cells (water-filled transparent containers to absorb heat) are no longer used today.

## Film projectors

Films present observers with a moving projected image. The eye is offered individual phases of movement in such rapid sequence that they appear to fuse together and give the impression of continuous motion. Projectors let each image from the film be projected briefly on to the screen as a still. The beam from the light source is interrupted while the next image takes over from the previous one. The film is moved by a so-called Maltese cross. The optical structure of a film projector is the same as that of a normal slide projector. High-performance projectors used in the theatre are fitted with xenon lamps, but tungsten halogen lamps and other daylight discharge lamps are also used.

140 Optical values for an image projection

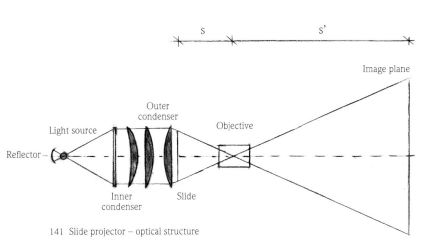

141 Slide projector – optical structure

Determining focal length f for a projection image:

f  = lens focal length
y  = $P_1 - P_2$ = slide size
y' = $P'_1 - P'_2$ = projected image size
s' = distance:
      lens focal point-projection plane
s =  distance:
      lens focal point-slide plane

These values have the following ratio:

$$\frac{\text{image size cm}}{\text{slide size cm}} = \frac{y'}{y} = V$$

$$= \text{enlargement ratio}$$

In addition: $\frac{y'}{y} = \frac{s'}{s} = V$

If the lens focal length f is needed, the following formulas are used:

$$\frac{1}{f} = \frac{1}{s} + \frac{1}{s'} \quad \text{or} \quad f = \frac{s' \times s}{s' + s}$$

In practice the following formulas are recommended:

$$f = \frac{s'}{V+1} \quad \text{or} \quad f = \frac{s' \times y}{y' + y}$$

(see also p. 186)

142 The scroller is mounted on the douser. The colour roll is wound on to the lower spool and can be wound upwards by remote control

143 The electronically remote-controlled douser is matched to lens size

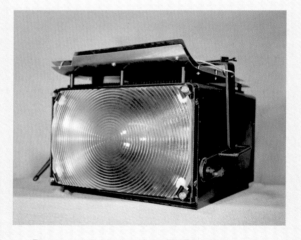

144 The special model from the front. The Fresnel lens was tailored to a longitudinal format. Heat dispersal plates are mounted on the top

145 Ill. top right: Three special 4,000 W HMI daylight spots. The housing had to be reduced to minimum size because of problems of space and set requirements. The ignition device is flange-mounted on the back of the spotlight, and the lanterns on the right and left are fitted with a scroller. The picture shows the colour starting to change from yellow to red-violet. This special model was a joint development by the Münchner Kammerspiele and Arnold + Richter

146 Both production photographs: J. W. von Goethe, *Faust, Part One* Director: Dieter Dorn Set designer: Jürgen Rose Münchner Kammerspiele, 1987

147 Schlieren method colour
photograph of a carbon arc

148 Schlieren method colour photograph of a candle flame

## BASIC VALUES IN LIGHTING TECHNOLOGY

Some basic definitions are necessary if we are to be able to decide how a light source relates to its surroundings.

### Luminous flux
Luminous flux is the luminous power of the light source for light emitted in all directions.
Unit: lumen (lm);
Symbol: $\phi$ (phi)

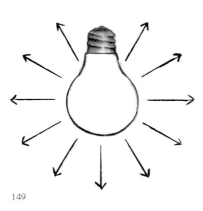

149

### Luminous efficiency
This gives the ratio between the luminous flux emitted and the electrical power consumed. Unit: lumen/watt (lm/W)

### Luminous intensity
Luminous intensity is the unit of light emitted in a specific direction. Candela, the luminous intensity, is an internationally agreed basic value. Distribution of light is represented in the form of a polar diagram.
Unit: candela (cd);
Symbol: l

150 Polar diagram

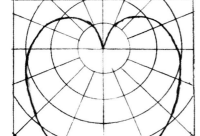

151

### Illuminance
This indicates how strongly a surface is illuminated in terms of the angle of incidence.
Unit: lux (lx)/ symbol: E
$1 \text{ lux} = 1 \text{ lumen/m}^2$

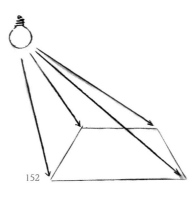

152

### Luminance
Luminance is a measure of the light radiating from a source or being reflected by a surface.
Unit: candela/m$^2$ (cd/m$^2$)
Luminance = luminous intensity (cd)/ luminous plane (m$^2$), taking the angle of sight into account.

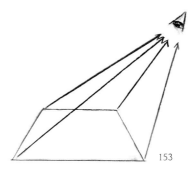

153

## WHAT IS AN INCANDESCENT LAMP?

Lamps differ according to their intended use with respect to mains voltage, power consumption, external shape and base, in the structure and position of the light source or the size and shape of the electric arc, in service life and luminous efficiency, and in the spectral energy distribution of their light. Lamps are divided into two groups according to the way in which their light is produced:

- incandescent lamps: luminous efficiency between 9 and 20 lm/W
- discharge lamps: luminous efficiency: between 30 and 190 lm/W

An incandescent lamp is a thermal radiator. A tungsten filament is heated to produce both thermal and luminous radiation. Only 5–10% of the electrical power consumption is converted into emitted light – the rest is heat!

### How does it work?
The light emitter is a tungsten filament, coiled one or more times. The length and diameter of the filament are adjusted to the desired working voltage, power consumption and incandescent temperature. In the presence of a vacuum or an inert gas, the filament is raised to a white heat (2,800°C). The tungsten filament melts at approx. 3,400°C or 3,650 K. The uncoiled tungsten filament in a 60 W household bulb is 1/100 mm thick and over 1 m long. As the temperature rises the luminous efficiency and colour temperature rise, but working life is shortened. This decline occurs because the filament material evaporates more rapidly at higher temperatures and becomes thinner and thinner until it melts at a particular point and the lamp no longer functions. Temperatures above 3,400 K are not possible with a tungsten lamp, as higher temperatures come too close to the melting-point of tungsten (see also colour temperature, p. 27).

The evaporated tungsten condenses on the bulb wall. This coating absorbs light and reduces the colour temperature, and the glass part of the lamp becomes increasingly dark.

The coil is differently arranged in theatrical bulbs. Usually the smallest possible point light source is desired, as the smaller it is, the better the optical images created. For this reason the tungsten filaments are neatly arranged in series next to each other. In a theatre projection lamp it is common to use a monoplanar coil to improve luminance, but biplanar coils are also used. In double ended lamps, the filament is defined as axial (segmented or nonsegmented). If a lamp has a low supply voltage, the coiled filaments can be arranged closer to each other.

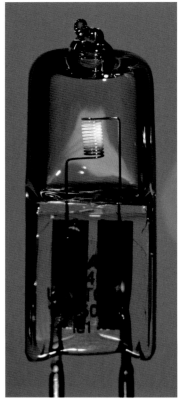

154 Low voltage lamp with axial coil

of blackening can also be reduced by increasing the size of the bulb. There are also special bulb shapes which cause the tungsten only to condense on surfaces that do not restrict light emission. In the case of very expensive lamps, such as projection lamps, the bulb used to be filled with buck shot to clean the bulb. This was in the lower part of the bulb when the lamp was in operation. If the lamp became badly blackened, the tungsten deposit could be removed by shaking the shot, which guaranteed a more constant colour temperature and luminous flux. Incandescent lamps are divided into three categories:

- vacuum lamp: no gas in the bulb, approx. 2,300–2,700 K
- gas-filled lamp: glass bulb filled with inert gas, approx. 2,600–3,000 K
- tungsten-halogen lamp: glass bulb filled with inert gas and bromine or iodine, approx. 3,000–3,400 K

ponents tungsten and halogen. The halogen is available to return to the cycle once more, the tungsten is deposited on the coil, where it tends towards the somewhat cooler, thicker parts, and not those that are relatively hot, thin and inclined to burn through.

To guarantee that all areas of the bulb's inner wall reach the minimum temperatures required for this cyclical process, the lamps have to be small and made of glass with a very high melting-point (quartz, Vycor, hardened glass). Higher gas pressures can be used in the small, stable bulb without risk to the user. This higher pressure reduces the speed of condensation at all points on the incandescent filament, even where it is thin and inclined to break. This means a longer service life, and the luminous efficiency is also increased.

Thus a tungsten-halogen lamp has the following essential advantages:

- constant luminous flux
- steady colour temperature throughout its service life

155 Tungsten-halogen double ended lamp with quartz bulb, linear filament, ceramic cap. This coil form is also manufactured with a segmented axial coil. In this case small, uncoiled sections are inserted at regular intervals, each with a small spacer to cushion the coil against the bulb inner wall

Condensation can be reduced by filling the lamps with gases (nitrogen, argon, krypton or mixtures of these) that do not attack the incandescent filaments even at high temperatures. The extent

156 Structure of an incandescent lamp

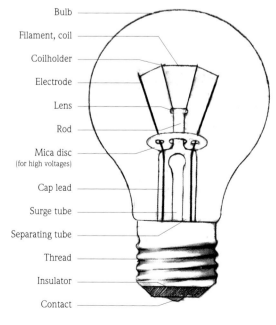

Bulb
Filament, coil
Coilholder
Electrode
Lens
Rod
Mica disc
(for high voltages)
Cap lead
Surge tube
Separating tube
Thread
Insulator
Contact

## THE TUNGSTEN-HALOGEN CYCLE

This process represents an important step in avoiding bulb blackening. Modern tungsten-halogen incandescent lamps have increasingly been used in all fields since the 1960s. At first iodine was the halide most frequently used, but now it is usually bromine or bromine compounds. In the meantime the tungsten-halogen lamp has become accepted in all power ratings. The following process takes place when running the lamp: tungsten atoms evaporated from the hot tungsten filament (up to approx. 3,000°C) reach a temperature zone below 1,400°C at a certain distance. Here they combine with the halogen atoms. This compound remains gaseous to 250°C, which means that the temperature of the glass bulb has to remain above 250°C. If a sufficiently small glass bulb is used, so that the inner wall rapidly reaches this minimum temperature, the tungsten-halogen compound is not precipitated on it. The thermal flow of the filler gas brings it back towards the hot coil, where it is once more broken down into its com-

- greater luminous efficiency and/or service life
- small dimensions

### Stage use
Spectators are not immediately aware of colour temperature, as the eye is not tuned to a standard temperature but is able to register differences in colour temperature. So if a candle flame at 1,500 K and a xenon lamp at 6,000 K are seen at the same time, the difference is particularly noticeable.

But this standard temperature is crucial for film and television. A uniform colour temperature for all light sources is needed for studio lighting. The colour temperature generally used for exposures in artificial light is 3,200 K.

The colour temperature of lamps represents a compromise between:

- long service life and low colour temperature
- short service life and high colour temperature

Lamps with a colour temperature of 3,000 K can achieve a service life of

Lamps and Light

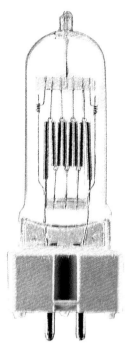

157 Tungsten-halogen lamp with quartz glass bulb, monoplanar filament, ceramic base and pins

approx. 600 hours; at 3,200 K the service life is only 300 hours, and at 3,400 K only 15 hours.

For this reason, lamps with a colour temperature of 3,000 K are good for theatre use. It is now easy to understand why photoflood lamps, for example, emit bright, white light but burn out after only a few hours.

Planck's curve shows the region of the spectrum in which the radiated light of a selection of important lamp types is to be found.

## INCANDESCENT LAMPS AS TEMPERATURE RADIATORS IN THE THEATRE

In contrast to lamps for general lighting purposes the following higher demands are made on special lamp types for stage work:

- high luminous flux (lm)
- high luminous efficiency (lm/W)
- constant colour temperature and constant luminous flux
- precise position and shape of the light source
- easy-to-use cap structure

Manufacturers list incandescent lamps up to 20,000 W, but 10,000 and 20,000 W lamps are not used in the theatre very much.

Higher luminous efficiency (lm/W) not only produces more light with the same power consumption, but also increases the proportion of visible light in relation to infra-red heat radiation. This results in a higher colour temperature. For example, if lamps for everyday use are compared with photofloods and incandescent lamps with the same current, we see that lamps for general use radiate about 80% more heat, which also means greater power consumption. In order to minimize discomfort to actors from unavoidable heat radiation, lamps with greater luminous efficiency are absolutely essential. When high intensity of illumination is required the disadvantage of a shorter service life for lamps with greater luminous efficiency is more than compensated for by the advantages of less discomfort from heat and lower power consumption.

158 CIE colour continuum with Planck's curve and Judd's scale for determining xy values of thermal radiators, with a selection of light sources that are used in the theatre

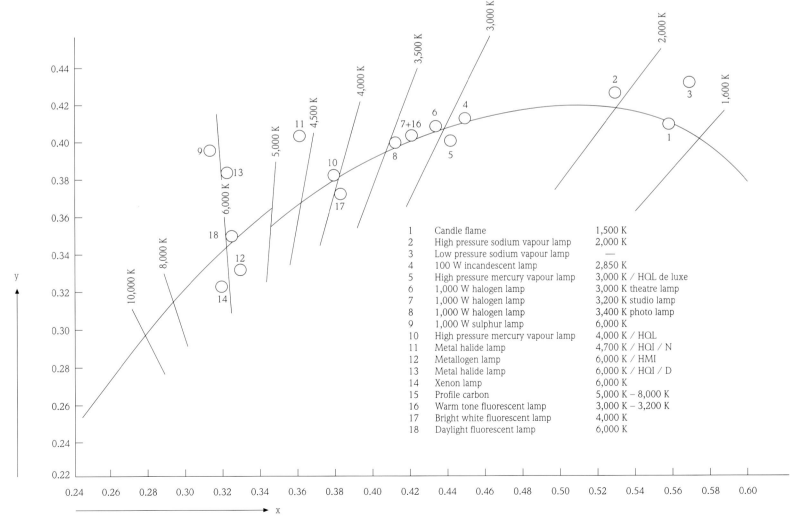

| | | |
|---|---|---|
| 1 | Candle flame | 1,500 K |
| 2 | High pressure sodium vapour lamp | 2,000 K |
| 3 | Low pressure sodium vapour lamp | — |
| 4 | 100 W incandescent lamp | 2,850 K |
| 5 | High pressure mercury vapour lamp | 3,000 K / HQL de luxe |
| 6 | 1,000 W halogen lamp | 3,000 K theatre lamp |
| 7 | 1,000 W halogen lamp | 3,200 K studio lamp |
| 8 | 1,000 W halogen lamp | 3,400 K photo lamp |
| 9 | 1,000 W sulphur lamp | 6,000 K |
| 10 | High pressure mercury vapour lamp | 4,000 K / HQL |
| 11 | Metal halide lamp | 4,700 K / HQI / N |
| 12 | Metallogen lamp | 6,000 K / HMI |
| 13 | Metal halide lamp | 6,000 K / HQI / D |
| 14 | Xenon lamp | 6,000 K |
| 15 | Profile carbon | 5,000 K – 8,000 K |
| 16 | Warm tone fluorescent lamp | 3,000 K – 3,200 K |
| 17 | Bright white fluorescent lamp | 4,000 K |
| 18 | Daylight fluorescent lamp | 6,000 K |

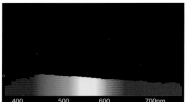

159 Daylight spectrum

160 Low pressure sodium vapour lamp

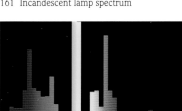

161 Incandescent lamp spectrum

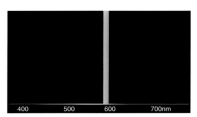

162 High pressure sodium vapour lamp

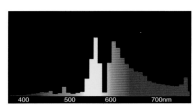

163 26 mm fluorescent lamp: colour 11 – daylight

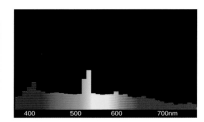

164 Metal halide lamp/Daylight

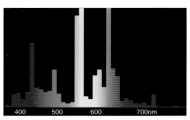

165 26 mm fluorescent lamp: colour 21 – bright white

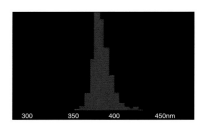

166 UV fluorescent lamp

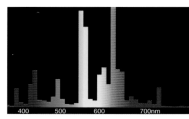

167 26 mm fluorescent lamp: colour 31 – warm tone

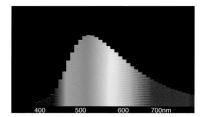

168 Sulphur lamp

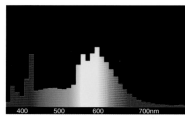

169 38 mm fluorescent lamp: bright white with ignition strips

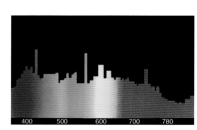

170 HMI Metallogen lamp

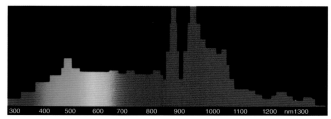

171 Xenon lamp

## TIGHTER AND BRIGHTER

### Luminance

The greater the luminance of a light source, the better the light it emits can be directed as desired by reflectors or lenses, thus reducing undesirable scattering effects. The luminous intensity of a spotlight increases with its luminance. High luminance can be achieved with small light sources. In practice, this is achieved by coiling the incandescent filaments and placing the individual parts such that they do not block each other in the direction of the main beam. This means that the individual filament sections are arranged on a single plane, a so-called monoplanar arrangement of the filament core. If a biplanar arrangement is used, the breadth of the light source can be even further reduced, which contributes to a further increase in luminance. But the individual filament cores still have to be far enough apart to prevent electrical arcing between filament sections. Thus the spaces are greater for lamps using a mains voltage of 230 than for low voltage lamps (e.g. 24 V), in which the filament lengths required are also shorter.

### PAR lamps

PAR lamps are reflector lamps (PAR = parabolic reflector). In this type the light source combines with the parabolic reflector as a unit. PAR lamps are available in various wattages, sizes and beam angles, from a very small angle spot to a flood or broad-beam fixture with a wide angle. PAR units are always replaced complete, and do not have to be refocused.

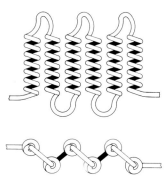

172 Monoplanar filament

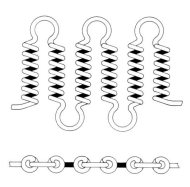

173 Biplanar filament

174 Quartz tungsten-halogen lamp with biplanar filament

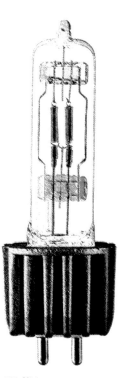

175 High power tungsten-halogen lamp with cooler cap

| Type | ø | Installation depth |
|---|---|---|
| PAR 36 | 114 mm | 70 mm |
| PAR 46 | 146 mm | 95–102 mm |
| PAR 56 | 178 mm | 114–127 mm |
| PAR 64 | 203 mm | 95–122 mm |

The filament is placed at the focal point of a parabolic reflector, which reflects the rays with slight divergence. As reflector, filament and lens form a unit (called a sealed beam), this compact lamp is particularly easy to use and has a long life.

| Surface structure | Radiation angle | Reference | Lamp base |
|---|---|---|---|
| Clear (transparent) | 9 × 12° | NSP/CP 60 | GX 16 d |
| Speckled | 10 × 14° | SP/CP 61 | GX 16 d |
| Corrugated | 11 × 24° | WFL/CP 62 | GX 16 d |
| Coarsely corrugated | 70 × 70° | EWF/CP 95 | GX 16 d |

Different beam angles are achieved by varying the surface structure of the front glass. Everybody who works with light now regards these lamps as a valuable addition for the field. The PAR 36 series in particular offers a number of interesting models, mainly in the low voltage range. They are used for numerous and varied effects.

176  PAR lamps sizes 64, 56 and 36

## DISCHARGE LAMPS

A discharge lamp differs from incandescent lamps – with the exception of sodium vapour lamps – in the following particular characteristics:

- daylight spectrum
- greater luminous efficiency
- low mechanical sensitivity
- a warm-up time to full luminous power with maximum of four minutes

Discharge lamps produce the light emission through the electrical discharge with gaseous, liquid or solid substances. The different colours of the emission are produced by the selection and combination of these components.

### Low pressure and high pressure lamps

There are three categories in this field:

- short arc lamp: As the name suggests, the electrodes are very close together. This means that the light source is dot-shaped and the luminance very high. A short arc lamp is usually a high pressure lamp.

- medium arc lamp: The electrodes are somewhat further apart in this lamp. The arc of light between the two electrodes is elliptical, and the luminance somewhat less than

in short arc lamps. This is usually a low pressure lamp type.

- long arc lamp: The electrodes are far apart. It is no longer possible to talk of a focal point, as the luminance is evenly distributed throughout the discharge field. These lamps are usually low pressure lamps.

### Low pressure lamps

Short definition:

- arc discharge with hot cathode (since 1854)
- large volume lamps
- average luminous flux
- long discharge tubes
- small tube diameter
- even, low luminance throughout the discharge field

Low pressure lamps are tubular and long. The largest group are the fluorescent lamps and also includes low pressure sodium lamps.

A mercury vapour discharge is used to activate the fluorescent substances in low pressure tubular fluorescent lamps, which are generally known simply as fluorescent tubes. At the saturation vapour pressure of the mercury, the temperature of the tube wall usually corresponds to an ambient room temperature of 25°C. A low pressure inert gas, usually neon-argon or krypton, is

often added to help ignition. The discharge takes place in a tube between two electrodes, which are usually in the form of incandescent coils. The inner wall of the tube is coated with a fluorescent mixture. UV radiation released by the mercury vapour discharge activates the fluorescent coating and makes it glow.

The two coils attached to the two pins of the cap are preheated by a heater circuit or separate filament transformers. This raises the emitter substance between the filament coils to an emission temperature of 600–800°C. Volume charges build up in front of the electrodes, which reduce the ignition voltage of the lamp below the mains voltage. This can also be brought about by an impulse of up to 1,500 V (starter circuit).

### High pressure lamps
Short definition

- arc discharge with a hot cathode (since 1906)
- small volume discharge tube
- high luminance
- narrow, concentrated arc

High pressure discharge lamps usually have short discharge distances. High pressure discharge in mercury vapour produces less UV radiation and more light than in low-pressure lamps. The higher discharge temperature produces higher pressure in the discharge tube.

The gas discharge is triggered by ignition between the electrodes. The filler substances needed to produce light – like mercury – have to be present in the lamp in appropriate proportions to be able to produce the desired light characteristics. Considerable improvement in colour and, in addition, increased luminous efficiency are produced by adding metallic iodide or 'rare earth' iodides. Lamps of this kind are called metal halide lamps.

A ballast is needed to limit the current in the lamps. Ignition is either by means of auxiliary electrodes built into the lamps or by separate ignition devices. Unlike fluorescent lamps, many high pressure lamps cannot be re-used immediately after having been switched off. The lamps have to cool before they can be relit. But brief application of very high voltages (up to ten times the working voltage), with the help of special ignition devices, make it possible to relight most lamps immediately, even when they are hot. High pressure lamps are temperature sensitive and require a sufficient bulb temperature for this.

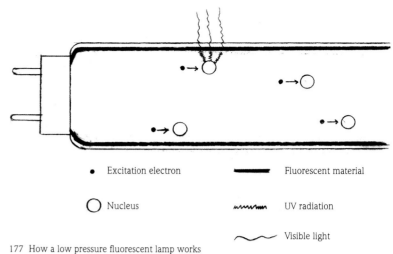

177  How a low pressure fluorescent lamp works

- Excitation electron
- Nucleus
- Fluorescent material
- UV radiation
- Visible light

## LOW PRESSURE FLUORESCENT LAMPS

These were described under low pressure lamps (p. 79). Gas discharge in the glass tube develops predominantly invisible intense ultraviolet radiation of 253.7 nm via the mercury vapour. The short wavelength radiation is transformed into longer-wave, visible rays by the fluorescent coating on the inner side of the discharge tube. The colour of the light can be varied through the composition of the fluorescent coating. A wide variety of different lengths, diameters, shapes and outputs are available. Light colours range from 2,800 to 6,500 K.

Luminous flux from fluorescent lamps is dependent on temperature, and such lamps reach their optimum performance at an ambient temperature of 20 to 25°C, with the exception of special lamps that reach their highest luminous flux at 35°C. The luminous efficiency of fluorescent lamps is three times greater than that of incandescent lamps, and the service life is 7.5 times greater.

| | |
|---|---|
| Power: | 4–215 W |
| Cap: | G 5, G 13, R 17 d, F$_a$ 6, 4-pin special |
| Position: | any |
| Immediate reignition: | yes |
| Start-up time: | none |
| Dimming: | yes |
| Service life: | 7,500–60,000 hours |
| Colour temperature: | depending on fluorescent coating: 2,800–6,500 K |
| Luminous efficiency: | 30–104 lm/W |
| Colour rendering: | depending on coating: levels 1–3 |

### Stage use
This 'popular lamp' is interesting but not entirely easy to handle. The versions that are of interest to lighting experts are the 65 W/150 cm and 40 W/120 cm types, 38 mm in diameter, and the whole range of 26 mm diameter tubes. The first two sizes mentioned are easiest to control. They can be so well regulated that a smooth non-flickering adjustment is possible when working from a lighting console.

### Brightness control
Unfortunately this is not so simple. Brightness cannot be reduced by lowering voltage (amplitude control), as a resistive load can. But it is possible with electronic phase control. If this is not available, special devices can be used, but they have the disadvantage that they cannot be built into the control operation. Most modern lighting boards work on the principle of phase control.

When dimming fluorescent lamps with a diameter of 38 mm, only half the dimmer's power rating should be used. The industry provides good accessories for fitting fluorescent lamps into the stage scenery.

### Steady brightness control for fluorescent lamps of 38 mm diameter
Any fluorescent lamp with a diameter of 38 mm can be controlled. Lamps with a smaller tube diameter (e.g. 26 mm or less) can be, too, but here a special circuitry is needed. The ideal types have already been mentioned, but lamps with a curved discharge tube (U-shaped) can also be controlled, though a rather complex system is needed to do this. When planning the set-up it is important that groups be made up containing the same lamp type, in order to avoid different brightness levels.

New fluorescent lamps sometimes have a turbulent discharge, caused by impurities in the discharge path. This can be cured by running in the lamp (between 10 and 50 hours).

Manufacturers also offer special dimmable fluorescent lamps containing an aluminium strip. Unfortunately these lamps are not available in all colour grades. Heater transformers are essential for dimmable fluorescent lamps, as well as the usual fluorescent lamp ballasts. These transformers have two separate secondary coils, each of which preheats one of the two lamp electrodes at a voltage of about 6.5 (high ohm coil) or 4 (low ohm coil), thus enabling striking an arc after each mains half-wave. In normal use this is done by the starter, which effectively short-circuits the fluorescent lamp after power reaches the ballast coil, creating a current potential surge in the ballast and lighting the lamp. The starter has to be omitted in dimmable fluorescent lamps, and the heat transformer takes over preheating the coil. A perfect contact must be made when attaching the lamp connections to the mains, because of the low voltage. Special holders are recommended for dimmable fluorescent lamps on the market for this reason.

Flickering also needs attention in order to produce consistently favourable results. Flickering is a function of phosphorescence, that is, of the afterglow in the fluorescent substance used, which differs according to light colours. Lamps that produce daylight-type light tend to flicker more than warm-toned lamps. Thus the latter are to be preferred for use in dimmer systems. An afterglow is necessary to bridge the current-free gaps between the mains half-waves. These gaps are larger when the lamp is dimmed than in normal use.

A capacitive ignition aid, which must be placed parallel to the discharge tube, is used for improved ease of ignition. More even field distribution and a higher capacitance with respect to the discharge column than with the standard ignition strip is achieved by adding an aluminium ignition strip about 10 mm wide, which is attached to the mid-point or neutral line terminal on the ballast end of the lamp. Commercial L-lamps L 65 W and L 40 with a diameter of 38 mm are available with an ignition strip.

To improve control quality further, it is recommended that users attach a constant load in the form of a resistive load to the output of a dimmer device. The most recent dimmer types, above all digital dimmers, no longer need a constant load. When designing large installations it is important to determine whether the fluorescent lamp coils are of the low or high resistance type

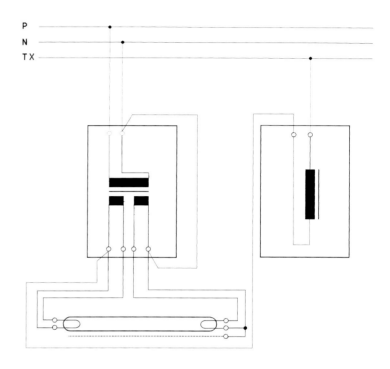

179 Circuit diagram for dimmable fluorescent lamps

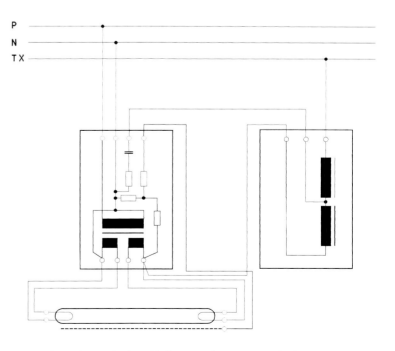

180 Circuit diagram for dimmable fluorescent lamps – runout circuit

178 Various fluorescent lampholders

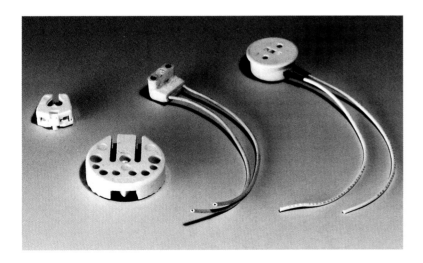

before specifying heat transformers. Unfortunately, reliable information is available only in the case of a few types, for example, for lamps with ignition strips (4 V heating potential). If a lamp from another series is used, caution is advised. Heat transformers for preheating coils are available for single or pairs of fluorescent lamps.

When planning stage installation equipment, several circuits for controlling fluorescent lamps should definitely be included. Here special outlets are needed including lines for electrode heating. The heating lines must be in phase with the regulated output. If a constant load is required – in the form of a resistive load (such as incandescent lamps) – it should be incorporated directly into the load distribution equipment.

### Dimming fluorescent lamps with a tube diameter of 26 mm

As lamps with 26 mm diameter tubes have such a high restriking voltage, they are unsuitable for dimming with the usual ballasts and transformers. In the meantime various manufacturers have developed electronic pulse generators to enable electronic brightness control.

The pulse generator described here is made by SE and called the VIP 90 (Varintens Intensive Pulser). This pulse generator delivers the required high-frequency pulsed voltage and heater voltage of 4, 6.5 or 8 V, and can be regulated from 0 to 100%. Used with a normal ballast (a coil) for current limiting, this combination can achieve a control ratio of 1:10,000. No additional ignition aid with ignition strips or grids is needed, nor is load resistance. This control unit can dim all 26 mm tubes of 2 x 18/36/38/58 W. To a limited extent, PL/Dulux lamps with four-pin caps and curved fluorescent tubes can also be controlled. Pulsed generators and ballasts should be mounted immediately adjacent to the fluorescent tube, and tubes with different power ratings should not be on the same line. To produce continuous brightness control, only lamps with the same power rating should be dimmed as groups. At present, this impulse generator is the only device that can be regulated from 0 to 100%. If regulation from 1 to 100% is adequate, there are further possibilities. Suppliers such as OSRAM, ABB or Zumtobel market devices called electronic ballasts. Brightness is regulated either by reducing the mains voltage or by phase control. The most recent development in this field is the digital electronic ballast, which operates at high frequencies between 25 and 70 kHz and can be run with a 1 to 10 V control voltage. This can be employed when lamps are used for indirect background lighting.

### Fluorescent lamps on stage

The fact that fluorescent lamps are expensive and difficult to control is tolerable because they have certain advantages. They can be mounted very close to scenery because they do not get very hot, and they do not take up a lot of room. They emit light through almost 360° and thus illuminate large areas over short distances. If space is limited or weight is a problem, the power supply (heat transformer, ballasts or pulse generators) can be fitted externally without any difficulty. So-called supply boxes can be set up for this purpose. The diffuse beams make almost completely shadow-free lighting possible.

Colour temperatures are in the range of 2,800 to 6,500 K. This shows the possibilities offered by this type of lighting. If the required colour is not available, colour gels can be used. They are simply wrapped round the lamps or laid over them.

### Lightstick

The lightstick is a small-scale fluorescent lamp. Its diameter varies from 2.6 to 4.1 mm according to its power, and its length is between 5 and 36 cm. This mini-lamp can be dimmed and is available in white, red, green and blue. The colour temperature is 5,400 K, and the voltage ranges between 0 and 12. It is obvious that the lightstick is particularly useful if little space is available – in the theatre perhaps as a special effect in elements of the scenery or as a 'magic wand' for the props department. In the latter case it is best powered by a battery. Its service life is given as 20,000 hours, which is extremely high for a lighting device.

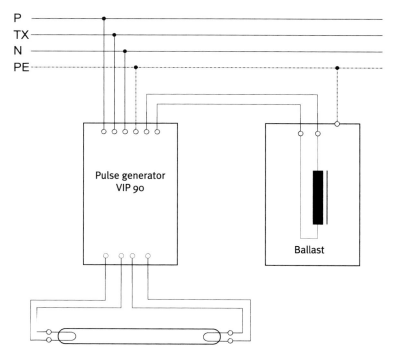

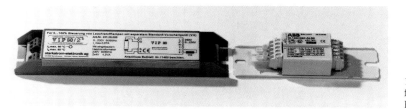

181 Circuit diagram for dimming a fluorescent lamp with a 26 mm diameter tube. Bottom: pulse generator with ballast

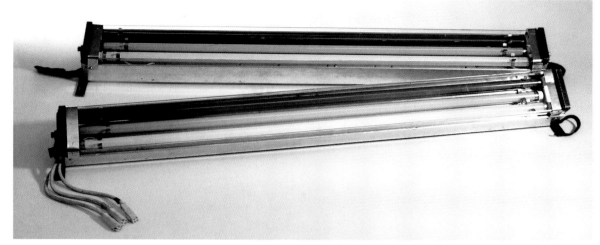

182 Fluorescent lamp segment for three colours with Macrolon cover

## LOW PRESSURE SODIUM VAPOUR LAMPS

When the lamp is cold, the sodium in the bulb is in a solid state. The vaporization process is initiated by an auxiliary discharge in the neon gas. The heat developed causes the sodium to vaporize slowly. All the radiation is in the yellow part of the spectrum (588–589 nm), in other words the area in which the human eye perceives the greatest brightness. In spite of losses in the switching device the luminous efficiency is extraordinarily high – up to 150 lm/W.

Light from a low pressure sodium discharge lamp is yellow; thus coloured objects appear only in various shades of yellow. Visual sharpness is high as there is no chromatic aberration and contrast is often much enhanced.

In this context we have to look very briefly at chromatic aberration. As the refraction of light in the lens of the human eye is a function of the wavelength, a chromatic aberration results. Shorter wave blue light is refracted more strongly by the eye than longer wave red light. The eye is short-sighted for blue light because the image plane is shifted, and far-sighted for long-wave

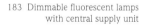
183 Dimmable fluorescent lamps with central supply unit

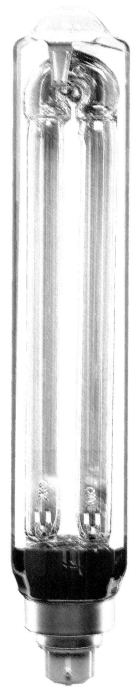

184 180 W low pressure sodium vapour lamp

## HIGH PRESSURE SODIUM VAPOUR LAMPS

These lamps work at a higher vapour pressure and gas temperature. The high pressure lamp creates a broad spectrum with a high ratio of radiation in the red

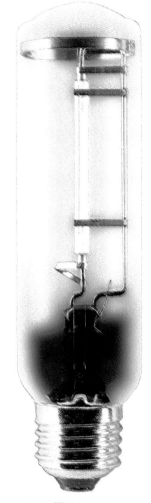

187  400 W high pressure sodium vapour lamp

185  Lantern housing for 4 x 180 W low pressure sodium vapour lamps. A douser for 50 cm daylight floods fits for dimming purposes. Homemade

red light. Thus vision is somewhat sharper when the illumination is from a low pressure sodium vapour lamp than with white light (e. g. street and tunnel lighting).

| Power: | 18 – 180 W |
| Cap: | BY 22 d |
| Position: | base down, horizontal |
| Immediate reignition: | depending on type: yes |
| Start-up time: | depending on type: 10 – 20 minutes |
| Dimming: | no |
| Service life: | approx. 10,000 hours |
| Spectrum: | 588 – 589 nm |
| Colour temperature: | 1,800 K |
| Luminous efficiency: | to 190 lm/W |
| Colour rendering: | none |

### Stage use

Low pressure sodium vapour lamps should be a component of any variable lighting inventory. Although they are difficult to handle, it is worth considering them as an alternative within the range of lighting available.

The greatest problem is integrating the lamp into different lighting states. The advantage of this type of light is that it is the only one to produce a monochromatic line spectrum that can still be used for stage lighting purposes. That is to say, we have a yellowish light as the sustaining light quality on the stage. Its low luminance makes this lamp ideal for surface lighting. The body colours of the costumes and set components are matt and dead, as though they do not exist. A red rose becomes black, a green tree turns grey. A wealth of expressive possibilities is offered.

field; the colour of the light is yellowish. Its luminous efficiency is lower than that of the low pressure lamp.

| Power: | 40 – 1,000 W |
| Cap: | Fc 2, RX 7 s, E 27, E 40 |
| Position: | any and horizontal |
| Immediate reignition: | yes, with double ended power supply and suitable ignition devices |
| Start-up time: | depending on type: several minutes |
| Dimming: | no |
| Service life: | approx: 10,000 hours |
| Colour temperature: | broad yellow orange block with red (at 600 nm)/ 2,000 K |
| Luminous efficiency: | up to 120 lm/W |
| Colour rendering: | level 4 |

186  400 W high pressure sodium vapour lamp, double ended

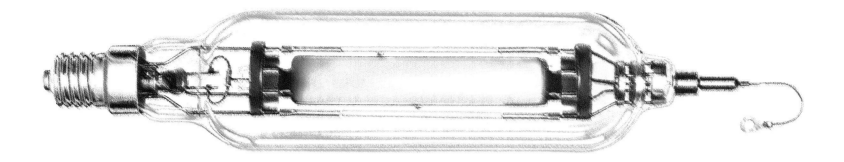

188 3,500 W metal halide
lamp for hot reignition

## Stage use

Because its spectrum is different, this lamp does not produce the monochrome colour impression given by the low pressure sodium vapour lamp. Its broad spectrum reproduces colours better. Its higher output makes it brighter and more powerful – at the expense of the surface colour transformations. Like the low pressure lamp, it cannot be dimmed.

## METAL HALIDE LAMPS

Metal halide lamps (HQIs) are an advanced form of high pressure mercury lamps. Adding tungsten-halogen compounds of various metals and 'rare earths' to the mercury makes it possible to increase luminous efficiency considerably (95 lm/W). In addition very good colour rendering can be obtained. As the ignition voltage of metal halide lamps is higher than the mains voltage, an ignition device or starter is needed as well as a current-limiting ballast. These lamps produce a very similar light to the Metallogen lamps used in the theatre. Since the lamp arc is very long, they can only be used in floodlights with symmetrical, asymmetrical or rotationally symmetrical reflectors.

A new metal halide lamp is now available to broaden the programme by adding metal iodides and 'rare earths'. A 150 W version has been created that radiates coloured light. Colours presently available are orange, green, blue and magenta. An additive mixture producing white can be made by using the colours blue, green and orange.

| | |
|---|---|
| Power: | 39–3,500 W |
| Cap: | E 27, E 40, Fc 2, RX 7 s, G 12 |
| Position: | vertical, horizontal |
| Immediate reignition: | single ended lamps: no; double ended lamps: yes |
| Start-up time: | 3–5 minutes |
| Dimming: | no |
| Service life: | approx. 6,000 hours |
| Colour temperature: | 4,700–6,000 K |
| Luminous efficiency: | to 120 lm/W |
| Colour rendering: | level 1 |

## Stage use

This is an interesting lamp for light design. Hung overhead and directed downwards, the lamps give a 'factory hall feeling'. But be careful – after an outstanding blackout there will be no light at all at first. The lamps can only be ignited again after a cooling down period (between five and twenty minutes depending on the type), and they need a three to five-minute warm-up period. The type of lamp that can be reignited immediately is easier to handle. Manufacturers offer extremely robust equipment for this kind of lighting, which stands up very well to rough use in the theatre. Unfortunately, as with many discharge lamps, the brightness cannot be regulated. Mechanical dimming with a shutter screen is the only way to integrate artificial daylight into lighting operation sensibly and variably. The lamp produces a hard, corporeal light, as the spectral composition produces a slight accentuation in the bluish-green range. High luminous efficiency means that you can see something as well. But the lamps that can be reignited immediately do not last very long, as the life of a lamp is reduced every time it is switched on. In other

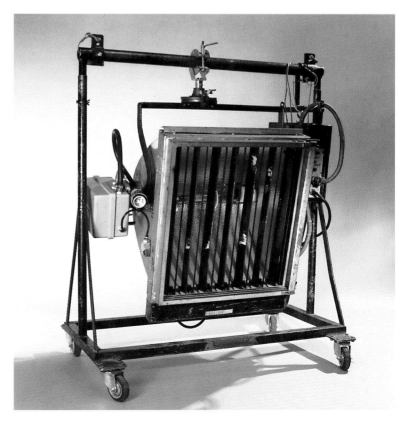

189 3,500 W metal halide lamp for hot reignition, in its housing with a mechanical dimming device

words, they are more suitable as continuous light source, which is what they were designed for. The advantages are definitely interesting, and anyone looking for a cold, slightly greenish-blue floodlight will be making the right choice with this lamp.

Insiders are also now aware of the excellent effects which can be gained through using the warm-up period. The metal vaporization process briefly produces a beautiful, ice-cold green. Effective use can be made of this physical process. The use of coloured metal halide lamps suggests itself particularly for architectural illumination.

## HMI METAL HALIDE LAMPS

In 1970 OSRAM launched a new lighting technology, the HMI® Metallogen lamp. OSRAM uses the abbreviation HMI® as a trademark. At present four different lamp forms are commercially available:

- single ended, without outer bulb
- cap on one end, with outer bulb (singled ended)
- double ended
- reflector lamps

The discharge chamber and lamp bulb are made of quartz glass, which encloses the electrode system and the circuit lines.

To produce light, the lamp is filled with an optimal combination of halides of various 'rare earth' metals: dysprosium, thulium and holmium. The tungsten-halogen cycle, familiar from the incandescent halogen lamp, prevents any vaporized electrode material from being deposited on the inner surface of the bulb. Other cycles ensure that the necessary high concentration of vaporized 'rare earths' is created in hot zones of the arc discharge. Because of the high temperatures involved, the elliptical or cylindrical discharge envelope and the lamp base are made of pure quartz glass. The glass has to be able to withstand a working pressure up to 35 bar and a thermal load of up to 950°C. Molybdenum bands fused into the lamp base are used for the power supply.

When the lamp is cold, the filler substances condense on the bulb lining (mercury usually in droplets, the halogenides as coloured deposits). These substances take about one to four minutes to evaporate after ignition. During this process arc drop voltage, electrical power and luminous flux gradually increase as they approach the rated value, while the lamp current and colour temperature are higher at first than in the lamp's steady-state operating mode. As the bulb temperature increases, the elements vaporize in the sequence indicated and produce a homogeneous gas-filling.

If the lamp is switched off, hot reignition is possible depending on the type used. This requires a voltage that is ten times higher: a 2,500 W lamp needs 5 kV when cold. If the lamp is reignited when hot, then 45–55 kV is needed. This high voltage can easily cause arcs elsewhere or in the base. But this happens only when there are faults in the envelope, or the connection between the lamp cap and the lamp holder is faulty. Cabling inside the lamp housing can also be a problem, but essentially, such problems today occur only within the lamp, above all, in lamps with a single ended holder.

Envelope filling
- first phase:      argon and mercury
- second phase:   mercury-iodide-bromine
- third phase:     thulium, dysprosium, holmium

HMI lamps have a lamp life between 300 and 1,000 hours, according to type. This is also affected by the number of times they are ignited. In any case the colour temperature decreases with the length of time they are used, on average by 50 K per 100 hours. This high pressure lamp has interesting technical specifications that make it a popular light source for film, television and theatre:

- similar light spectrum to daylight
- excellent colour rendering qualities
- high luminous power and luminous efficiency

## DOUBLE ENDED HMI LAMPS

This series includes lamps with a rating of 125 to 24,000 W. The lamps combine high luminous efficiency (80–100 lm/W) with a relatively short arc, which makes it very easy to control the light emitted and thus creates ideal conditions for using the lamp in very many ways. This applies particularly to the improved 'GS' version lamps introduced in 1986 (GS = gap shortened, i.e. a shorter arc). The maximum admissible cap temperature in the lanterns should not exceed 230°C.

| | |
|---|---|
| Power: | 125–24,000 W |
| Cap: | X 515, SFc 10–4, SFc 15.5–6, SFa 21–12, K 25 s, S 30 x 70 |
| Operating position: | depending on type: horizontal, vertical |
| Immediate reignition: | yes |
| Warm-up time: | 2–4 minutes |
| Dimming: | limited |
| Average service life: | 200 W = 350 hours 575 and 1,200 W = 750 hours 2,500 and 4,000 W = 500 hours 6,000 and 12,000 W = 350 hours 18,000 and 24,000 W = 250 hours |
| Spectrum: | daylight white |
| Colour temperature: | 5,600–6,000 K |
| Luminous efficiency: | up to 100 lm/W |
| Colour rendering: | level 1 |

### Stage use

Daylight lamps are now in general use in the theatre. They were first used in slide projectors, then as a theatrical spotlight, then finally in musicals. Projectors are available in versions up to 12,000 W and Fresnel spots up to 24,000 W, but reflector devices are also offered. Follow spots go up to 4,000 W, but the 1.2 and 2.5 kW profile spots are more common and easier to use. Very sophisticated slide projectors using this technology are available, but they require a complex operating technology. All this equipment is dimmed by dousers or wedge filters. The light produced is corporeal and forceful, exposing everything in its path. Correction gels make it possible to adapt the colour temperature to tungsten-halogen light, and despite a reduced light intensity, double the luminous efficiency of tungsten-halogen light is achieved. A visible ignition phase can also be built into the lighting concept with this kind of lamp. If it is used this way, the ignition impulse should be mechanically screened, either with a hand screen or with a douser.

### HMI ON STAGE

Various logistical conditions have to be met in order to use this lighting technology properly. As has been explained, the ballast is operated by an on-off (non-dim) device. It makes sense to try to use ballasts with a DMX connection (DMX = digital multiplexing, which means simultaneous digital transmission of several messages via one transmitter; see p. 125). This eliminates the need for separate switching gear. Because they are noisy, these electrical components

190  HMI 1,200 W metal halide lamp

have to be accommodated in an extra space away from the stage, ideally kept together in so-called ballast pools. If the dimmer rooms in a theatre are divided up into local groups, this is a suitable place to accommodate the spotlight ballast equipment. The lines between lanterns and ballasts run through acoustic baffles, to ensure that the loud switching sounds cannot be heard on stage.

As daylight type lanterns need a warming up period, this phase has to be masked by a douser. But it is also possible to make deliberate use of this phase as a lighting effect.

The brightness is regulated by means of a mechanical shutter, controlled by hand or a motor. When using a slatted shutter, care should be taken that the slats are set at 90° to the electrodes. If the arc is parallel to the slats, a strong

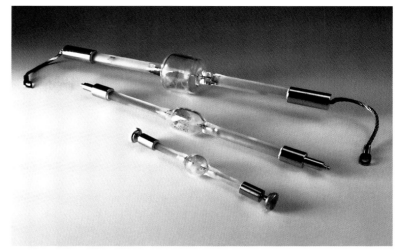

191 Double ended metal halide lamps, from front to back: 575, 4,000 and 12,000 W

192 Double ended 575 W metal halide lamp and knurled nuts for clamping in the holder

image of them will be projected on the stage (slat projection). The arc is vertical in a single ended lamp and horizontal in a double ended lamp. Here it must be mentioned again that all discharge lamps provide a unique opportunity to create a real blackout on stage. The weak afterglow from the electrodes is almost imperceptible, and 'cut images' can be produced by reigniting the lamps.

The noises made when working with these lamps is a ticklish point. This kind of switching is very disagreeable for theatre work. The lines to the apparatus can be 50 m long. This length also depends on the cross-section of the lead, and on the condition of the plugs and the lamp.

193 4,000 W HMI lanterns with colour changers and dousers in use on stage. The lanterns are lighting a white reflecting surface that throws the light back on to the white shirting tent. Indirect lighting makes it possible to achieve extremely homogeneous light distribution

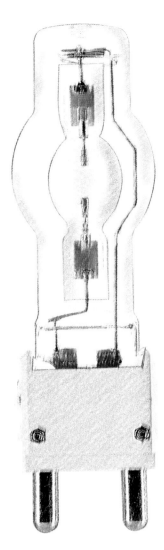

194  2,500 W metal halide lamp, single ended

### Regulating HMIs

It is not possible to regulate these lamps 100% electrically. Limited regulation is possible from 70 to 110%. Below 70% of the lamp's output the colour temperature changes visibly, and this is probably not in the best interests of the user. The best devices for this manipulation are electronic ballasts. Because complete dimming as a soft, homogeneous process is not possible, I find it preferable to work on perfecting mechanical dimming devices. This has the advantage that the lamp remains at the correct working temperature even when it is not emitting much light, thus avoiding colour changes.

### SINGLE ENDED HMI LAMPS

Single ended HMI lamps opened up new ground for spotlight manufacturers. The G 38 cap is commonly used for this purpose.

These lamps can be smaller in size, which gives the manufacturers greater design scope. Versions from 21 to 12,000 W are available at present. These almost all have a double bulb structure, i.e. the discharge envelope is surrounded by a second glass envelope. An electrode connection is run to the ignition envelope between the two glass walls. The intermediate volume is usually filled with nitrogen.

| | |
|---|---|
| Power: | 21, 125, 250, 400, 575, 1,200, 2,500, 4,000, 6,000, 12,000 W |
| Cap: | FaX 1.5, GZY 9.5, GZZ 9.5, G 22, G 38 + special |
| Operating position: | any, 45° tilted |
| Immediate reignition: | yes |
| Warm-up time: | 2 minutes |
| Dimming: | limited |
| Average service life: | 125 W = 150 hours |
| | 250 W = 200 hours |
| | 400 W = 650 hours |
| | 575 W = 750 hours |
| | 1,200 W = 750 hours |
| | 2,500 W = 500 hours |
| | 4,000 W = 500 hours |
| | 6,000 W = 300 hours |
| | 12,000 W = 250 hours |
| Spectrum: | daylight white |
| Colour temperature: | 5,600–6,000 K |
| Colour rendering: | level 1 |

195  1,200 PAR 64 metal halide lamp

### PAR-HMI REFLECTOR LAMP

This lamp is fitted with a parabolic reflector that produces slightly diverging light, similarly to the function of a PAR 64 incandescent lamp. The key advantages of the PAR-HMI lamp are its greater efficiency as a lighting unit and its ability to focus light. It is thus particularly suitable for all uses in which large throw distances are required. The reflector has a dichroic coating and is thus permeable for most radiated heat. This type of reflector is technically referred to as a cold reflector.

The PAR-HMI lamp has become less important recently, as the development of single ended HMI lamps has meant that spotlights with axially mounted HMI lamps are available that offer the same effective light and can also be focused to a limited extent.

The angle of dispersion can be altered by the use of various supplementary discs that can be attached to the housing:

| | |
|---|---|
| Narrow spot: | 7° x 8° |
| Medium flood: | 26° x 56° |
| Wide flood: | 26° x 56° |
| Super wide flood: | 47° x 47° |
| Power: | 200 W – PAR 36 |
| | 575 W – PAR 46 |
| | 1,200 W – PAR 64 |
| Cap: | G 38 + special |
| Operating position: | any, lamp horizontal |
| Immediate reignition: | yes |
| Warm-up period: | 1–2 minutes |
| Dimming: | limited |
| Service life: | approx. 1,000 hours |
| Spectrum: | daylight white |
| Colour temperature: | 6,000 K |
| Colour rendering: | level 1 |

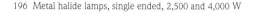

196  Metal halide lamps, single ended, 2,500 and 4,000 W

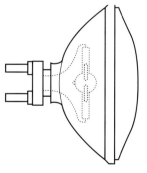

197  1,200 W PAR lamp. The lamp is a sealed unit inside the PAR housing

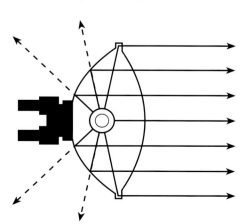

198  1,200 W PAR lamp with beam path. The cold reflector allows the heat radiation to pass out through the back.

199 400 W HTI reflector lamp

## HTI LAMPS

There are two main versions of this discharge lamp, one with an integral cold reflector and one without. The optimum combination of ellipsoidal cold reflector and lamp system gives this lamp extraordinary spot brilliance, combined with high luminous efficiency and luminance, created by the very short arc (short arc lamp). This lamp type is preferred for small, compact scanners, which usually offer the possibility of rapid, complex colour changes. HTI lamps are also used often in fibre optics technology.

200 Beam path in a reflector lamp, ellipsoidal cold reflector

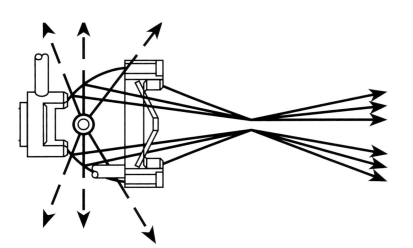

| | |
|---|---|
| Power: | 150–2,500 W, with cold reflector 250–400 W |
| Cap: | single or double ended |
| Operating position: | any |
| Immediate reignition: | depends on type |
| Warm-up time: | 30 seconds |
| Dimming: | limited |
| Service life: | 250–700 hours |
| Spectrum: | daylight white |
| Colour temperature: | 4,500–6,500 K |
| Colour rendering: | level 1 |

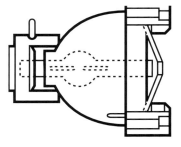

201 Lamp position in an HTI reflector lamp

202 400 W HTI reflector lamp

## XENON LAMPS

The discharge envelope is ellipsoidal or spherical and largely free of streaks or bubbles. It is made of pure quartz glass because of the high thermal load. The xenon gas filling is compressed and rises about threefold when the lamp is on. Two tungsten electrodes are placed opposite each other in the discharge envelope. The cathode (negative electrode) is considerably smaller and thinner than the anode (positive electrode), which gets much hotter than the cathode due to the physics of the discharge process, and thus needs a larger surface area in order to disperse the excess warmth by radiation. Each electrode is attached to a tungsten rod that also links it to the relevant cap. The lamp ends are also made of quartz glass and mounted in metal sleeve caps.

Xenon lamps need direct current, which is supplied by special rectifiers. These power supply devices have to deliver a no-load voltage that is at least three times the lamp's working voltage. The xenon gas in the cold lamp is to a certain extent an electric insulator that becomes a conducter during the ignition process. A high-frequency, high-voltage charge (20,000–40,000 V) is put through the lamp for a few tenths of a second to trigger the gas discharge. The tips of the electrodes are 2 to 9 mm apart (short arc lamp). The arc is generated here after ignition. Light intensity can be controlled over a wide range by changing the current strength. In contrast with most other light sources, this does not change the spectrum and the colour temperature. The lamp produces outstanding colour rendering and daylight white light.

As the luminous efficiency is only approx. 30 to 40 lm/W, xenon lamps are no longer very popular for stage use and have been largely replaced by metal halide lamps, which produce between 60 and 105 lm/W. But xenon lamps are still standard light sources for film and video projections (eidophor process).

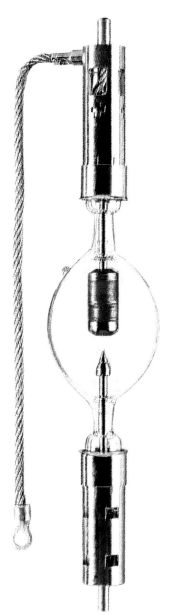

204 Xenon lamp

| | |
|---|---|
| Power: | 75–10,000 W |
| Cap: | PSFa 25–10, PSFa 25–12, PSFa 27–10, PSFa 27–12, PSFaX 27–13, PSFaX 27–14, Sfa 30 |
| Operating position: | vertical, horizontal |
| Immediate reignition: | yes |
| Warm-up time: | none (no vaporization process) |
| Dimming: | yes |
| Service life: | up to 2,000 hours |
| Spectrum: | daylight white |
| Colour temperature: | 5,600–6,300 K |
| Luminous efficiency: | to 40 lm/W |
| Colour rendering: | level |

203 1,200 W HMI lamp, shortly after switching on

### Stage use

Xenon devices are made as follow spots, profile spots, cyclorama wash lights and also as projectors. They are enormously expensive to run, as a direct current supply is not cheap and the luminous efficiency relatively low. This technology has been increasingly displaced by metal halide lamps. The German firm Altmann Lichtoptik recently started making profile spots again using this technology. The lanterns have been restructured and fitted with an innovative mechanical douser.

## SOLAR 1000/SULPHUR LAMP

This lamp is filled with sulphur-argon gas and its spectrum is in the daylight field. This new lamp technology involves ionizing the sulphur-argon mixture with microwaves and thus making it glow. The glowing plasma, which is enclosed in a quartz glass chamber, emits flicker-free, daylight quality light, with unusually little associated heat radiation. The lamp bulb is rotated 3,400 times per minute when in operation. The lamp life of approx. 60,000 hours seems to lie in the realms of fantasy. The life span of the magnetron, which

205 Sulphur lamp. The sphere is approx. 3 cm in diameter. The lamp with the glass tube is rotated by a motor

emits the microwaves that generates the light, is given as approx. 15,000 hours.

This lamp is used mainly in combination with a fluorescent tube placed in front of the lamp reflector to distribute the radiated light evenly throughout the tube. The plastic tube is 25.4 cm (10 inches) in diameter and is effective over a length of up to 20 m. The inside of the tube is covered with a special reflecting foil that distributes and transmits the light evenly.

| | |
|---|---|
| Power: | 1,425 W |
| Cap: | none |
| Operating position: | horizontal and vertical |
| Warm-up time: | a few seconds |
| Immediate reignition: | no |
| Waiting time for reignition: | approx. 5 minutes warm-up time, 4 seconds after switching on, 20 seconds to 100% |
| Dimming: | to 20% |
| Service life, lamp: | approx. 60,000 hours |
| Service life, magnetron: | approx. 15,000 hours |
| Colour temperature: | 6,000 K |
| Luminous efficiency: | 95 lm/W |
| Colour rendering: | level 2 |

## HIGH VOLTAGE DISCHARGE LAMPS (NEON LIGHTS)

Lamps of this kind are made in every possible shape, in various lengths and many colours. The glass tube can be shaped as desired and is also available in various colours.

| | |
|---|---|
| Glass tube: | 9–35 mm external diameter and up to 3 m long, wall thickness 0.9–1.2 mm |
| Clear glass: | colourless glass tube, suitable for all luminous colours |
| Filter glass: | in yellow, blue, red, transparent; suitable for green, blue-violet, red and yellow luminous colours |
| Luminous substances: | over 40 different luminous colours |

### Luminous substances

Tubes in clear and filter glass without luminous substances offer a restricted range of colours, mainly shades of blue and red. The gas discharge is visible as different colours in the peripheral zones of the glass tube. Similar to low voltage tubes, many neon tubes have a

### Neon tube

The power supply to the gas column is via a wired electrode melted into either end of the system. The connections are in the form of copper strand or wire. The gas filling is either neon alone or an argon mixture combined with mercury. The lamp position is as desired, and the length of the tube depends on the electrode positioning, normally up to 3 m long. A long lamp life of over 10,000 hours allows an economical operation.

### Electrical supply

Mains voltage is not sufficient to run neon tubes. Several systems are used in series for high voltage neon tubes. The high voltage is delivered by a high-reactance transformer. Transformers are available for induced voltages up to 10 kV and tube currents of 15 to 200 mA. Smaller transformers are also used. In Europe the large units have to be housed in a safety casing, and there are detailed regulations. To reduce expense and effort, a voltage under 1,000 is recommended; small transformers producing 990 V and 40 to 250 mA are available.

Approx. 230 V are necessary for 1 m of neon tube. This depends on whether the discharge is red or blue, and on the shape and diameter of the neon tube. Around 150 V per system have to be added for electrode loss, and 50% of the tube and electrode voltage on top of this for the ignition voltage.

| | |
|---|---|
| Power: | 23–40 W per m |
| Voltage: | approx. 570 V for 1 m length and a tube diameter of 20 mm |
| Cap: | bolted or clamped connection |
| Operating position: | any |
| Immediate reignition: | yes |
| Warm-up time: | none |
| Dimming: | yes |
| Service life: | approx. 10,000 hours |
| Glass tube diameter: | 9–35 mm external diameter |
| Ambient temperature: | optimum 25°C |

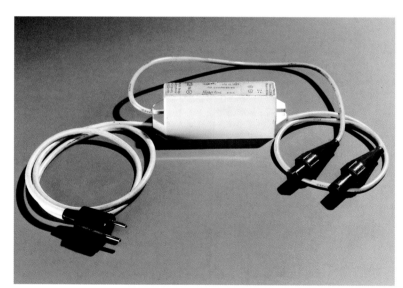

206  High voltage transformer to 990 V with high voltage plug connection

### Stage use

At present there is no ideal lantern. This is mainly because of the lamp's inadequate luminance. But it is a light source that can be used excellently for illuminating buildings. A design using a fluorescent lamp system could be very effective on the stage, as it has never yet been possible to illuminate such a long transparent plastic tube evenly.

fluorescent layer of luminous material consisting of halogen phosphates, silicates, tungstates or other substances on the inner wall of the gas tube. The gas discharge takes place in a gas mixture containing mercury and an inert gas as the basic gas. The mercury vapour radiation contains a strong ultraviolet component that is transformed into visible radiation by the luminous coating.

### Stage use

Neon lights can be regulated well from lighting consoles, and they are flicker-free provided the tubes are not too long. Like the low voltage tube, this system is very susceptible to mechanical stress, but the aesthetic lighting effect that it can produce is often required. As a neon light has very low luminous power it is not exactly suitable for lighting a surface, but it is ideal for

207 Sheet metal housing with two 4,000 W high voltage transformers

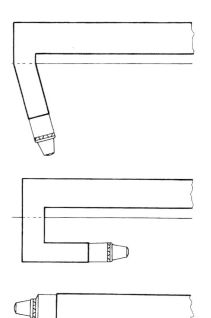

208 Neon tube with differently shaped electrodes

making a distinctive mark. As it can be manufactured in most shapes and produces very beautiful colours, it offers the stage designer a large range of possibilities. These tubes are very good for creating a long, thin line of light. If the electrodes are angled, all that is between the individual lamps is the material thickness of the neon tube. In this case a thin layer of high voltage insulation tape should be inserted between the tubes. Reasonably priced accessories such as fixing clips and high volt-

| | |
|---|---|
| Power: | 4–125 W |
| Cap: | G 5, G 13, E 27, E 40 |
| Operating position: | as desired |
| Immediate reignition: | as a fluorescent lamp: yes; as a high pressure mercury vapour lamp: no |
| Warm-up time: | as a fluorescent lamp: none; as a discharge lamp: 3 minutes |
| Dimming: | none |
| Service life: | approx. 1,000 hours |
| Colour rendering: | none |

## SPECTRAL LAMPS

Spectral lamps are discharge lamps that emit line spectrums of inert gases and metal vapours with high irradiance. They consist of a glass or quartz glass lamp containing the desired inert gas or a basic gas and the metal whose spectrum is to be created. These lamps are used in the field of optics, medicine etc. Matching the gases and metals to the appropriate spectral line is necessary and significant.

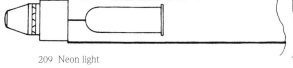

209 Neon light

age cable for self-assembly, and also high voltage insulation tape are available. The transformers are not exactly cheap, but they do last for many years.

## ULTRAVIOLET LAMPS

UV lamps have little to offer, with the exception of one special feature: they emit only ultraviolet rays. As we know, this radiation is outside the visible light range. The lamps have a black glass bulb that absorbs all visible light.

### Stage use

These lamps can be used on stage, but as UV radiation can only be used effectively in a dark area, the stage would have to be almost in black in order to do this. This can produce exciting after-effects. It makes white colours, nylon or similar artificial materials visible, but, for example, teeth and finger nails as well. Two types of illumination effects have to be distinguished here: phosphorescence and fluorescence. The former effect allows a short-term radiation storage, whereas fluorescent light is present only as long as the lamp is turned on.

### Stage use

These 'outsider' lamps are not powerful enough for theatrical use. At best they are used for mysterious, spiritualistic stage presentations.

Important spectral lines

| | | | |
|---|---|---|---|
| Thallium | = violet | 380 | nm |
| Mercury | = violet | 404.7 | nm |
| Hydrogen | = violet | 435.0 | nm |
| Mercury | = violet | 435.8 | nm |
| Hydrogen | = blue-green | 486.1 | nm |
| Mercury | = green | 546.1 | nm |
| Mercury | = yellow | 577–579 | nm |
| Helium | = yellow | 587 | nm |
| Sodium | = yellow | 589 | nm |
| Hydrogen | = red | 656 | nm |
| Helium | = red | 706 | nm |

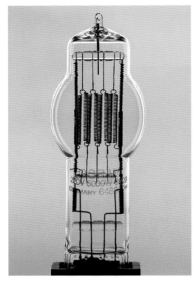

210 5,000 W tungsten-halogen lamp with biplanar filament

211 Xenon lamp

## LAMPS, LAMPS AND MORE LAMPS

There are many more interesting special discharge lamps that are almost exclusively for theatre use. The trend is unequivocal: This lamp technology is increasingly in demand in the theatre and in the field of entertainment. If a discharge lamp is used, the person using it must be familiar with its characteristics and know the kind of light it emits. In addition he must also be able to handle its technology and know why the desired daylight effect cannot be produced by other means. The following is a guide to the qualities:

| Solid-state lamp:  | 3,200 K, 28 lm/W |
| Real lumens:       | approx. 4 lm/W   |
| Metal halide lamps: | 6,000 K.<br>100 lm/W |
| Real lumens:       | approx. 11 lm/W  |
| PAR-HMI:           | 6,000 K, 91 lm/W |
| Real lumens:       | approx. 45 lm/W  |

Illustration of colour temperature adjustment: converting from 3,200 K to 5,600° reduces illuminance by a factor of 2, i. e. from 4 lm/W to 2 lm/W.

## LAMP CAPS – LAMPHOLDERS

All solid-state and discharge lamps need an electrical power supply. A lampholder is used to transfer this to the lamp with the least possible resistance. Its job is to hold the lamp in the intended operating position and to conduct the current to the filament or the electrodes. This is done via the power feed, which is hermetically sealed or pinched into the bulb.

As a rule, lampholders are made of metal or ceramics, and the lamp bodies are made of glass. A distinction is made between soft, hard and quartz glass.

As all materials expand differently when heated – for example, quartz glass has a very low coefficient of expansion, hard glass a higher one and metal expands even more when heated – the joint between the glass bulb and the lamp cap is a particular problem.

A lamp is held in the lampholder in the intended position by the cap. Usually lamps have a single cap. Tubular lamps have two ends, which always have the same type of cap. A good contact, and especially a contact with a large surface area between the cap and

the lampholder is absolutely essential, particularly with high power ratings, as this can also help to conduct heat away, which is very good for the lamp's thermal situation.

The glass bulb has to be connected with the tungsten filament or the electrodes via the cap. Generally the connection between glass and ceramics is cemented. The cap provides a suitable metallic contact with the holder. The holder's function is first and foremost to supply the necessary current and conduct the resultant heat away. The latter function is particularly important, as overheating of the pinch in the lamp can damage the electric circuit material. Air is emptied from the bulb which is then filled with an inert gas or halides before the two parts are connected.

### Cap types

SINGLE ENDED: Lamps with caps at one end only are the most widely used in the theatre. This type runs from simple, small signal lamps to high voltage metal vapour lamps.

DOUBLE ENDED: Double ended, tubular lamps have the same cap at each end. The usual cap for halogen tubes is the R 7 s cap (recessed single contact). For more powerful lamps (from 2,000 W), cable caps are used.

GLASS CAPS: The simplest cap construction. The mounting and contact is effected directly through the molybdenum pins of the pinched-in current supply. The usual pin diameter is 0.7–1 mm. This cap is used only for low voltages and wattages.

CERAMIC CAP: The pinched-in bulb is cemented into a ceramic recess, and the molybdenum pins are attached to the contact pins in the cap. A ceramic cap makes the lamp easier to handle and stabilise in the holder.

METAL CAP: The most versatile cap. Lamps for general use, car lamps and high-powered lanterns are fitted with them.

– The screw cap has one contact in the screw thread and the other is the centre contact.

– Low voltage lamps with metal sleeve caps make electrical contact via the metal sleeve and a central contact or two insulated base contacts.

– For lamps with a high power rating, the power supply is via two insulated leads or, in the case of double ended caps, directly via the metal caps.

212 Ill. p. 95: Various lamp caps

## Screw caps

These are often found in general use but are quite rare for stage use, and then only when the coil does not have to align to a reflector or lens system, for example in low voltage lamps.

E 27          E 40

## Bayonet cap

The pins on the cap make it possible for the body of the lamp to be placed in a predetermined position. Corresponding holes in the holder ensure that the lamp sits firmly. B and BA caps are only used for low power requirements.

BA 20 d      BA 21s–4      BA 24 s–3

## Prefocus cap

The broad cap base flanges guarantee better seating in the holder than bayonet cap lamps. The cap flanges are differently shaped to prevent the lamp from being fitted incorrectly.

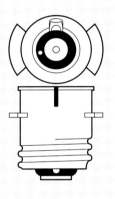 

P 40 s          P 28 s

## Pin cap

This is the kind of cap most used in the theatre. They make excellent electrical contact and guarantee a perfectly aligned position in the holder. Pin caps with pins of unequal thickness make it impossible to fit the lamp incorrectly. These caps are used from tiny low voltage lamps to 10,000 W solid-state lamps and 4,000 W HMI lamps.

GZX 9.5      GX 9.5      GY 9.5      GX 16 d

G 38          G 22          GY 22          GY 16

## Locking caps

These create contact with the holder by the application of mechanical pressure. Contact is made either by mechanical contact pressure from the holder contacts, by a cliplock or by a milled nut. The connection is both the mechanical mount and the electrical contact. This cap is used for the smallest lamps and discharge lamps up to 4,000 W.

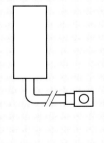

SFaX 27–10      R7 s / RX7 s      SFa 21–12      SFc 10–4 / M4 thread

## Cable caps

Cable caps are used for single and double ended lamps. Here the lamp mount is separated from the power supply. Separate electrical contact via cable lugs guarantees a particularly good electrical contact. This cap is used for high powered lamps.

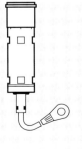 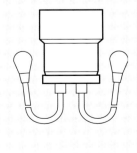

S 30 x 70      K 24 s      K 39 d

### Cap categories for solid-state lamps

This system simplifies the identification of lamp caps.

• Component A:

This is made up of one or more capital letters explaining the type of cap. Here are the most important letters:

G: base with two or more protruding contacts like pins or pegs.

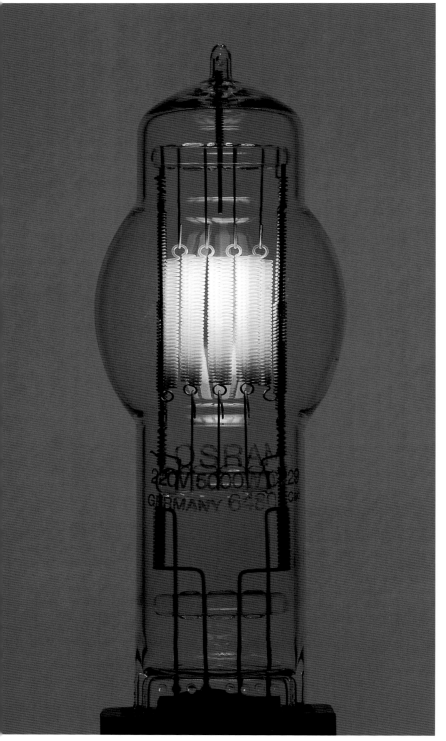

G caps are also called pin caps. Common examples include G 4 in the low voltage field and G 22 in the high voltage field. (G = originally derived from glass cap)

P: prefocus or adjustable cap for tight tolerance systems: lamp-cap-holder
K: cap with cable connection
R: cap with sunken, recessed contacts (R = recessed)
B: bayonet cap

If one letter is not sufficient to describe a cap, several can be used, with the most important characteristic first. A PK cap would be a prefocus cable cap. If the one-letter characteristics are not enough to distinguish between caps, the letters X, Y, Z and U are used alone or in combination. Example: G 6.35 – GY 6.35, GX 9.5

• Component B:

This is a number identifying the cap's most important approximate dimension in mm.

| For G caps: | the pins' distance |
| For P caps: | the size of the sleeve |
| For K caps: | the diameter of the cup sleeve |
| For R caps: | the diameter of the ceramic ring (not of the recessed contact, e. g. the R 7 s cap) |
| For B caps: | the diameter of the cap sleeve |

• Component C:

This is a lower case letter describing the number of contacts or connections. The following key letters are used:

s: one contact (single)
d: two contacts (double)
t: three contacts (triple)
q: four contacts (quadruple)
p: five contacts (penta)

• Component D:

After a hyphen, i. e. after the basic definition of the cap (which is adopted for the holder), come additional features that are often only mentioned in order to avoid confusion.

• Components E and F:

After component D, it is possible to add additional measurements, after a slash and one underneath the other, linked by the multiplication sign ×; these describe secondary characteristics of the cap, for example length (height) and the diameter of sleeves or flanges.

### Discharge lamp categories

The first three letters identify the type of lamp: HMI, HMP, HTI, HSR, HSD.

D: durable
H: abbreviation for mercury
I: halide compound (iodide, bromide)
M: metals ('rare earths'), e. g. dysprosium, holmium, thulium
P: projection
R: rare earth metals (see M)
S: safe, simple handling
T: daylight

The letters after the power details identify particular construction features.

C: cable, with connector cable and plug
D: double, usually capless lamps with pin contacts
DE: double ended lamps with setscrew
GS: gap short (reduced distance between electrodes)
P: projection
PAR: lamp with parabolic reflector (sealed unit)
S: short, a geometrically shorter version of the standard lamp (different light centre position)
SE: single ended lamp

213  5,000 W tungsten-halogen lamp with biplanar filament

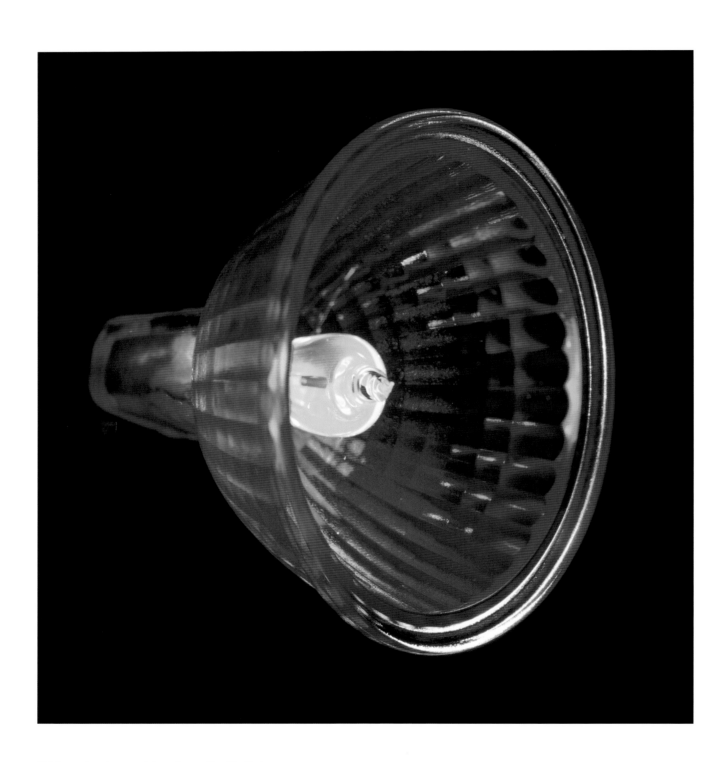

215  Low voltage tungsten-halogen lamp with cold reflector

# Colour Plates and Colour Gels

White light is not always agreeable. There are various ways of changing white light into a colour. For example, a lamp can be operated at a higher or lower voltage, which will mean that the colour temperature of the light source changes. The light still gives the impression that it is white, but if the incandescent coil takes on a reddish-yellow tinge because the voltage is being lowered, the quality of the light will become slightly reddish. But it is not possible to make a significant colour change by this method. Fundamentally, we have two basic means at our disposal for changing the original colour of light: with colour plates and colour gels. These filters change the colour of a light source by subtractive colour mixing.

## COLOUR PLATES

Until the plastics industry was able to make colour gels, stage light was coloured by coloured glass plates. Some lanterns still use colour plates if heat or mechanical durability is a factor. The advantage of a glass plate is that the chosen colour remains constant throughout the life of the plate. The disadvantages are weight, fragility and price. Only pure chemicals are used as starting materials for colouring glass. Different colours are achieved by adding chemicals such as copper, chromium, manganese, iron, cobalt, vanadium, titanium, neodymium, and so on. These metal ions are added to molten glass and change the colour of the material. Another process is so-called mordant dyeing. Here the surface of the white glass is colour-treated at a temperature of 400 to 600°C.

As the quantities needed for the different colour shades are relatively small, these filter plates are still hand-blown. The glass is blown into a cylinder by the blowpipe, and this is then cut up and heated to form a flat sheet. The various formats are then cut out of this sheet.

Hand-blowing inevitably produces variations in thickness within the sheet of glass, which may lead to differences in colour. The most common thickness is between 2–3 mm. Colour filter plates are cut into small strips approx. 25 mm wide for better heat durability. The glass strips are held next to or above one another in a metal frame and slid into the lantern magazine. As well as about 50 different types of colour plates, several textured glasses are available which produce interesting light patterns by refraction.

It is becoming increasingly difficult to buy coloured glass. Glassworks that specialized in its manufacture found that it was not economically viable. Thus, machine-made glass is usually the option now when glass plates are required. There are not as many colours available, but one great advantage of machine-made glass is that all the various thicknesses have the same colour saturation.

Ultraviolet glass plates are still important in the theatre. UV colour absorbs almost the whole light spectrum and thus gets very hot. For this reason, only an UV plate can be used when filtering out UV rays in solid-state and discharge lamps.

## SPECIAL PLATES

• Heat Shield Filters: These plates withhold infrared radiation and thus reduce heat radiation. Filters of this kind are mainly used in large projectors and in fibre optics technology.
• Correction Filter Plates: These are used where gels are too imprecise and too heat-sensitive. They regulate the colour temperature adjustment between daylight and incandescent light.
• Uv Plates: Almost the whole of the visible spectrum has to be negated to filter UV radiation out of light. In the case of solid-state and discharge lamps this can only be accomplished by using a glass filter.

## COLOUR GELS

Colour gels started to be made as the plastics industry developed. The polymers (or plastic bases) currently used include, in approximate order of heat resistance, acetates, vinyls, polyesters and polycarbonates. Acetates and vinyls have the lowest melting points, polycarbonates the highest.

We are familiar with three different processes for combining the colour with the filter base material: colour can be applied to the base, incorporated into the surface of the base material or distributed completely throughout the gel material.

Adequate filter gels can be produced on a base of animal gelatines. These are reasonably priced, but they dry out after a time in the lantern and become brittle. In the case of acetates or vinyls this process can be delayed to a degree, but they are more flammable.

Polyester and polycarbonate materials are heat and deformation-resistant from 126 to 143°C. Polycarbonate plastic has the best combination of qualities of the available modern resins as a base material, as it does not lose its shape until the temperature reaches 149 to 163°C. This type of colour filter is self-extinguishing.

The user will not necessarily want to know all about these different manufacturing techniques when choosing gel colour qualities. He has to choose a gel that meets the requirements of the responsible local authority. This means: extreme heat resistance, non-combustible, clear, versatile colours, water-resistant and very flexible.

There are only a very few gel manufacturers in the world. The leading firms are ROSCO and LEE. Both offer a good assortment of colours with rich colour values that meet the highest quality requirements.

Filter material in rolls is very practical, available in lengths up to 15 m and 61 cm wide. Other roll sizes are also available, for example 6 m long and 120 cm wide.

Individual colour sheets are good for smaller purchases. There is a broad colour range with over 50 shades, and various versions of diffusion filters. These filters change the consistency of 'white light', but not its colour. Interesting changes can be made by using different 'texture filters', for example polarization gels, which allow light with only one direction to pass.

Correction filters have an important part to play. Here a distinction is made between:

- colour temperature correction filters:
  incandescent light to daylight
  daylight to incandescent light

- correction filters for colour brightness
- colour filters for correcting both: adapting colour temperature and colour brightness

Colour temperature correction filters are required to change the colour tem-

perature. This is physically not possible, as nothing about the lamp can be changed. Light can be corrected towards blue or reddish-yellow by filtering out certain colour components. It is thus possible to adapt the colour temperature of HMI spotlights to incandescent light or vice versa. This means

| Gel colour | LEE filter | Y% = Transparency | A = Absorption | R% = Reflection | x-Axis | y-Axis |
|---|---|---|---|---|---|---|
| Medium blue | LEE 132 | 8.27 | 1.08 | 82 | 0.13 | 0.10 |
| Peacock blue | LEE 115 | 35.22 | 0.45 | 49 | 0.13 | 0.29 |
| Dark green | LEE 124 | 29.71 | 0.25 | 55 | 0.11 | 0.62 |
| Yellow | LEE 101 | 80.00 | 0.97 | 12 | 0.45 | 0.50 |
| Flame red | LEE 164 | 17.97 | 0.74 | 68 | 0.65 | 0.30 |
| Magenta | LEE 113 | 10.92 | 0.96 | 80 | 0.56 | 0.21 |

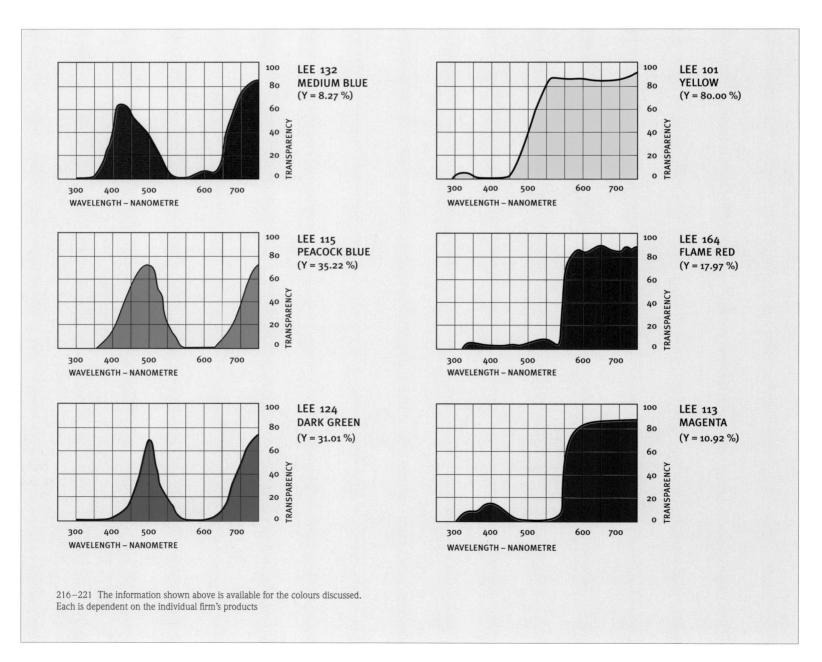

216–221 The information shown above is available for the colours discussed. Each is dependent on the individual firm's products

Colour Plates and Colour Gels

correcting small intermediate stages, not just the whole colour temperature field.

Correction filters for colour brightness reduce the brightness of the light in various stages and are used when the colour value of the filter has to be somewhat darker.

Correction gels combining both change factors are also available. As well as these three main possibilities, there is a large range of special gels that permit further light corrections. All gel manufacturers offer their collections in small sample swatch booklets. Some of them also give more precise information about transparency, how a gel relates to the colour space, and absorption.

## DICHROIC FILTERS

Dichroic colour filters are interference filters. Various oxide layers are vacuum-deposited onto heat-resistant borosilicate glass plates, which are usually 2 mm thick. The thickness of the layer (1/1000 mm) makes it possible to decide which wavelength sector (nm) will be allowed to pass through the plate. Unlike normal colour plates or filters, which absorb all colours that do not correspond with the selected colour shade, dichroic filters reflect the remaining light (Greek *dichroma* = two-colour). Each filter divides the light into a portion that is allowed to pass through and a portion that is reflected. Highly efficient processes make it possible to determine colours to an accuracy of ± 5 nm.

The filter's position and angle in the beam path determine the precise effect on colour values, and thus also for the additional colour variants in a CMY colour mixing system. For example, if a dark blue dichroic filter is tilted at 22° from the vertical, the colour changes in the direction of lavender, at 80° to a reddish pink.

Dichroic filters have several advantages over all other filters:

- up to 20% more efficiency with respect to colour intensity
- long-term colour stability
- extreme colour differences and colour saturation
- not sensitive to heat up to 400°C
- easy to clean and handle
- higher colour transmission (in gel colours this value is only 50–60% of the inherent colour)

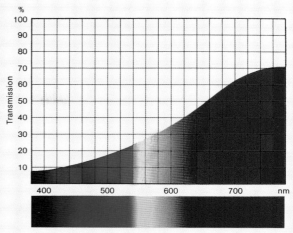

222  This diagram shows the way a normal filter works. The filter colour is identical with that of a dichroic filter (see ill. 223). The colour separation is not very great, and the rest of the spectrum also passes through the filter. This shows that this filter can never achieve the luminosity and colour intensity of a dichroic filter

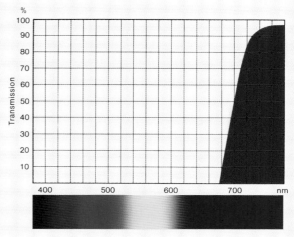

223  This diagram shows how a dichroic filter works. The area of the spectrum that is not required is reflected away and a very pure colour remains. Most dichroic colours yield 90% of the colour value. Thus the colour of the light that passes through a dichroic filter is very intense

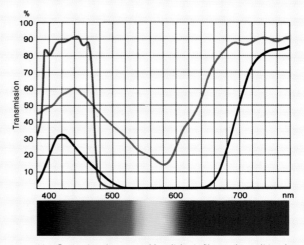

224  Comparison between a blue dichroic filter and a traditional gel filter. The red line shows a filter that allows almost 100% of the blue light to pass through; the green next to it is 100% filtered out. The blue line shows a new, unused colour gel that allows only 60% of the blue light and large parts of the red spectrum. Despite this it looks dark blue to the human eye. The black line shows the same filter after being placed in front of a PAR 64 1,000 W spotlight for one hour. Now only 30% of the blue spectrum is allowed to pass through, while the rest is absorbed in the filter

225 Anton Chekhov
*Uncle Vanya*
Director: Hans Lietzau
Set Designer: Ezio Toffolutti
Münchner Kammerspiele, 1987

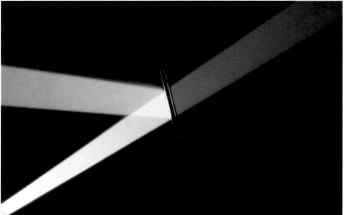

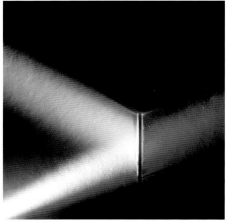

226 A beam of white light falls on a blue dichroic filter.
It is clear that unwanted light is reflected and not absorbed

227 Here the reflection process is illustrated
by a beam refracted by a prism

It is obvious that filter plates of this kind cannot be treated as normal colour plates, as a normal filter glass or gel still has to be used to change the colour of a 5,000 W spotlight with an incandescent lamp. Dichroic filters are particularly useful in 'intelligent lighting' and in colour changers that can be placed in the relatively thin beam of a focused, optically controlled system.

## COLOUR LACQUER

Lacquer does not have a lot to offer in this context, as it does not provide a very heat-resistant coating. The lacquer is applied to the glass that is to be coloured as a transparent layer and thus changes the basic colour. But it can only be used to colour bulbs that do not emit very much heat.

Lacquer is available in yellow, orange, red, blue and green. Other required intermediate tones have to be mixed.

## USING COLOUR FILTERS

If coloured gels or plates are used the light emitted by a lantern is 'filtered'. Colour components that are not desired are 'left' in the colour filter, that is, the filter absorbs them and becomes warm. This warming is considerable in the case of dark colours and makes great demands on the filter material.

Along with the colour change the strength of illumination is reduced. For example, in the case of yellow the light emitted is reduced by approx. 20%, in the case of magenta by approx. 90%. Absorption is greater in glass plates, as the material is many times thicker than colour gels.

229  1,000 W halogen flood with diffusion filter and barn-doors

## LANTERN SELECTION

A large range of lanterns is needed to execute the ideas evolving from a lighting plot. There are basic guidelines about the types of lantern needed to equip a venue. In German theatres this basic rig is already available, so all that has to be decided for a particular production is whether any additional lighting equipment is needed – and, of course, this has to be tailored to the money available.

### Floodlights
### (reflector lanterns, floods)

The simplest version of this lantern is a light source combined with a reflector, which emits a broad beam of light. Several such reflector lanterns are often put together to form banks of light, and used for border lights or footlights. Nowadays lanterns of this kind usually consist of a tungsten-halogen tube combined with a trough reflector. Aspherical (asymmetrical) reflectors are used in particular for ground rows or cyclorama lanterns intended to light large back-cloths or rear projection screens. Very few floodlights have adjustable beam spreads, and the adjustment available is minimal, as it can only change the vertical spread. They are used in various combinations, typically as border lights and footlights. The light is emitted 'in a flood', and used where even coverage is needed. Only glass colour filters can be used, as these lanterns do not have a heat-absorbing lens, and the distance between the lamp and the filter-holder is often minimal.

Colour gels can be used, however, if they can be placed at least 15 cm in front of the lantern. This is done either by using a wire attachment, or the gels are attached to the barn-doors with clips or magnets. Unfortunately these improvised solutions are increasingly common, as it is becoming more difficult to get hold of suitable coloured glass in appropriate shades.

Types: 100–5,000 W

Spotlights are technical devices for modifying light emitted by a lamp. Each type of spotlight has a special role, for example, for lighting an area, for special effects, profile lighting, moving light and projections. Fundamentally, a spotlight is constructed as follows:

An appropriate lamp is built into a sheet-metal or cast housing (nowadays mainly in aluminium). The lamp is fixed in the desired position in the housing by a lampholder. Light emitted towards the back is reflected forwards by a reflector. If a spotlight is intended to concentrate the beam of light, it is focused by a glass lens placed in the front of the lantern. Typical reflector spots are the exception to this. There are slots at the front to hold colour filters. They will also take barn-doors, which can adjust the outward path of the beam somewhat. The lantern has a fastener attached to the housing so that it can be mounted in the desired position.

228  Ill. left: Lamp carriage with 6,000 W daylight lamp, double ended with reflector

230  5,000 W halogen flood with forced ventilation

231 Four-colour footlight unit with asymmetrical reflector

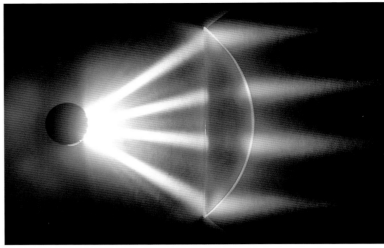

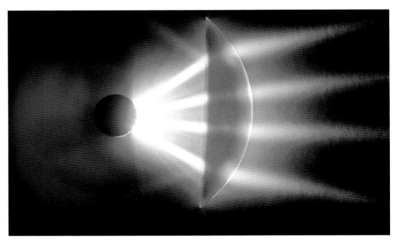

232/233 Change of aperture angle in a spotlight

## Lens spotlights

This is the simplest way of concentrating the light emitted. The distance between the lamp and the lens is changed by shifting the lampholder on the optical axis. The lens is usually plano-convex and made of clear glass. The light refraction in the lens causes a slight secondary spectrum on the periphery of the beam. Light emitted to the rear of the lamp is caught and reflected by a spherical reflector. This does not substantially increase the luminous power, but makes the beam of light more even. Emitted light between 4 and 78° can be expected, depending on manufacturer and power rating.

Also available are spotlights with lenses in which the lens is slightly corrugated or contains tiny prisms. These lenses have the advantage that the refraction error (coloured edges) produced by clear plano-convex lenses is no longer visible. In principle, the effect is the same as that generated by slight diffusion screen.

Types: 100–5,000 W

## Fresnel spots

The construction principle is the same as for a conventional spotlight, but the plano-convex lens is replaced by a Fresnel lens (see p. 69). The optical principle behind this lens means that very large diameters can be used. Aperture

234 2,500 W Fresnel spot

235 Miniature spotlight with 2 x 250 W 120 V flood reflector lamps

236 2,500 W plano-convex lens spotlight with barn-doors

237 5,000 W Fresnel spot, theatre model with colour frame box and offset centre of gravity

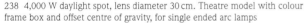

238 4,000 W daylight spot, lens diameter 30 cm. Theatre model with colour frame box and offset centre of gravity, for single ended arc lamps

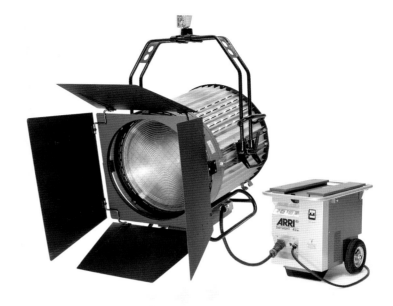

239 6,000 W daylight Fresnel spot (ø 50 cm) with barn-doors and ballast, for double ended arc lamps

adjustments work in the same way as a conventional spotlight; the beam spread is between 6 and 65° depending on manufacturer and power rating. The light is diffuse, and colour errors are no longer visible on the edges; the beam produced is soft-edged. Conventional and Fresnel spots can be used in widespread applications. They can be used everywhere and are the cheapest form of 'directed' light. They take normal incandescent lamps and discharge lamps.

Types:
100–10,000 W for incandescent lamps
21–24,000 W for discharge lamps

### Parabolic reflector spots

The classic parabolic reflector spot is a reflector spot without a lens. The lamp filament is placed at the focal point of the reflector system. The light emitted is parallel with the reflector axis and produces a narrow beam with high luminance. There is not much variety of beam size, but a little can be achieved by slightly adjusting the light source horizontally. Low voltage, mirror-domed lamps are used to produce high luminance. The metallized reflector on the lamp works conversely: light beamed forwards is reflected to the reflector. This type of lantern can be used very successfully in battens, but it is also used individually in most theatres. If it is used in a group, the most common practice is to mount nine parabolic reflectors in two rows to form a segment; these are so-called Svoboda units, which are named after their inventor, Josef Svoboda.

The narrow light beams from the individual reflectors produce a curtain of light with high luminance. Electrically speaking, the nine low voltage incandescent lamps are wired in series and can thus be run on 230 V. Parabolic reflector spots are used for effect lighting but also as follow spots. They are often selected to cover an area from a great distance. This particular application makes lighting changes less fluid, as the thick incandescent coil makes the light react slowly to regulation. The precision of the beam of light depends on the quality of the reflector and thus also on the price. A silvered glass reflector is always better than one made of aluminium, but a dichroic reflector is even better. The low voltage used, 12 and 24 V, needs a transformer as part of the basic equipment, and this is built

240 500 W parabolic spot with mirror-domed reflector lamp and integral transformer

into the housing in the smaller models. Circular baffles are often used to minimize light dispersal; these consist of concentric sheet metal rings.

Types are available from 100 W/12 V to 1,000 W/24 V, with various intermediate power ratings.

This lantern is not likely to have much of a future, with the exception of the very popular Svoboda units. Similar effects from single lanterns can be achieved more cheaply and rapidly with PAR spots.

Great progress has been made recently in the field of daylight parabolic reflector spots at all outputs. Beams of light can be modified by attaching lens adapters, the different surfaces of which create the appropriate effect on the light emitted.

Types: 21–12,000 W

241  125 W daylight spot with parabolic reflector. The light is conveyed to an optically focused endpiece by a fluid light conductor

242  6,000 W daylight spot with parabolic reflector and supplementary beam adapters, model ARRI-SUN

243  Middle left: Segment of a bank of lights with parabolic reflectors and curved 250 W reflector lamps, with circular baffles removed

244  124 W daylight spot with parabolic reflector, barn-doors, ballast and supplementary beam and colour temperature adapters

Lanterns, Special Lights, Additional Equipment

245 PAR 64 spot

246 PAR spot system with PAR 64 reflector lamp

## Parcans

The PAR or moulded glass lamp spotlight is a further development of the parabolic reflector spot. The traditional and most common size (lamp diameter) is the PAR 64 spot, but there are also spotlight housings on the market for PAR sizes 16, 36, 46 and 56. The optical system, consisting of incandescent coil (arc in the case of discharge lamps), a reflector, holder and front lens (sealed beam versions available), is made up as a fixed unit and is simply mounted in the housing. The PAR 6 lamp is an exception; it is a reflector lamp with a cold reflector, 12 V low voltage and a GU 5.3 cap. Other PAR lamps are connected to the power supply either by a screw-on system or by a plug device fixed to the external contact.

This lantern produces an oval beam, and the outer edges of the beam are not entirely sharply defined. The focal length is determined by the choice of lamp and cannot be altered. The lantern is usually available in four dif-

247  1,200 W profile spot with condenser optics, zoom lens

## Profile spotlights

The profile spot is a most convenient type of lantern. It offers abundant optical variants and is attractively versatile. The great difference to a lens spotlight is that the lamp no longer has to light beam vertically and horizontally. All three planes for modifying the beam are placed closely behind each other, so that with the objective fitted – consisting of one or more lenses – the sharpness of the light circle has to be

248  575 Ellipsoidal reflector spot with long focal length, type Source four

ferent models with different beam angles: narrow beam (9 x 12°), medium beam (10 x 15°) and wide beam (11 x 24° and 70 x 70°).

Variations in the beam angles are created by the surface of the front lens. Thus, for spots the lens is transparent and clear, while for floods it is heavily corrugated. Remember when using this beam that ellipsoidal beams, unlike normal round beams, can be precisely directed. Turning the lamp in the lamp housing determines and sets the desired position.

The PAR 64 size is also available in a daylight version. The reflector lamp has a clear front lens. Various beam angles are achieved by attaching adapters with different surfaces.

be adjusted to change the size of the beam. The lamp is fixed in the spotlight housing, which prevents the light source from being jarred when size changes are made. Two design types are available:

• ELLIPSOIDAL REFLECTOR SPOTS
Ellipsoidal reflector spots use an ellipsoidal reflector to focus the light. The light source is placed at its rear focal point, and the reflector produces an image at the front focal point. The light circle diameter is changed by an iris diaphragm placed as close as possible to the front focal point. Near the iris diaphragm are the shutters and gobo slots typical of the ellipsoidal reflector spot. Moving the shutters restricts the

adjusted for one of the three projection planes. The shutters are available in two versions: the four shutters are placed either on four or two different planes. The gobo slot is an additional image plane. The beam can be transformed by the use of gobos to produce any desired shape (e. g. in the form of a window). The material used for the negative mask must be highly heat-resistant. Aluminium foil 0.1 mm thick is suitable for making these gobos yourself and is easy to work with. Of course, masks made of other heat-resistant metals can also be used, but these are less suitable for making your own. However, the lighting industry has a wide range of gobos available for sale, and many of these are quite good.

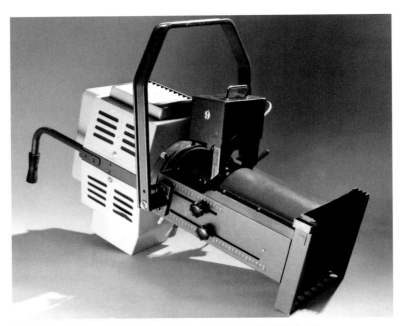

249 1,200 W daylight profile spot with condenser slot, zoom lens with plug-in holder for mechanical dimming

**Gobos**

Template masks – called gobos – have become more important recently, particularly for structural and motif patterns for intelligent spotlights.

In profile spotlights the template motif is placed in a holder in the slot intended for it, in multifunction spotlights it is placed on the gobo wheels.

The full range has become quite diverse and also includes glass plates with coloured motifs, logos and photographic illustrations. Coloured gobos are usually made of dichroic colour plates. The advantage of this is that they can also be used in more powerful lanterns. The motif plates are made of highly heat-resistant stainless steel 0.2 mm thick, with a relatively long life span. But you can make plainer motifs yourself. Aluminium foil 0.1 mm thick is sufficient for this, and it is easy to work with.

Classic standard gobo sizes for profile spots are:

Size A:
Outside diameter:    100 mm
Inside diameter:     68–75 mm

Size B:
Outside diameter:    86 mm
Inside diameter:     64.5 mm

Size M:
Outside diameter:    65.5 mm
Inside diameter:     45–49.5 mm

Interchangeable lenses for changing the focal length mean that this lantern can be used over practically any distance, because the focal length can be selected to suit the site chosen.

These lanterns have recently become even more efficient through the use of zoom optics. This kind of beam control originates in incandescent lamp technology. The wide range available is complemented by metal halide and xenon lamp versions.

Incandescent lamp models:
300–2,500 W
Metal halide lamp models:
2,500 W

- PROFILE SPOTLIGHTS WITH
  CONDENSER OPTICS

In profile spotlights with condenser optics the light emitted by the lamp and the spherical reflector is focused by a lens. The beam is changed mechanically, as in the case of an ellipsoidal reflector spot, by the use of an iris diaphragm, shutters or a gobo. Interchangeable lenses can also alter the focal length of this profile spotlight.

Zoom profile spots offer an improved and more convenient way of changing the focal length. Here lenses are no longer changed, but an adjustable lens is used to cover a greater range of beam angles. For example, fields can range from 12–22°, 16–30° and 28–40°. This varies according to the spotlight version and manufacturer chosen.

Both kinds of spotlight are available in many power ratings, from a 100 W miniature version for shop window

lighting up to 5,000 W for large stages. This technology is also used for discharge lamps up to 2,500 W. Follow spot versions are additionally fitted with a colour changer, improved bearings for balance and a blackout shutter. Carbon arcs are also used in special follow spots.

Incandescent lamp models:
300–5,000 W
Metal halide lamp models:
250–2,500 W

| Rosco gobo sizes | | |
|---|---|---|
| Size | Outside diameter | Inside diameter |
| A | 100 mm | 68–75 mm |
| B | 86 mm | 64.5 mm |
| M | 65.5 mm | 45–49.5 mm |
| D | 53.3 mm | 40 mm |
| E | 37.5 mm | 28.13 mm |
| G for Golden Scan | 66 mm | 45 mm |
| J | 38.8 mm | 25 mm |
| VLI | 25 mm | 18.75 mm |
| VL2B | Vari*Lite VL2®/28 spot luminaire | Available if required |
| Cyberlight | 44.5 mm | 36 mm |
| HPE Glass | 51.8 mm | 45 mm |
| Metal | 66 mm | 45 mm |
| CP Miniscan | 37.5 mm | 24 mm |
| Intellabeam | 25 mm | 18.75 mm |
| Martin PAL | 53.3 mm | 40 mm |
| Martin 1220 | 37.5 mm | 28 mm |
| Martin 518 | 25 mm | 13 mm |
| C Size | 150 mm | 112.5 mm |
| E Glass | 81.25 × 37.5 mm | 24 mm |

### Gobo wheels

A gobo wheel is used to rotate gobos. The motif disc is fitted onto the wheel instead of in the usual gobo holder. It can rotate at various speeds, and the direction can be changed. The device is controlled by a DMX signal.

### Fluorescent lamps

Fluorescent lamps (see 'Lamps and Light', pp. 80–83) are normally used on stage for borderlights or to light the cyclorama. As such lamps emit a great deal of light and do not need to be a great distance from the object, they can also be used in other ways. Footlights or mobile ground rows can be put together using a modular system. Colour corrections apart from the fundamental decision about colour temperature can be made by using coloured gels. These are made up as tubes and simply slipped over the individual lamps.

253 Single ended fluorescent lamps in a lantern housing

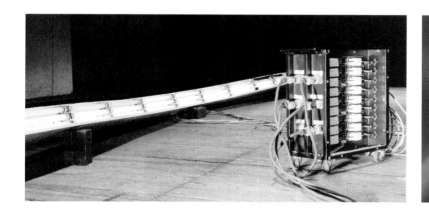

254 Left: Fluorescent footlights with three colours divided over six circuits, mobile supply unit with drivers

255 Right: Fluorescent lamp segment with dimmable fluorescent lamps

## SPECIAL EQUIPMENT AND ADDITIONAL DEVICES

### Follow spots

Brightness control alone is not always sufficient for the entire lighting operation. In order to fit them into the ambient light more effectively performers are 'followed' by their own individual light. Spotlights intended for use in this way are almost always profile spots.

These are specially balanced so that following can be done smoothly.

### Mechanical dimming devices

Indifferent light sources, initially known only as general light sources for street lighting and factory, have, in the meantime, become an established part of theatre lighting. The versions of these industrial lamps that designers most frequently use are high pressure mer-

cury and low pressure sodium vapour lamps. As we have already mentioned, both have the disadvantage that they cannot be dimmed electrically. The 'disadvantage' of all discharge lamps (the phase in which the light develops until it is up to full strength), is now often regarded as especially interesting and attractive in terms of colour and is therefore adopted as part of lighting design.

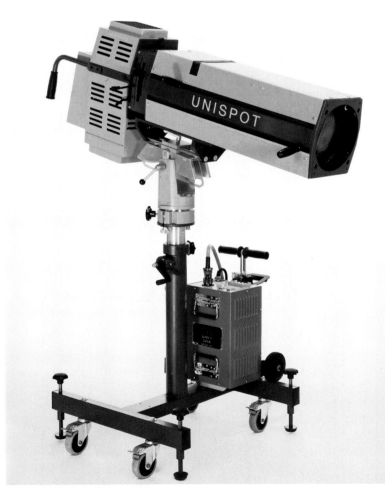

256 1,600 and 2,000 W xenon follow spot. Traditional follow spot for long throw distances, fitted with cold reflector, zoom optics and colour changers for six colours

257 2.5. kW HMI profile spot for use as a follow spot, with ballast. The stand is fitted with special fixing devices to guarantee the best possible balance

As these light fittings are not intended for theatre use, the designer has to be fairly inventive to build them into a lighting system. Increased flexibility can be gained by developing mechanical dimming systems or by using dimming devices available for spotlights.

Industrial lamps are not the only devices needing mechanical dimming, however. Metallogen and xenon lamps used in the theatre also cannot be dimmed to blackout electrically and need mechanical aids.

## Louvred dimmers (dousers)

Mechanical dimming for lens spotlights is usually done by using louvres. The frame containing these louvres is mounted on the front of the spotlight housing, the seams being as lightproof as possible. These devices can be controlled electrically. Sophisticated versions can also be radio-controlled.

In practice, the positioning of the louvres in relation to the light source needs careful attention. If a douser is being used, the assumption is that the

258 4,000 W HMI Fresnel spot with douser

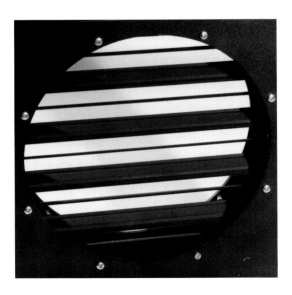

259 Louvred dimmer to be placed in front of a lens

Lanterns, Special Lights, Additional Equipment

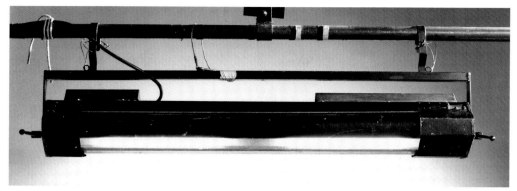

260 Coaxial dimmer. Two motorized semi-circular metal sheets running one inside the other close round the light sources. Made in-house for dimming low pressure sodium vapour lamps

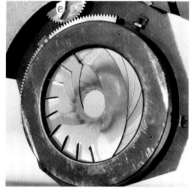

From left to right:

261 Segment shutter: This mechanical dimmer is used mainly in daylight profile spots. It is quicker than an iris diaphragm as it has fewer leaves

262 Iris diaphragm: These diaphragms are used mainly for dimming daylight profile spots. They are arranged either in front of the objective or in the beam path within the objective

263 Neutral wedge filter: A glass plate running from light to dark is used to control brightness in projectors. There are also versions with two glass plates running counter to each other

264 Cat's eye shutter: This consists of two metal plates with a negative V notch. The motorized plates move towards or away from each other

light source will always be a discharge lamp. The arc between the electrodes is elliptical. The louvres must always be positioned at 90° to the arc, as they will otherwise create an intense projection during the dimming process.

**Intelligent light**

For a long time light for stage purposes was neither intelligent nor stupid. Lighting technicians had only lanterns to work with and were delighted about every small technical development.

Today the speed with which electronically controlled spotlights develop does not leave us much time to rest. All operations involving movement, and also beam spread, changes of colour and motif, are programmed and set to run during the performance. Control is either by a firmware signal or the DMX 512 data protocol.

But these high performance lanterns are not the only intelligent ones. Any lighting rig that can carry out remote controlled changes of position and colour, motif movement, brightness and beam angle adjustment is sophisticated. All these are technical operations executed outside the normal lighting system.

Essentially the categories are divided into two main systems: scanners and moving lights.

Scanners are systems in which the beam can be rapidly and precisely directed by a reflector. The body of the lantern remains static in a fixed position. Focus, light structure, colours and special effects are all developed within the lantern housing.

In the case of moving lights, the whole lantern moves horizontally and vertically, so that the light is guided directly towards the playing area and not via a reflector.

The VARI∗LITE Production Services company invented technically intelligent spotlight technology and introduced it to the public with the rock group Genesis in 1981. It all stemmed from the development of a colour changer for a Parcan. The final result looked a little different. The first innovations were a colour changing system with diochroic slides and the use of Metallogen lamps, along with two motors for horizontal (panning) and vertical (tilting) movements.

In the meantime VARI∗LITE have come up with a number of new and innovative products, but some other notable manufacturers are now producing similar products of this quality. Moving lights can be divided into two groups: projectors and floods.

• PROJECTORS (SPOTLIGHTS)

These automatic spotlights have two main parts: the stationary base housing with the electronic controls and the drive for the spotlight yoke, containing the lighting device itself. The inner life of such a spotlight (its head) involves an ingenious system. The light source consists either of a reflector lamp or a lamp within an ellipsoidal reflector. Two gobo wheels are positioned in the image plane of the beam, one of them for fixed motif projections (up to nine motifs depending on manufacturer). The second gobo wheel is fitted with rotating gobos, which allows the motifs to turn on the spot. Normally an additional two rotating wheels with various diochroic colour filters are placed in the beam path, so that almost any colour can be created by changing their positions relative to each other (CMY colour mixing). A zoom facility is almost standard (from 5–50% depending on manufacturer). Brightness is regulated either by a metal diaphragm or a light/dark glass filter with variable shading. Special effect filters, such as a rotating prism, may be placed in the beam path, depending on the version.

The latest VARI∗LITE product, the VL7™ spot luminaire, is again a moving light with a 600 W HTI reflector lamp. Their increasing technical sophis-

265 VARI*LITE VL6™ spot luminaire, 400 W daylight lamp, automated profile spot

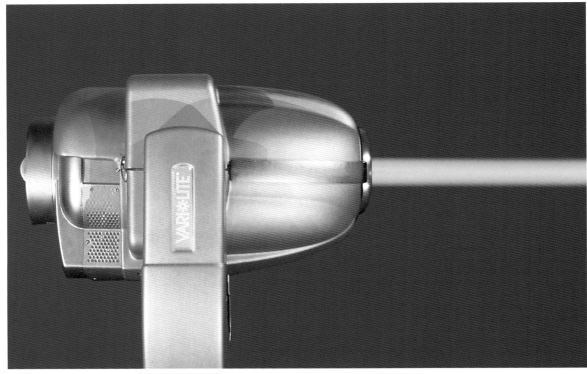

267 VARI*LITE™ VL7 spot luminaire, 600 W, 6,100 K, CVF™ colour system, beam angle from 5 to 40°

266 VARI*LITE VL5™ wash luminaire, 1,000 W, 3,200 K

tication, enormous power and precise projection make these lanterns a genuine alternative for any lighting expert. The new CVF™ colour system makes it possible for the first time to use continuously variable colour changes, from pastel shades to highly saturated colours. The 8-fold zoom facility, with a continuously variable focal length from 5 to 40°, makes variable precision use possible for many lighting jobs. A par-

ticular feature of this lantern is that all its functions are designed for fast as well as slow movement sequences. Like all new VARI*LITE products, this spotlight can also be controlled by the DMX 512 protocol.

• FLOODLIGHTS (WASHLIGHTS)
Essentially these are intelligent Fresnel spots, producing a soft-edged beam of light, but some new technical details

of the broad range available make them particularly interesting. VARI*LITE's VL5™ lantern has a built-in, continuously variable colour changer that could theoretically produce 100 million colours! The CMY dichroic colour filters are arranged behind one another on three levels in turbine form and are responsible for colour mixing and brightness control. The front lens on this lantern consists of 200 individual

268 VARI*LITE VL5™ wash luminaire, lamp/reflector unit open. View of Dichro*Tune™ colour changer

'honeycomb cells', which together make up a concave lens. If the beam angle is changed, a special fluid is pumped into the honeycombs. This turns the concave honeycomb into convex cells that can achieve a vergence of up to 17.5%. Normally a traditional Fresnel lens is used, and colour changes are effected by a rotating disk with dichroic filters. The beam angle is fixed by the focal length of the front lens, and cannot be changed. Both systems are very rapid in their movements, which means that many moving light combinations are possible. Almost all the products are available in incandescent and daylight versions.

- MOVING MIRROR MULTIFUNCTIONAL SPOTLIGHTS (SCANNERS)

A scanner is a multifunctional spotlight in which light is directed to the acting area by a moving mirror. The body of the lantern is in a fixed position. Usually these lanterns are more powerful than moving lights: up to 2,500 W daylight, and have either a reflector or arc lamp in an ellipsoidal reflector. These spotlights have Metallogen lamps almost without exception. In some models the light can also be used to produce patterns with gobos. Two wheels, one with fixed gobo motifs, the other with rotating gobos, provide the light structure. Colour is selected by a colour wheel fitted with dichroic filters. Brightness is regulated either mechanically or by a light-dark shaded glass filter. Focal length can be altered within the manufacturer's parameters.

In comparing the two multifunctional lanterns, attention has to be paid to mobility, speed and the amount of light emitted.

All these lanterns can only work with a digital control signal. Some models have their own special control signal. This means that they cannot be operated from lighting control consoles. If many such lanterns are involved in a lighting design, then it makes sense to save the automated lighting program in a separate device and run it parallel with the conventional standard lighting control desk.

271 Colour-mix module in a scanner

| Scanner | | Moving light |
|---|---|---|
| 280° | Horizontal movement (pan) | 360° |
| 80° | Vertical movement (tilt) | 270° |
| | Per second speed | 110° |
| 110° | In 0.3 seconds | |
| 1,200 W | Daylight | 600 W |
| approx. 65 kg | Weight up to approx. 30 kg | |

269 Gobo module with iris diaphragm. One modular wheel with rotating gobos, one with fixed motifs

270 1,200 W daylight scanner with internal view

**Colour changer**

The traditional colour wheel has held its own here for a long time. This was fitted in front of a lantern or into the colour cassette unit. These devices were chosen when an ultra-rapid visible colour change had to be executed, or when the colour for the next scene was prepared with the lights out.

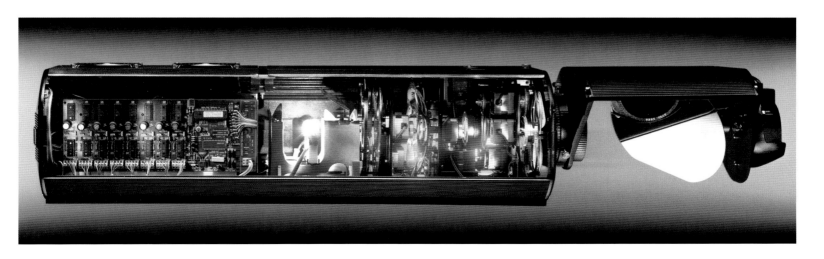

For follow spots, magazines can be fitted with several colour filters in frames stored one behind the other. The colour selected is pivoted into the beam as desired. The colour changing systems have now been developed to produce a completely different construction, the colour scroller.

The colour scroller consists of a sheet metal case in which two rolls of colour gel move past the beam. Depending on the lantern opening (lens diameter), up to 20 colour gels can be stuck one after the other with transparent tape. In simple roller colour changers the selected colours are fixed directly to the cylinder drives. The method of fitting the colour rolls into the scroller is standard. But in repertory theatre flexibility runs out very quickly, as there is often little time for taking out the old colour combination and fitting a new one if a large number of colour sequences is needed.

In repertory theatre the use of roller colour changers rapidly becomes a problem, as a daily change of performance and additional rehearsal work often require new and different colour sequences. Here the MAG MAX® colour changer with colour cassette offers greater flexibility and convenience. In this system the basic unit, consisting of the motor drive and electronic controls, remains on the lantern. Colour cassettes with colour gels are put into the base unit magazine. While a colour combination is in use, a second maga-

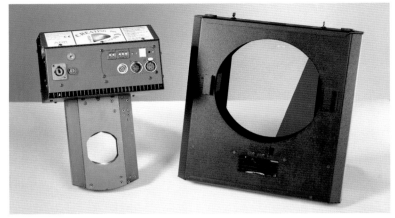

272 Left: CMY colour changer for inserting in a light beam; right: scroller colour changer for fitting in front of a light source

zine with a new combination can be prepared in the workshop. The work can be carried out more carefully and circumspectly, which means that sticking errors are easier to avoid. LT colour changers are made for lens diameters from 20 to 50 cm. This colour changing system has the following features:

- up to 20 colours, depending on size
- individual colours can be as long as desired (limited by the maximum colour strip length)
- DMX 512 USITT or analogue (+10 V)
- time control: one colour change between 1 and 600 seconds
- DMX ventilator control; ventilator power as wished
- LCD display for DMX addresses and data; illuminated
- user guidance in several languages
- dark colour mode; protection for dark colours. The device recognizes dark colours automatically, which means that dark colours can be moved slowly back and forth between two fields

For stage use it may well be important to consider whether colours should not only change quickly, but also very slowly. An open colour change, that is, one that is visible on stage, can be a very important component of a lighting cue. But it can only be considered if a slow, open colour change can really be slowly and smoothly executed.

### CMY Ingenio colour changer

This colour changer was developed for profile spots. The device is placed in a lens tube and can be used for fixed

273 Colour scroller with cassette system. The basic unit with DMX setting panel remains on the spotlight, the colour cassettes can be changed

focal lengths as well as for zoom lenses. It is suitable for all profile spots up to 2,500 W using daylight and 2,500 W using incandescent lamps. When used in a daylight spot the Ingenio also replaces the mechanical dimming shutter, in the form of a cat's eye. Colour mixing is produced by dichroic coated filters using the CMY colour mixing system. Ingenio can be attached to any lighting control desk by a DMX signal, and needs five channels for all function controls. There is one channel each for colour, colour saturation, brightness, diffusion (soft focus) and speed. Brightness can be controlled down to complete blackout. Very slow and very fast colour changes are possible.

Unlike other CMY colour changers, Ingenio produces high colour saturation which can sometimes have the quality of monochrome light.

The device can also be used just for dimming, for example, with additional conversion filters and a diffusing screen.

### Motorized yokes

A motorized yoke is a mechanical mount for a lantern – mostly Fresnel daylight or incandescent spots – which can move horizontally and vertically by remote control. It should be able to pan up to 300°. This is often achieved, but for normal use only 180° of pan are necessary. Tilt movement up to 60° is adequate. A greater degree of tilt is often outside the tilt tolerance of a solid-state lamp.

Other interesting options provided by a remote controlled motorized yoke are focusing for Fresnel spots and barn-door operation. The four flaps on the barn-door can be moved, and the whole unit can sometimes be turned as well. Up to 11 DMX channels are needed to use all the features of this remote control technology. Using this kind of

274 Motorized yoke with a Fresnel spot

remote control system often requires the additional control of a dimming unit for daylight lamps and a connection to control a colour scroller. It is only worth spending so much money if the combination remains in the same place. Another technical addition is a remote controlled telescoping boom. In addition to all the possible movements mentioned, a further alternative is to change the vertical position of the lantern. A complete system of this kind is more likely to be found in a television studio than on stage. Some manufacturers also offer radio controls. But there is one thing that always has to be done by hand: changing an incandescent or arc lamp that is defective.

On a theatre stage there are positions that are very suitable for a set up of this kind: on border light bars, for back lighting, or in some parts of the fly galleries. Various positions in the auditorium are also suitable. Investment of this kind is recommended when the particular lantern does not have to be moved daily.

The motorized yoke is an alternative to multifunctional spotlights. As these spotlights do not produce a very great deal of light, it is often desirable to use more powerful Fresnel spots for general or directed light.

### Fibre optics

Transporting light exactly as we wish is something that designers have always wanted to do, particularly around corners. Modern technology makes this possible in various interesting ways. The first experiments in this field were undertaken in 1870 but not used commercially until 1927, and the technology was christened 'fibre optics' in 1956. Many of us can remember the glass fibres that adorned television sets,

among other things, in the sixties. Today this lighting technology is very advanced, and fibre optics have become an essential part of data and image transfer. Fibres for use in lighting must be able to carry all visible wavelengths of light, unlike the fibres used for communications technology, which usually have to carry only one wavelength. But the light energy that is fed in is not transported without loss; some of the light is lost by absorption and diffusion in the fibres. These losses are known as attenuation. The use of fibre optics is particularly interesting and important when light from a single source has to be emitted from a number of points. Fibres emitting light laterally allow the realization of separate, glowing lines of light, so that architectural outlines can be heightened or simply made up using the contours of the fibre.

Ideally the light source that feeds the light into the fibres is a short arc discharge lamp with a reflector and a colour temperature of 5,600 to 6,000 K. Also very popular of course are 3,200 K incandescent lamp projectors in low voltage tungsten-halogen versions, but they are not so efficient in terms of brightness. There are also manufacturers who use sulphur lamps as a source for this technology.

The light can be fed in either from a reflector lamp or from a small optical system. The lamp and its optical system are in a housing, together with the power supply (transformer or ignition device) and with different features such as heat filters, colour wheel and structure wheel. The coupler for the glass or plastic fibre bundle is placed centrally on the axis of the light emitted. The light is fed in at 65° for glass fibres, and

275 Light generator for 20–50 W for connecting end or side light emitting fibres. Lamp housing separate from the electronic transformer

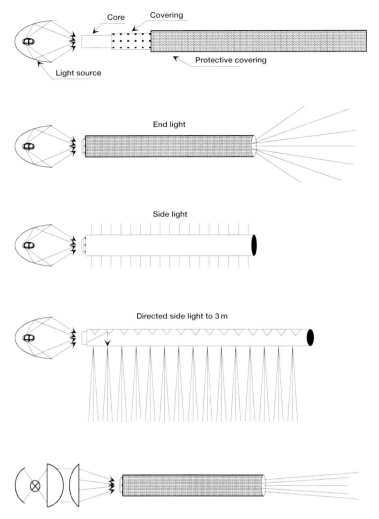

276 Fibre optics set-up

at 61.4° for plastic fibres, and leaves the fibre at the same beam angle. There is also special equipment on the market to enhance the optical design possibilities available, which can work with up to four fibre couplings, for example.

A distinction is made between glass fibres and plastic fibres (PMMA).

Glass fibre optics includes light conductors of a diameter from 5 to 200 mm; 50 mm has become standard in the lighting field. Great numbers of these very thin fibres, 100 to 100,000 single fibres, are bundled together. Plastic fibres are 1 mm in diameter.

Remote source technology has the advantage that the light source can be positioned accessibly; in other words it does not have to be at the lighting location and does not convey either ultra-violet rays or electricity. The maximum fibre length depends on the light source. Low voltage solid-state lamps are suitable for up to 30 m. If a longer distance has to be covered, the fibre bundle can be supplied with light from two sides. The principle is based on total internal multiple reflection. The light is either conducted to the end of the fibre and

adjusted to the correct angle by an optical endpiece. Unless an optical end-piece is used, the exiting light is always at an angle of 65°. Or it is continuously directed outwards along the whole length of the fibre. An optical device can be attached to the end to focus or disperse the light; a decorative plastic or glass element can be used as a light source, depending on the area in which the device is being used. The direction within a fibre is determined exclusively by its surface qualities.

Normally a light conductor system is made up of several fibre bundles, rather than just one. These come together to create a bundle of light, then they are stuck or fused together and joined to the light source by a coupler. The light source is structured or coloured as desired by colour or gobo wheels inside the unit. Depending on cable diameter, up to 400 single fibres in the case of glass and about 800 plastic fibres can be served by one generator. The radius of

277 Lamp block with parabolic reflector. The tube is placed on the reflector when the light pipeline is used

curvature depends on the number of single fibres and their diameter. Given three single fibres 1.8 mm in diameter in a protective tube, a curve with a 5 mm radius is possible and with 75 fibres 8 mm in diameter in a protective tube, a radius of 20 mm is possible.

The light can be conducted to the end of the fibre or emerge from it laterally. The cable bundle is twisted for lateral light emission. Here, too, the fibre bundle is protected by a transparent covering. The usual diameters are 9–17 mm. Here a curve with a radius of 50 mm is possible. Thin single fibres without covering can be used for certain special effects.

It is also possible for light to be emitted, efficiently controlled from one side of the fibre only.

The decision to use glass or plastic fibres relates directly to the wear and tear demands made on the material. Glass fibres have the following additional characteristics:
- longer lasting
- resistant to higher temperatures
- lower fire risk
- better resistance to acids and alkalis
- more pressure resistant

Plastic fibres are always preferable for theatre use because they are less expensive.

Summary:
- The radius of the curve in the fibre bundle is dependent on the overall diameter
- 4–6 mm is the usual bundle diameter. For example: 19 plastic fibres give a cable diameter of 5 mm
- End light fibres can be up to approx. 10 m long with incandescent lamps, up to 30 m with daylight lamps
- Lateral light fibres can be up to 17 m long with a single-sided feed, 40 m with a double-sided feed

278 Luminous sheeting in use. Arthur Kopit, *Road to Nirvana*, director: Dieter Dorn, set designer: Jürgen Rose, Münchner Kammerspiele, 1992

279 Lamp block with motor drive for the sulphur lamp and cage for microwaves

### Solar 1000

This lighting unit is a combined light source and a reflector. This new lamp technology is described in detail in the 'Lamps and Light' chapter (see pp. 91–92). The light source, a sulphur lamp, is set inside a parabolic reflector. The sulphur generated luminous core is not small enough to produce light parallel to the axis using the optical qualities of the parabolic reflector.

The light emitted is either distributed over a broad area by a reflector or conveyed in a light conductor system consisting of a plastic tube with an internal prismatic foil. These tubes are 25 cm in diameter and available in 2 m sections. An overall length of approx. 22 m is possible without significant light loss.

### Luminous sheeting (light pad)

Lighting designers have had a new device at their disposal since 1991: electro-luminescent sheeting, or light pads. This new light source is available as tape approx. 1 mm thick or as plastic or glass sheets 4 to 12 mm thick. The other dimensions of these luminous sheets also vary. The foil version even offers the possibility of cutting it to your own requirements.

This luminous sheeting is increasingly used in the theatre as it is easy to paste on parts of the set. Various sheet sizes are available, and also long luminous strips and cords. The light can be controlled continuously throughout its range and – with a converter (frequency transformer) and battery drive – can easily be built into mobile elements, for

example, luminous props. The material is greyish when switched off and does not take on its actual colour until switched on. On request it can be supplied in the same shade when on and off. The material is impact-resistant, durable and flexible within 2 to 5 cm.

| | |
|---|---|
| Power: | approx. 200 VA/m$^2$ |
| Voltage: | 230 V/50 Hz or 110 V/60 Hz |
| Standard: | 0–180 V/ 300–1,000 Hz |
| Luminance: | approx. 200 cd/m$^2$ |
| Uniformity: | > 95% |
| Colour temperature: | 3,200–6,000 K |
| Dimming: | yes, from 0 to 100% |
| Service life: | > 10,000 hours |
| Standard colours: | white, yellow, red blue, green, pink; other colours available on request |

280/281 Following double page: Henrik Ibsen *John Gabriel Borkman* Director: Hans Lietzau Set Designer: Jürgen Rose Münchner Kammerspiele, 1989

Lanterns, Special Lights, Additional Equipment

282 Botho Strauß
*Schlusschor* (Final Chorus)
Director: Dieter Dorn
Set Designer: Jürgen Rose
Münchner Kammerspiele, 1991

## CABLE–PLUG CONNECTIONS

All electrical equipment has to be connected to the lighting console's control circuits. Experience shows that this sort of plugging is often handled carelessly. Successful and effective lighting requires that all connections be secure. In addition to the earthed, heavy duty household plug, which is not protected from accidental disconnection, special plug connections are available for theatre use. The 'Eberl plug', which was considered standard for a long time, is being replaced by CEEFORM (CEE) connections. These models are significantly safer to use, but unfortunately somewhat bulky.

A large number of special versions are available according to the voltage and current requirements for various specific connections and are suitable for the many tasks they have to perform.

### Multicore systems

Load is normally conveyed to the appliance by a cable with an earthed heavy duty household plug, Eberl or CEE connectors. In other words: a lot of appliances, a lot of cables. This kind of power supply can be handled more efficiently by taking the power in one cable to a distribution substation (power distribution pool). In this case several circuits – six as a rule – share one cable and then separate out into individual connections again (multi-strand). A connector system of this kind guarantees time-saving when setting up and

283 CEE power plugs, at right an Eberl plug

284 Distinctive plugs from various manufacturers

285 Harting input, 6 household outputs

286 Harting input, 6 household outputs, Harting output

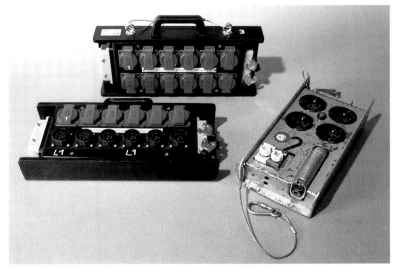

287 6 CEE inputs, Harting output

288 Socket units
Top: Harting input and output,
12 household outputs
Bottom: Harting input and output, 6 household outputs, parallel with these switching connections for dimmable fluorescent lamps
Right: Eberl input, 4 household outputs

289 Mobile DMX distribution box for controlling motorized yokes, colour changers, mechanical dimmers etc. with power supply for the drive units

striking different kinds of lighting equipment in theatres and for shows. The most used electric connection system at the moment is the Harting programme. This has proved its worth by its reliable workmanship, robust housing and tight locking clamps. It is particularly popular with firms that hire out and sell lighting equipment.

The German standards regulations require that all plug connections have to be locked and that, in case of a fault, the supply must have an all-pole shut-off which is activated by a residual-current operated device.

290 Plugging box. Top left: Eberl and CEE 32 ampere connection with switch. Centre: Dimmable fluorescent lamp connection with multipole plug connection, 16 and 63 ampere connection. All three plugging options are connected to one lighting circuit. Bottom left: Special receptacles for control devices

| Multicore variants | | | | | | | |
|---|---|---|---|---|---|---|---|
| | 3 × 5,000 W 4 mm²/30 m long | | | 6 × 2,000 W 1.5 mm²/50 m long | | | |
| Rated power | 25 amperes | | | 10/13 amperes | | | |
| Circuits | 3 | | | 6 | | | |
| Number of strands | 7 | | | 13 | | | |
| **Contact assignments** | | | | | | | |
| Channel | 1 | 2 | 3 | 1 | 2 | 3 | 4 5 6 |
| Phase | 1 | 3 | 5 | 1 | 2 | 3 | 4 5 6 |
| Neutral lead | 2 | 4 | 6 | 9 | 10 | 11 | 12 13 14 |

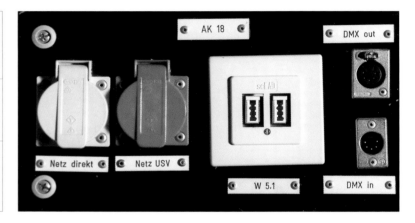

291 Ill. above:
Fixed connector box for control functions. From left: Direct socket, independent power supply for data distributors and transponders, Ethernet connection for networking lighting consoles, monitors and printers; DMX input and output sockets

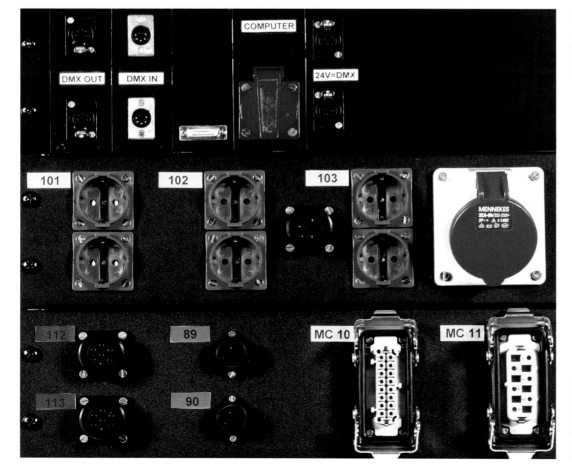

292 Plugging box, latest model: DMX input and output, DMX 24 V, CEE plugging devices, multiple pole connections for dimmable fluorescent lamps, multicore-multipole connections for six 2,000 W circuits and three 5,000 W circuits

Making a connection with an electrical plug does not always mean that the work is over. For example, there is a special ribbon cable used for lighting battens that is stored in a basket (Hauck basket, see ill. 298). Other variants are available, as well as this flexibly laid connection. Cable drums, which can handle only a small number of circuits, are mounted at the highest point of the movable span. The cable ribbon is taut and connected to the batten and the winding drum. If the batten with the lantern fastening is moved downwards, the cable automatically unwinds from the drum.

Chains of the kind shown in ill. 297 are very interesting and, above all, can be developed further. The plastic chain consists of many small, box-shaped links. The cables run inside them, and the chain is attached at the upper and lower ends of the greatest possible distance to be travelled.

As well as being connected electrically, the lanterns and other accessories have to be fixed at their particular positions. If a tripod cannot be used, then hanging positions have to be installed. They should be solidly built and afford adequate securing devices to prevent them from being disarranged. The trade offers a wide range for the various desired applications.

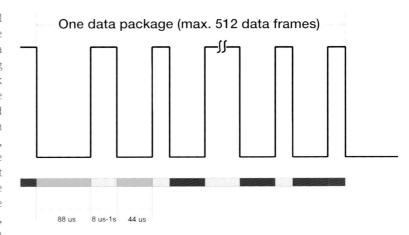

One data package (max. 512 data frames)

88 us    8 us-1s    44 us

■ Reset with interruption signal and start code
□ Interruption signals between 0 and 1 second
■ Data frame DMX 1-512
■ Interruption signal between 2 data packages

294 DMX data frame

293 Ceiling-mounted cable drum, three circuits

### DMX – DMX addressing

Before digital signal transfer was introduced, control leads had to be provided for every unit to be regulated – for example, motors or relays – as the signals were analogue. The information is transmitted to the receiver as a voltage level. As several devices – some of them with different control units – usually have to be driven from the same lighting console at the same time, this

technique is not only very arduous but also very expensive. Also, analogue control technology is highly susceptible to faults. The disadvantages of this data technology can be greatly reduced by using a digital system.

The control technology most used in theatres and studios is the standard DMX 512 (digital multiplex 1 to 512 circuits). The DMX 512 standard protocol transmits the electrical signals digitally in serial form. This means that the data from all 512 lighting board channels can be transmitted one after the other on a single lead. The number of leads is dramatically fewer than needed for analogue technology. They are also less susceptible to faults, as there are only two states in which data is transmitted: active and not active.

However, in addition to this data signal, an energy supply for the end user is also needed unless a so-called booster (signal amplifier) is used to provide the motors directly with a 24 V direct-current supply from the same plug. Solutions of this kind are specific to the manufacturer and do not comply with standards. But they do obviate the necessity for additional power supply leads.

For the various devices controlled by a DMX signal to be able to filter the correct information out of the data sent, each device has to have an address and each function has to be separately identified. These channels are allotted directly by a control panel on the device. As a maximum of 512 channels are available, it is sensible to put individual functions such as panning or tilt-

ing by motorized yokes on to the same channel; they will then work in parallel. Here is a brief summary of DMX 512 data transfer:

A level between 0 and 100% can be set at the board for each of the 512 channels. This level is coded from the board as a digital word consisting of 8 bits. Each digital word (byte) is assembled from the determined number of 8 bits. In this context, active means that a DC voltage between $-12$ and $+12$ V is present; not active means that no current is present. Levels from 0 to 255 correspond to 0–12 V. A byte is also accompanied by a start bit and two stop bits. Each individual bit signal requires 4 µs, so that a byte takes 44 µs ($\mu$ = one millionth of a second).

Devices are supplied with data by transmitting a DMX data package, consisting of a start sequence and up to 512 data frames.

The start sequence begins with a reset signal, which sets the data stream to not active for at least 2 byte cycles (88 µs). This is a preparatory phase for data reception for the devices attached. The start code follows after a short interruption signal, followed by the transfer of the information for the 512 data packages in chronological order.

The addressed devices wait for their data to be transmitted and process these into a usable form so that they can carry out the various functions – for example, moving dimmer louvres, transporting colour gels in colour changers, activating ballasts or relays, moving motorized yokes and all

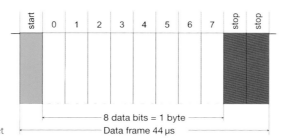

| start | 0 | 1 | 2 | 3 | 4 | 5 | 6 | 7 | stop | stop |

←——— 8 data bits = 1 byte ———→
←——————— Data frame 44 µs ———————→

295 DMX data packet

motorized tasks for multifunction spot-lights. After the last data frame (512), the data package ends with an inter-ruption signal.

Data transfer should be effected via a shielded, twisted pair lead. The leads must have a 5-channel XLR plug con-nection. With a 5-channel standard plug connection, a second DMX 512 control lead can also be operated (see pin assignment, right-hand column).

Although data transfer is possible for lead distances of up to 1,200 m, the rec-ommended length for a data lead should be not more than 300 m. If the supply is shared between a number of devices along the line, even shorter connector leads should be used.

Despite the fact that DMX 512 stand-ard data transfer has established itself firmly in practice, users are often faced with the problem of combining DMX devices with older analogue lighting boards. The trade offers appropriate electronic adapters for this, called 'de-multiplexers'. They make it possible to drive dimmers, ballasts, motors, relays and all kinds of effects devices using the DMX protocol.

This technology does have its disad-vantages, however. As the individual devices are usually connected in series, in the case of a line interruption subse-quent devices would not receive sig-nals. For this reason, it is recommend-ed that a maximum of 20 devices be connected in series to a data strand. The various data lines are split up in a distributor box. In addition, the data lines have to be concluded at the last user with a terminator resistance of 120 ohms, to minimize interference and signal reflections.

Because the devices used are becom-ing increasingly more complex, the fundamental disadvantages of DMX data transfer today are the limited number of channels, lack of check-back signals and of protection against gen-eral signal interference.

This transfer standard is now being developed to include bidirectional data transfer (Ethernet, see glossary), which means that the devices connected can send status messages back to the board. This data transfer protocol can also con-vey information more rapidly and in greater quantity for longer distances without errors. Data can also be trans-ferred by a fibre optic cable (glass fibre). 5-channel XLR plug connection:

| Pin | Function |
|---|---|
| 1 | ground (shield) |
| 2 | DMX− |
| 3 | DMX+ |
| 4 | free, or 2nd DMX− connection |
| 5 | free, or 2nd DMX+ connection |

plug: receiver
socket: transmitter

## Patching circuits

In older lighting systems the electrical connections between controller, dim-mer and socket outlet are clearly fixed, that is, the three components together make up a fixed unit. Computer con-trolled lighting consoles have opened up new and more flexible combination possibilities within this rigid connec-tion system. These are hot patching and soft patching.

• Hot patching applies to the way in which sockets and dimmer channels are linked, i. e. patching on the high voltage side, involving spotlight con-nections and dimmers. In principle this is a more modern version of the old patch panel.

• Soft patching applies to the way in which the numbered keys on the lighting console and a dimmer connec-tion are linked. In this case a circuit number is allocated to a corresponding dimmer. This is done on the low volt-age side.

## DMX multicore

DMX multicore leads are flexible multi-core leads for various data transfers (e. g. 1 x 230 V, 1 x DMX and an inter-com connection). This kind of cabling makes sense if an extra command pos-ition has to be set up, for example a working board in the auditorium. This means that the power supply for the lighting console, the connection for the DMX control of dimmers, multifunc-tion lanterns, scrollers, shutters etc. and the connections for the essential communications equipment can be neatly installed and ready for immedi-ate use in the shortest possible time.

## SPECIAL EFFECTS

There are many ways of putting ideas into practice here, but it is essential that the designer have the appropriate technical knowledge and skill so that special effects can be executed on de-mand not just once, but always.

• SMOKE MACHINES have covered up many an inadequacy. Three main kinds of vapour are available: dry ice fog, thick fog produced with other chemicals, and mist from cracked oil. Dry ice has the advantage that the vapour stays at ground level for a long time, is very dense and can be blown over a given area in large quantities. There are all sorts of chemical thick fog generators available. The machines are often set up offstage, and the mist is directed on

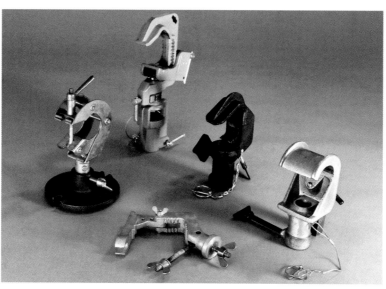

296 Various hook clamps for lanterns

297 Chain-type power supply line guide

300 Hanging smoke machine

298 Motorized lighting battens with lantern power supply leads sewn into fabric ribbon cables and Hauck cable storage baskets

- STROBOSCOPES do not really have to be described in detail. Several stroboscopes should be connected to a central control panel, where the desired effects can be programmed.
- FILM LOOPS AND EFFECT DISKS are accessories that are attached to the front of a projector. Interchangeable films or disks are available for the different effects that can be inserted in the respective device. The desired image size is determined by the objective lens.
- LIGHTNING EFFECTS are somewhat difficult to achieve. It is essential for the

299 'Cracker' mist machine

to the stage through tubing. Radio-controlled smoke machines are also very useful.

Machines that produce haze create an interesting effect because the haze is much less dense than normal fog. Vapour in the air makes the spotlight beams clearly visible and helps to enliven the scene as an optical design element. The use of smoke is not entirely without its problems, as the ambient temperature and the ventilation in the space considerably affect whether the smoke remains on the desired level or floats off towards the audience.

301 Smoke machines. Back: dry ice machine; front left: high-powered smoke machine; front centre: hand-held smoke gun; front right: small remote controlled smoke machine

302 Left: Optical flash attachment; right: flash unit with parabolic reflector, special quartz flash tube for connection to a flash generator

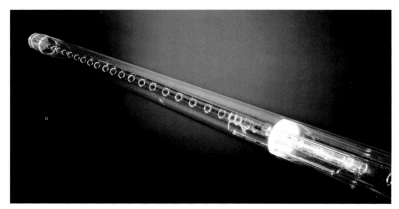

303 Flash tube, 2,110 mm long, 60 mm ø with 2 pyrex flash tubes (xenon gas) 900 mm long, for connection to a flash generator

theatre to be dark if the flash is to be effective, and this hampers the lighting before and after the lightning is used.

A 'dream lightning' flash in zig-zag form can be produced with a light-box, a slide or a gobo projection. The effect of a lightning sequence, that is, of moving light, can easily be achieved with photoflood lamps or the increasingly rare flash bulbs, above all if the individual sockets are programmed to fire in sequence. Fundamentally, light sources without incandescent coils are physically better for short flashes of light. These include fluorescent lamps, neon tubes, carbon arc equipment and xenon lamps.

A fluorescent lamp can be fired either for a short time electrically by the usual system or directly with 1,000 V per 1.2 m or 1.5 m of tube length. Gun cotton is most impressive, but it and other pyrotechnic effects have the disadvantage that they can rarely be used in confined spaces.

### Xenon high output flash

Given the problems with flashes, there is an understandable desire to produce as bright and brief a flash of light as possible. At the Münchner Kammerspiele we have developed a very high output flash. The basic equipment for this flash construction, called 'Big Bang 4,000', includes the following parts:

- power supply unit for single flashes with operating panel
- back-up dolly for short periods of extended use (approx. 10 minutes)
- lantern housing with 4,000 W xenon lamp

The lantern housing is fitted with a 4,000 W xenon lamp with a horizontal burner. The light source of the short arc lamp is set at the focal point of a para-

bolic precision glass reflector. The light aperture, 35 cm in diameter, is covered with a thermopane filter and can be additionally secured with a sheet-metal shutter. Three 390 x 390 mm slots for coloured glass filters are available. The flash device can be used in three ways. The desired mode and type of flash are preselected on the main dolly. The selected mode can be triggered from the main preset panel or on the lantern housing itself. The triggers can also be remote-controlled, and the combination is set up in such a way that all functions can subsequently be set for remote control as well.

The intensity of the flash depends on the length and sequence of flashes. For the brightest, shortest flash the lamp takes 800 amperes for a flash lasting two-tenths of a second. The light is daylight-type, blueish-white, hardly greater than the colour temperature of the xenon lamp when used for continuous light. Two other flash levels are available:

- 500 amperes lasting 1 second
- 350 amperes lasting 2 seconds

The 5 large batteries each delivering 12 V/210 Ah (ampere-hour) can produce a light at 120 amperes for about ten minutes of continuous duty.

However, such use is possible only if the lamp has forced air-cooling. The flash sequences can be produced without cooling. The battery dollies can be trickle charged for long-term conservation and last for approximately four to five years. Of course the power supply can also be from the mains, but the effort necessary for good direct current is considerable and can only be used locally. Certainly this high output flash does not mark the final stages of development, but the present possibility for putting such a heavy load on xenon lamps for a short time offers a lightning accentuation, even with a relatively high ambient light. Swivelling mirrors or a divided glass surface could further improve the beam or broaden its range of uses. The following levels for the lamp have been measured:

| Distance: 20 m, light circle diameter: approx. 1.2 m | | | |
|---|---|---|---|
| Continuous use at | 120 amperes: | 50,000 lux | 5,500 K |
| Flash 0.8 sec. | 250 amperes: | 140,000 lux | 5,500 K |
| Flash 0.8 sec. | 500 amperes: | 433,000 lux | 5,780 K |
| Flash 0.2 sec. | 800 amperes: | 610,000 lux | 5,780 K |

and more light for the acting area. Four power circuits were needed, connected by a multi-plug unit. Sightlines meant that the ring for the small lamps had to be built in on a perspective line. Such distinctive light can be integrated into the general lighting.

Both snow and rain create their own difficulties. There are snow machines that blow swirling white flakes on to the stage. If light snow has to fall for a longer period, a larger device is necessary, unless artificial snow is thrown by hand from the proscenium lighting bridge, or from even higher up.

304  4,000 W high-powered xenon flash with power supply dolly

## CUSTOM-MADE LIGHTING EFFECTS

For one production we developed a 'duck shot'. Low voltage incandescent lamps were hung in a certain pattern from a batten. Each lamp was individually controlled, and they were switched on and off automatically at the chosen speed and in the appropriate sequence. When the last lamp was on, a neon tube aimed diagonally at the last lamp triggered a brief flash intended to be understood as a shot. A flash lamp was fired immediately after this. The whole sequence was run by trick switching and stored as a cue.

If a lampshade is used in a room on stage, it should emit the most realistic light possible, which means that using a single lamp is certainly not enough. The photograph (ill. 306) gives a good idea of how the lamps can be arranged. The centre lamp shines straight down,

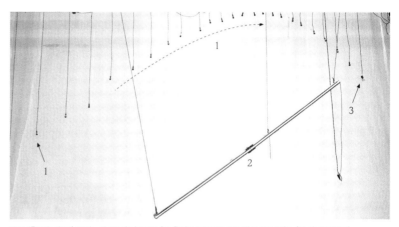

305  'Duck shot' trick: 1) single lamps for flight movement; 2) neon tube for shot signal; 3) flash lamp

and three household bulbs are used for general lighting and to make the shade transparent. Then several 12 V/ 50 W reflector lamps are fitted on an outer ring, each pointed to the opposite side, in order to produce a brighter light

306  Lampshade with four built-in circuits: two circuits for performers, one each for the lampshade and the table

307  Snow machine, confetti rolled up in a cloth. The drive roller turns very slowly, and the confetti trickles slowly out of the cloth on to the stage

308 Rack
of 52 PAR 46,
6.4 V/30 W
spotlights.
The spotlights are
arranged on several
levels so that
their beams do
not cross

309/310  Ill. left and top:
*Le Roi Arthus*
Bregenz Festival, 1996

Beams of light from an imaginary
point first light 52 chairs arranged
around a table (the number of
chairs is reduced in the course
of the production). The stellar
arrangement of beams here was
chosen deliberately. The non-
visible light source means that
the point of origin cannot be
located as a specific area, but
suggests a central light source
high up in a void

311  Edward Bond, *Summer*
Director: Luc Bondy
Set designer: Erich Wonder
Münchner Kammerspiele, 1983

Ill. 312–316 (left, from top to bottom) show changing light on a row of
houses. In the production, an island with houses on it was shown in
the background. The house façades were built with two separate light
zones that could shine through the transparent front 'from the inside to
the outside'. The impression to be given by the light was setting sun and
lights at night. Tiny lamps were mounted in a kind of grid, so that the
light was visibly separate. In the brightest lighting state the houses were
lit from the front, and a very slow change made the steadily fading daylight most realistic

312  Island lit only from the front

313  Twilight. Lights in the houses start to come on

314  The sun at its lowest point. Built-in 'sharp shadows' faded in.
Front light on the houses reduced

315  Front light faded out completely. No window lights,
only contrasts between light and dark

316  Night. Only isolated lights in the houses

317 *Summer*
Münchner Kammerspiele, 1983
In the foreground is the
darkened acting area,
in the background the
town at night

318 *Reigen*
Théâtre de la Monnaie
Brussels, 1993

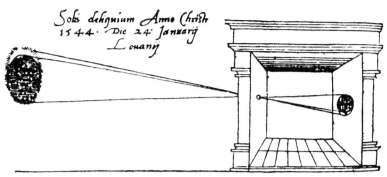

319 Camera obscura dating from 1544

## HISTORY

The first known illustration of the CAMERA OBSCURA (Lat.: dark chamber), the original form of the camera, dates from 1544. Gemma Frisius was watching an eclipse of the sun through a hole in a wall and noticed that the image was upside-down and reversed. Shortly after that attempts were made to improve this technique with a lens. Initially full-size rooms were set up to observe the phenomenon, but the first portable equipment did not appear until after 1620.

The invention of the LATERNA MAGICA (Lat.: magic lantern), the original form of the projector, was the start of it all. Visitors to public picture houses were fascinated by colour images and image sequences. In these pioneering years some admirers of this form of projected entertainment were reminded of magic and occult powers. The first magic lantern made was described in the mid 17th century as 'a light source whose beam is reflected and directed through a concave mirror with two biconvex lenses in an objective. A transparent picture is pushed in between them.'

In principle this description is still valid. Even when technological developments were made there was very little change in the way images were produced – except in refinements of the construction. The long projection insertions could be put together to form a pictorial record made up of several sequences of individual images. Paul Hoffmann, probably the best-known 19th-century projection artist, painted whole stories on glass plates which at that time were framed in wood. This art form became an industry around 1850. Travelling projectionists presented themes from natural history as well as topical material. Around 1900 photographic slides replaced hand-painted

320 Illustrations of various versions of the Laterna magica, c. 1794

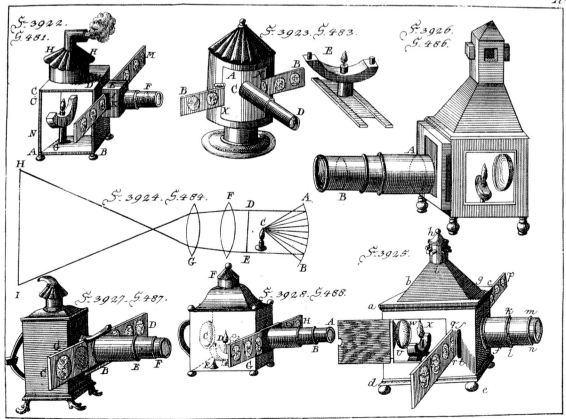

pictures in projectors. Unfortunately these slides were only used in black-and-white form at first. It is interesting that pioneers of this projection development were already working with the technique of crossfading. This was described as follows:

323 Laterna magica with projection slide for pictures painted on glass, 1720

The apparatus for fog pictures consists of two (or even more) projection lanterns that are set up in such a way that the circles of light they produce cover each other on the wall. It also consists of the dissolver, a device that switches the lanterns off alternately, or allows both to work at the same time. The effect is based on the fact that the image from the first lantern (e.g. a landscape by day), gradually fades into the image from the second lantern (the same landscape by night). The image from the first lantern has to be dimmed very slowly for this to work, and at the same time the image from the second lantern has to be cast more strongly to just the same degree, until the first image has disappeared and the second lantern is working at full power. The level of brightness on the wall must become neither greater nor less during the change if the effect is to be a good one. Besides this, it is essential that the second image, into which the first one is to fade, should be correctly adjusted so that the outlines of the images match precisely during the change. A second effect, also quite powerful, is achieved by projecting into the image. The first lantern shows an image, for example,

of Jacob sleeping in the field. Now a picture is placed in the second lantern, showing the ladder leading to heaven and the angelic host about which Jacob is dreaming. The second lantern is then faded in, and in this way creates a wonderful effect on the wall: Jacob's ladder, with the angels, gradually appears, as if forming in the mist – and in just the same way it slowly dissolves in the mist, when the second lantern is slowly faded out.

Translated from:
Hoffmann and Junker,
*Laterna Magica*, Berlin 1982

This crossfading technique was needed because in those days the light sources consisted mainly of candlelight, oil lamps or gas. The dissolver system mentioned performs the same function as a neutral wedge filter today. This consists of a glass plate, which is graded in various shades of grey down to complete black, which obscures everything. Pushing the dimmer slide into the beam path gradually fades the light out mechanically. The original dissolver

324 Wooden slide with pictures
painted on glass

consisted of a jagged metal leaf, and a similar dimming system is still found today in stage lighting. Mechanical dimming can be achieved with overlaid fine-mesh grids in varying densities.

These picture-shows included an enormous range of projection techniques. Mirror tricks with their mystifying apparitions were also often used (ill. 331). Even today this kind of projection can be found in variety shows.

326 Simple sheet metal lantern with glass image strip inserted, 18th century

## PROJECTION AND PROJECTION MATERIALS

Projection means representing something on a surface. This surface is a necessity for all projection techniques: at home on a screen or white sheet, in the theatre on backcloths, cycloramas, panoramas, gauze, and so on. Objects are always projected from slides by an optical enlargement process. The simplest form is a Linnebach projection, which is described in the chapter 'The Development of Stage Lighting' (see. p. 153). This uses light and dark contrasts to present different light intensities. A theatre spotlight using ellipsoid or condenser technology is to be seen as a projection apparatus. In this system the object to be depicted is placed in the beam path, using a heat-resistant material.

A projector using normal projection technology was used for the photographic illustrations on pages 140 and 141. In the theatre this projection implies depth of field. Pictorial sequences can be presented one after the other by putting images from several projectors together and then doubling the number of instruments crossfading from one group to the other. As fabric or projection screens are needed as the basic material for the pictorial surface, only a very limited range of creative theatrical invention is possible. Total projection (e.g. a cyclorama as the projection surface) is used by very few stage designers. This is, above all, because in this kind of presentation it is a matter of taste whether something so abstract is suitable for a production. This form of stage design also needs a very special staging concept, and there are very few designers who have the graphic skills for creating slides.

The standard projector position for large pictorial projections is often high

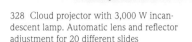

328 Cloud projector with 3,000 W incandescent lamp. Automatic lens and reflector adjustment for 20 different slides

329 Cloud projector for 20 different sets of material with 10 x 1,000 W cinema lamps, reflector adjustment by direct current motors with speed controls; c. 1958

327 Projection apparatus for a starry sky. There is a low voltage lamp behind every lens; constructed in 1935

up in the stage tower and on the proscenium lighting bridge. Back projections are projected from the rear on to a matt-transparent sheet.

If no ideal location is available, a distortion factor has to be built into the slides. When they are being made the positive picture is transferred to the base material in a distorted form. A grid system makes it possible to place the object points on the glass slide, taking the distortion into account. The dimensions involved are usually 13 x 13, 18 x 18 or 24 x 24 cm for large image projections. The light passing through is always slightly smaller than the size of the plate itself. Photographic material is often used, as well as hand-painted motifs. The aforementioned projec-

330 From the early days of colour projection: image projected using three slides for additive colour mixing

331 Pepper's ghost: a projection using Henry Pepper's system; c. 1862

tion plates for large projectors are made of special glass with high thermo-mechanical stability and which are heat-resistant up to 300 to 400°C. The motifs are painted on the glass with heat-resistant Repro-Lux colouring. Thinners and stoppers can be used to change the way in which the colour behaves on the glass plate. If film material is used

for slides, for example when projecting photographic subjects, various types are available. The choice should be agreed upon with a specialist lab which will make up the slides.

Even more interesting than static projections are moving images, which have a magical effect. German theatres were once renowned for inventing special projectors. Recently such sophisticated devices have disappeared from use or are gathering dust in storerooms, as these machines are no longer bright enough to hold their own at the stage lighting levels used today.

## PRACTICE

Usually an object is projected on to a surface in such a way that the image is as parallel as possible to the surface on to which it is being projected. This avoids distortion of the image. In so-called front projection the image is projected from the spectators' side on to a vertical surface. Positions for this in the

332 Cyclorama cloud apparatus using shadow projection with a low voltage lamp, 24 V, 1,000 W. The picture to be projected was applied to perspex foil; c. 1955

333 Benjamin Britten, *Peter Grimes*, director: Willy Decker, set designer: John Macfarlane, Théâtre de la Monnaie, Brussels, 1994

334 Cyclorama cloud projector with painted glass ball; *c.* 1955

theatre are the projection box, the auditorium and proscenium lighting bridge and the perch towers.

If there is plenty of room, rear projection is extremely versatile, as the surface can be lit with different intensity from the other light on stage. This is also possible to a limited extent with front projection, but a material that is luminous in its own right always makes a better visual effect. In a case like this the projector is placed behind the surface to be lit, which usually means that focal lengths will be very short.

If projection is for dramatic purposes in a production, the material to be used is likely to come from the designer. The lighting expert has to deal with positioning the projector correctly and selecting an appropriate focal length.

But projectors can also contribute to lighting designs without the use of slides, as projectors are able to light large surfaces evenly. If we are faced with the problem that the focal length of a profile spot is no longer sufficient, a projector with its variable objective lenses can be a great help. The light can easily be shaped by applying opaque paint to a hardened glass plate or by cutting out a piece of aluminium foil and slipping it between the glass plates.

335 Drive film for loops

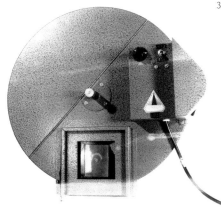

336 Effects wheel. Revolving, painted glass disc

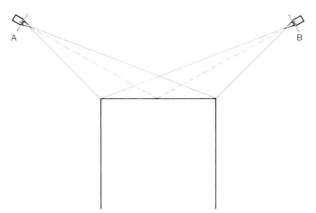

337  Plan view of projector positions for back projection

## PROJECTION IN ACTION

The rear wall of a real, constructed interior is replaced with a projection screen. Our intention is to make the room look larger, in other words to increase the sense of depth. The real space at the front is lit with two different kinds of light, which means that similar lighting has to be created for the virtual extension of the scene. The screen is lit using the aforementioned grid system, after the position of the projectors has been fixed. The rear section that is to be created is produced in a distorted version and manipulated on the slide.

If the difference in angle between the first and last edge of light is too great there will be problems with the depth of field. For this reason the projection angle should not be too wide.

Picture sequence, from left to right:

338  Room mock-up without projection

339  Projection plate for projector B

340  Rear wall of room changed to a projection screen, room extended by back projection

341  Room mock-up without projection

342  Projection plate for projector A

343  Rear wall of room changed to a projection screen, room extended by back projection

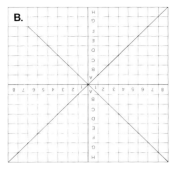

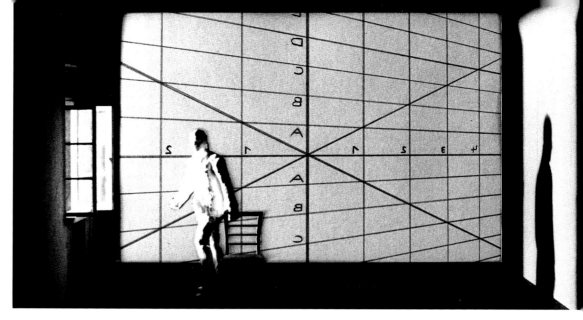

344 Grid system for a projection plate. The lettering on the plate must be legible for the user. The grid is upside down and reversed

345 Ill. right: Projector position B: grid distorted as a result of oblique projection

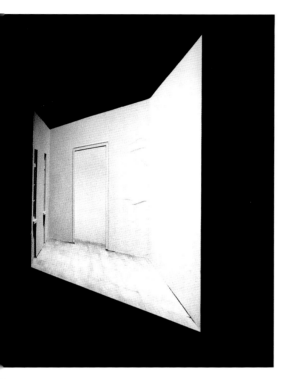

## Graphic distortion correction

The starting position for our graphically calculated construction is again the sample room in which we have replaced the rear wall with a projection screen 500 cm wide and 340 cm high. The projector is placed so that the optical axis runs at a height of 150 cm parallel with the stage floor.

Simple distortion can be calculated by using the following example and system:

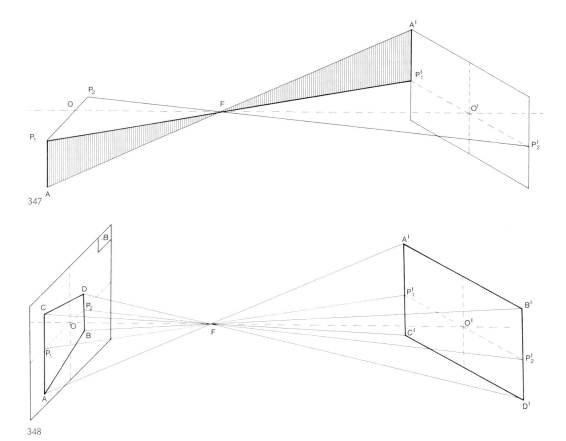

346 Accurate plan with projection area $P'_1$ and $P'_2$, slide $P_1-P_2$, for plate B

347

348

- draw scale plan view of projection area and objectives focal length F:
$\overline{P'_1 P'_2} = 500$ cm
- draw in optical axis O'F
- measure s': O'F = s' = 645 cm

- calculate f:   $f = \dfrac{s'_1}{V + 1}$

- $V = \dfrac{340 \text{ cm}}{16 \text{ cm}} = 21.25$ cm

- $s'_1$ = shortest distance from the projector to the projected area
$\overline{FP'_1} = s'_1 = 445$ cm

- $f = \dfrac{445 \text{ cm}}{21.25 + 1} \approx 18$ cm

  f = 18 cm
- calculate object width s

- $\dfrac{1}{f} = \dfrac{1}{s} + \dfrac{1}{s'}$,   $s'_1 = \overline{O'F} = 645$ cm

  $\dfrac{1}{18} = \dfrac{1}{s} + \dfrac{1}{645}$

  $\dfrac{1}{s} = \dfrac{1}{18} - \dfrac{1}{645}$

  $\overline{OF}$   s = 18.5 cm

- draw in picture plane $P_1$, $P_2$ at right angles to the optical axis at distance
- the distances $\overline{OP_1}$ and $\overline{OP_2}$ produced in this way can now be transferred to the projection plate illustrated in ill. 349
- to find the distance $\overline{P_1 A}$ the distances $\overline{FP_1}$ and $\overline{FP'_1}$ must first be measured on the plan
- then the calculation is made using the following formula $\dfrac{\overline{AP_1}}{\overline{FP_1}} = \dfrac{\overline{A'P'_1}}{\overline{FP'_1}}$
- $\overline{A'P'_1}$ is derived from the height of the projected wall and the distance of the optical axis from the floor:
(340 cm − 150 cm = 190 cm)

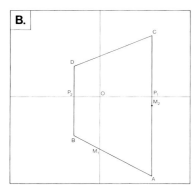

**B.**

349 Projection plate B with distorted borderlines

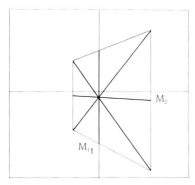

350 Creating the main diagonals and drawing in the lines meeting at intersection M1 or M2

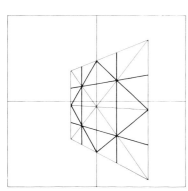

351

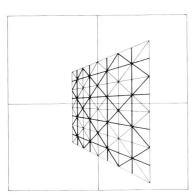

352 Further divisions created by drawing in diagonals in the squares produced and joining their intersection points (ill. 351 and 352)

- points B, C, D are calculated in the same way, using the following formulae:

- point B = $\dfrac{\overline{BP_2}}{\overline{FP_2}} = \dfrac{\overline{B'P_2'}}{\overline{FP_2'}}$

- point C = $\dfrac{\overline{CP_1}}{\overline{FP_1}} = \dfrac{\overline{C'P_1'}}{\overline{FP_1'}}$

- point C = $\dfrac{\overline{DP_2}}{\overline{FP_2}} = \dfrac{\overline{D'P_2'}}{\overline{FP_2'}}$

Note that for $\overline{C'P_1'}$ and $\overline{D'P_2'}$ the real projection height of 150 cm must be used. The values found in this way are transferred to the projection plate. To transfer the appropriately distorted grid system on to the plate we need the points that bisect the respective side lines of the projected area.

The centre M1 is given by the intersection point of the line AB with the centre axis:

- M2 halves the line AC

Ill. 350–352 shows how the grid density is increased. The more complicated the image to be projected is, the more intricate the grid has to be.

**Computer aided slide manufacture**

A projection simulator is used to determine size. Usually this is the projector with an objective lens. A special tracing paper is fitted into the objective. The outlines of the projected area are drawn in pencil. This produces the angles of distortion of the projected area and the angle of distortion of the lens. This is then read into the computer with a scanner and can be processed with a graphics program such as Photoshop. Be careful to use the correct slide format when doing so.

An essential element of professional projection is the picture dot resolution, usually set at 300 x 300 dpi. For details or realistic photographic motifs the figure increases to 600 x 600 or even 1,000 x 1,000 dpi.

The completed picture can be prepared with a printer, for example on Multitec Inkjet Projection Film, or it is processed by a specialist lab on suitable film stock.

If you are using slides you have made yourself, the colours of the slide material should be protected using a UV stop filter. Care should also be taken that the forced ventilation is aimed at the slide surface as much as possible.

## PROJECTOR POSITIONS

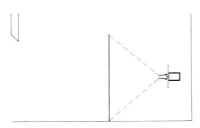

353 Rear projection

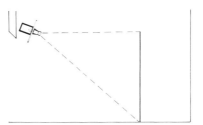

354 Front projection from the proscenium lighting bridge or the perch towers

355 Front projection from a projection booth

356 Total projection on to a cyclorama with three projectors to create a full image

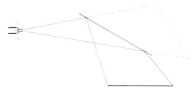

357 Deflection is important if the distance between the projector and the projected area cannot be covered directly on the shortest possible path. A reflector can be used to deflect the projected image

358 Simplest version of a slide projector, 650 W

## PROJECTORS

The industry has a wide range of projection equipment available. We can choose from a varied programme, from the familiar amateur models to high performance projectors. Selection criteria are based on the intended use, performance and budget. There are any number of 35 mm slide projector manufacturers. Large image professional models are supplied mainly by Pani or Reiche & Vogel. Useful projectors for the theatre range from 250 to 10,000 W with solid-state lamps, 1,200 to 12,000 W using daylight technology. Special projectors, above all for 35 mm and medium slide formats, are also available in very good versions with xenon lamps.

359 Optical arrangement of the projector illustrated above

360 2,000 W tungsten-halogen incandescent lamp projector for 18 x 18 cm slides, with motorized slide changer and magazine for 15 slides

361 2000-W-HQI-architectural projector with douser. The light source has a particularly long service life

362 Bottom left:
4,000 W HMI projector with automatic slide changer for 32 slides. Sequence and exposure duration can be programmed

363 Bottom right:
2,500 W HMI projector with motorized zoom optics

## LOOKING TO THE FUTURE

As well as its traditional stage lighting range, the Pani company has been working on special projectors for architectural lighting purposes since 1998. This is equipment designed for long-term use, and it requires durable materials and a high degree of freedom from maintenance. The architectural prototype is the ARC II, a projector with a HQI lamp and a set of interchangeable lenses and filters. Unlike earlier HMI projectors, the optical parts are fitted into the projector with simple plug connections and can be changed quickly without special tools.

Pani is now further expanding its range by developing the Pani 2000 series, which can project both traditional slides and also special effects. Pani is breaking new ground both in terms of its optical system structures and also in developing effects projectors and addressing the temperature problem. If this is solved, a large number of projection media will become available for use.

## STAGE PROJECTION IN THE IMMEDIATE FUTURE

Modern stage requirements for control, handling and flexibility as well as the demand for new effects and moving

364  6,000 W HMI projector

365  12,000 W HMI projector

images mean that new concepts are needed for projector design. As with other technologies, modular structure is an important feature for all sorts of reasons in order to be able to address future developments. In the case of projectors, the hanging device is the key point at which the essential elements of the projector – such as the lamp housing, slide position and effects module 1, along with the projector objective lens and effects module 2 – are connected with each other. This concept is open-ended in many directions. For the first time it will be possible to change the lighting unit if a different luminous power level is needed. Thus, a flexible modular system has been created.

The new generation of projectors are being built according to the most up-to-date scientific methods and in time will have an even higher level of luminous efficiency. For the time being the proven HMI lamp system is still in use, because it is simple to handle, works reliably and colour values can be perfectly adjusted to the rest of the stage lighting. But the new projector concept is an open system. When technical innovations come along, there will be an appropriate reaction, which has the advantage that users can adapt their modular system quite simply.

Handling also has a high priority in the new projector concept. In future, it will be possible to change the projector from stand use to hanging use with a few simple steps. A reduction in weight can also be expected. A welcome improvement is the quick-release system for attaching effect equipment. This, combined with power focusing, will mean that quick conversions can be achieved. With respect to the controls, all functions will essentially be designed for DMX 512 or other contemporary protocols.

### Breaking new ground

If we permit ourselves to question previous practice and are prepared to take other technological approaches, quite interesting solutions to problems can ensue, although serial production remains laborious, expensive and risky. This also applies to the field of projection. Nevertheless, we can expect that in the next few years there will be new projector systems with other possibilities that will not replace current ones but complement them sensibly. Thus

366  7,000 W xenon high powered large image projector for 18 x 18 cm slides. The basic apparatus can be fitted with a hand-operated or an automatic changer taking up to 40 slides. By fitting a scroller, it is possible to use transparencies stuck together as a film up to a length of 30 m. Picture transport can be adjusted between 0 and 80 cm per second. Individual pictures can be shown for as long as wished. The changer can be pivoted horizontally. A double scroller can be used to project two films one behind the other, e.g. a framing mask in the back and the motif in front

projections will be better able to enhance the stage design.

New developments will tend towards combinations between video projection and slide stills, so that dynamic elements can be combined with large-size slide projections. Co-operation in the fields of holography and laser technology will continue.

367  W. A. Mozart, *Così fan tutte*
Director: Dieter Dorn
Set Designer: Jürgen Rose
Bayerische Staatsoper, Cuvilliés-Theater,
Munich, 1993

# Lighting Consoles

The 'central nervous system' of any lighting installation is the lighting console. It has evolved along with other technical developments in the theatre as the hub of an elaborate combination of individual items intended to co-ordinate and regulate the various lighting functions. Ill. 368 shows how a small analogue system works and ill. 369 a possible approach to controlling lighting with a DMX signal.

Another development for incorporating lighting consoles in a lighting network is the Ethernet connection (ill. 370). This latest technology means that even complicated drives and multifunctional spotlight control are no longer a problem. Of course all these components have to be linked up very carefully, as there are many potential sources of error.

Modern lighting boards contain dimmer operating systems, which makes them easy to place in the theatre and in the lighting control booth, as they do not occupy a great deal of space. Which of these lighting control units to buy is often a matter of taste, operating philosophy and, not least of all, money. In any case, the right thing to do when deciding on a new system is to give the highest priority to the technical lighting requirements of the institution and the size of the stage. Only after such considerations should a decision be made about which kind to choose, and here, too, ease of use, precision, reliability and servicing should be balanced against the price. Electronics are developing at an enormous speed, which means that the sector has an immense range of new possibilities to offer. There

are many types and makes of lighting consoles, from small mobile systems to the large, permanently installed ones. In any case, digital technology is nowadays preferable for the dimmer device, and drive and memory technology should also be computer controlled. DMX controls also deserve serious consideration because they make it much simpler to include additional functions within a lighting concept.

## WHAT DOES THE CONSOLE DO?

The lighting board is used to identify individual lanterns and fix their intensity by means of individual faders, fader wheels or a numbered keyboard. A combination of different intensities is brought together to create a lighting

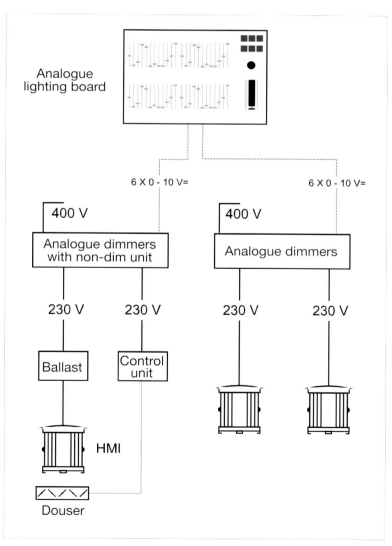

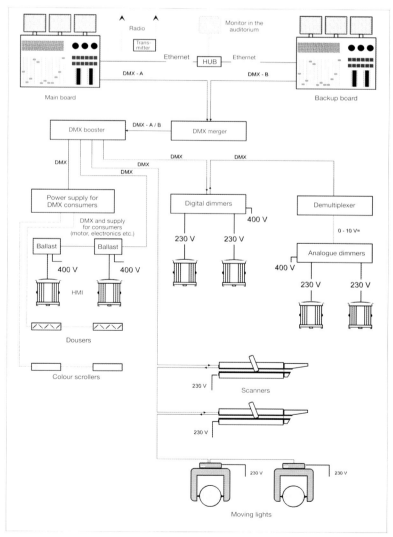

368 Schematic diagram of an analogue lighting console

369 Schematic diagram of a DMX lighting console

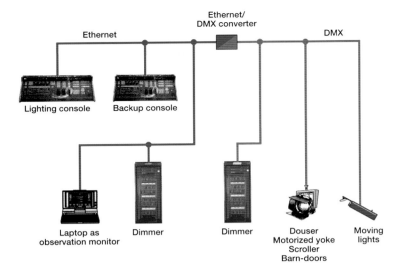

Ethernet/
DMX converter

Ethernet                                    DMX

Lighting console    Backup console

Laptop as          Dimmer        Dimmer    Douser        Moving
observation monitor                        Motorized yoke lights
                                           Scroller
                                           Barn-doors

370 Set-up for an Ethernet network

state and then stored. The results can be recorded by jotting down the circuits used or by storing the data electronically. The accumulated states for a particular production are then saved on disk.

When using older, smaller systems, each lighting state made up of lights set at various intensities and the speed at which they reach their final level is noted in a lighting schedule. The state is then faded in or out using a master dimmer lever. Most boards have preset levers with which the lighting channels can be selected and their intensity fixed. A fader is then used to fade between these two lever settings.

In simpler systems, the stages of the production are reproduced from the written notes, and presets and fades are executed by hand. This manual approach is considered antiquated today, but it does require a degree of empathy

from the operators that more modern systems often do not require.

A computer lighting operator has to watch the technical operation of the lighting on a monitor, which shows brightness levels, fades with development times, colour changer operating details and information about moving lights and action cues. Usually a lighting state is called up with a keyboard, which also makes it possible to correct any aspect of the process. Computer technology offers major advantages in producing complicated cueing operations. Once such combinations have been established, they can be repeated as often as desired, and corrected, and then stored in the memory. These systems also need automatic logging facilities, so that the process described can be followed clearly and effectively. The lighting states and important information about electrical circuits, brightness levels, times for fading in and out and special notes can all be printed out. A record of this kind provides the operator in the booth and other lighting technicians involved with a complete summary of the production, which can either be corrected off-line or stored for further reference.

Many lighting people find it difficult to get used to new lighting booth techniques. Earlier they had an adjustable fader or a mechanical lever when following an action on stage. The operator knew by looking at his controls that if something was moved it would change the brightness of the lights. Today, all that changes are the control data on the monitor. But it would be wrong to assume that a system like this does not offer ample ways of adapting to a sudden change in what is happening on stage.

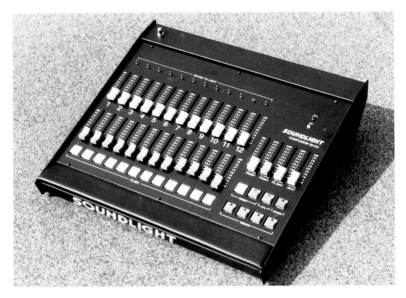

371 Small analogue self-assembly lighting console: twelve channels, four masters and one preset, flash buttons for each channel and each group

372  Mobile digital dimmer racks

373  Panther lighting control system, AVAB with monitors, for up to 4,000 channels, function selection by icon, fully integrated controls for scrollers, scanners and other DMX equipment

374  Contor 96/DMX lighting board for up to 512 circuits with monitor control, ADB system

375  Feeds and power outlets behind the mobile dimmer racks

Modern systems permit every manipulation or correction, but the operator has to know how to use the keyboard.

Demands on lighting technicians have increased considerably. As already mentioned, it's not just about fading spotlights up and down in a certain rhythm, but above all about linking up all the additional automated systems with their individual behaviour patterns to create a lighting state, or even using some of them independently from the main state. But the real difficulty for the operator is linking all these functions to create a harmonious lighting change. The operator's skill is a crucial factor for the success of a lighting concept, as it is possible to attach single channels to single circuits, or to let several lighting states run parallel or into each other. In any case, lighting consoles for medium and large stages should be suitable for operating all the new types of equipment. Controlling moving lights and scrollers from a central point makes lighting console work easier and improves operational reliability.

376 DP90, digital dimmer for 2.5 kVA. Various characteristic curves can be adjusted over 4,096 levels

377 Mobile digital dimming unit for 6 x 5 kVA or 12 x 2.5 kVA. On the right is a backlit display with data on the B19 operating status

378 VARI*LITE ARTISAN® Plus, control console for VARI*LITE products and DMX compatible equipment. The board is designed for 1,000 channels and 2,000 lighting states per channel. It is used mainly for rock concerts

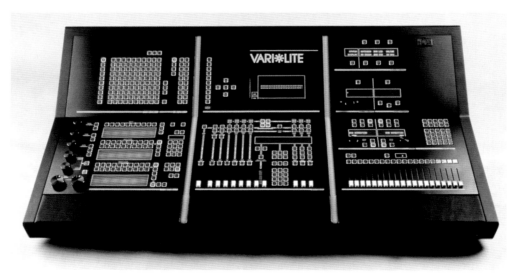

## THE LIGHTING CONSOLE OF THE FUTURE

### A modified approach

The lighting board of the future will be much more result-oriented than its predecessors. The lighting operator will no longer have to wonder how to achieve certain effects, but will simply tell the system what he wants to have. The main aim of this changed approach is to have the highest possible level of working efficiency. Graphic presentations, along with topographical plans and automated logic diagrams will make operations easier to grasp and to carry out. The control menu on the screen will change according to the particular situation (focusing, performance, rehearsal etc.). Some operations may even be activated from touch screens. Multifunction keys could then be programmed as desired.

Handling will be simplified. There will no longer be any difference between normal dimmers, scrollers, moving lights etc. when using the system. Operational elements will become universal; for example, there will no longer be any need to distinguish between master levers and crossfade controllers. Functions could be allocated according to situation, and thus the number of operating elements will be considerably more manageable.

The whole lighting system will be configured from a menu, rather like using a modern PC. Many of these menus will be in graphic form. This visual presentation of the components to be selected, in the form of block and circuit diagrams as well as other graphic devices, will be infinitely more direct than long lists and notes. 'Starting image', for example, will be a block diagram of the whole installation. Click-

ing on the 'dimmer' icon leads to the next menu page, which shows the various dimmers in the system. The next click takes you to a particular dimmer, where parameters such as characteristics, kind of input and so on can be set. It will be possible to feed in information quickly and simply in a similar way about the type, number and arrangement of instruments and equipment, load attributes and all the other necessary data. New equipment may also be brought in by choosing an appropriate depiction. An equipment library will also contain all the lanterns, scanners, yokes, telescopes etc. available. For example, a click on the mouse will open up a list of all the lanterns, and choosing one will be like choosing a printer driver on the PC.

This kind of new approach will make almost any individual configuration possible; ideally one will even be able to set the degree of complexity of the operations. An experienced lighting expert will also be able to custom-build his own user interface on the same equipment.

### Comprehensive networking

The system of the future will be part of a complex network. Hierarchically arranged computer units will be linked by bus systems and share the jobs to be done. PCs may be linked and possibly manage control functions too, allowing the visualization of lighting scenarios or work on lighting design off-line. Input terminals will be set up as wished, with the range running from radio control via laptop and PC to convenient, ergonomic, graphically prepared operations with a touch screen monitor. Attached databases may contain equipment libraries, for example. Connection to the Internet will simplify software updates and make direct service possible, along with remote trouble shooting.

### Improved operational reliability

Building up the entire lighting control system from a number of components and then interlinking them will make a new approach to backup provisions possible. Distinguishing between the main system and a backup system that is usually not used at all will become a thing of the past. All the components can constantly be in use, and computing and control work will sensibly be distributed by databus. At the same time, these computer terminals will serve as mutual backups (an active reserve). If a component fails, the

tion. Changes will be shown on the screen in real time.

This realistic, three-dimensional simulation of an entire lighting scenario will also mean that the production can be designed and planned far away from the actual stage. The lighting technician will do most of the lantern set-up on any PC, or on a laptop while he is travelling. He will be able to call up a list of all the lanterns and other equipment needed for the chosen lighting design, which will simplify production planning considerably. After that, all that will be needed on stage are the corrections.

Despite all these prospects one thing holds true: Technology must serve, and never determine, art.

379 Professional lighting console with backup board and flat-screen monitors. System: Prisma NT, Transtechnik. Ethernet and professional bus interface; designed for 4,096 DMX combinations on eight channels, and controls scrollers, moving lights and scanners

remaining stations will take over without affecting anything else.

### Conclusions

The console of the future will offer users hitherto unknown standards of working efficiency. Operation will be result-oriented; 'how' something is done will largely be left to the system. Graphic interfaces will make it possible to implement design ideas directly and effectively. Designing lighting scenarios will be simpler and quicker, and no longer tied to a particular location. A modular approach means that lighting control hardware and software can be rapidly adapted to individual needs.

The lighting technician will be able to devote himself to his prime role: creative lighting design which perfectly supports the effect of a theatrical production in its entirety.

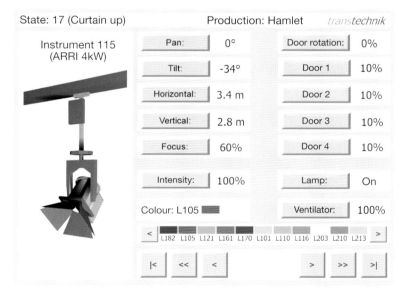

380 Design study for a new operating interface. After selecting a circuit on the keyboard, the above image appears on a touch screen let into the surface of the board. It shows all the possible settings that can be addressed from the touch screen. Changes are shown simultaneously on the left in the illustration

### FORECAST

Rapid developments in the fields of both hard and software, with ever greater computing power in an ever smaller space, will radically change lighting design in the future. The lighting expert will have a realistic image of the whole stage and lighting installation on his console computer screen. He will be able to run through the scene, examine every point from any angle and correct the lighting at any time. If he wishes he will be able to see the effect of what he has done on the monitor beforehand and decide whether to incorporate the modifica-

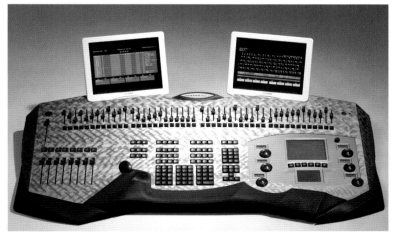

381 Professional lighting console, Obsession II system, designed for up to 3,072 DMX channels

382  4,000 W HMI Fresnel
for the theatre with douser and
scroller magazine

# The Development of Stage Lighting

383 Gas control unit with valves for individual gas pipes for auditorium lighting, footlights, border and proscenium lights, 1880

Gas lighting was first used in the theatre in 1803. This very dangerous kind of stage lighting reached a particularly advanced stage of development in England with amazing effects. Complicated mechanical cable controls were used to turn or pull coloured plates or gauzes around the gas flames to produce colour effects. The gas supply was provided by valves, which even at that time were grouped together in a 'lighting centre'. Large theatres used up to 2,000 gas flames to light the stage.

Gaslights were placed mainly at the front of the stage, as footlights. Side lights behind the proscenium arch and a few border lights helped to cast more light on the centre of the stage. Protagonists quite naturally met downstage, where they were very well lit by the footlights. Clearly this diffuse lighting did not produce any major dramatic effects. Even in those days there were discontented theatre critics who had a thing or two to say about this simple and relatively ineffective stage lighting.

Until that time, the 18th-century backcloth had held its own on the stage, and a backdrop with flat wings was still standard. Directional light, lighting angles and shadows which could not be achieved with gas lighting were painted on the set. The diffuse shadow-play of the many gas burners and lighting effects painted on the set to create an illusion produced a chaos of different impressions. An important development in stage lighting came with the invention of the carbon arc lamp.

This new kind of light was introduced in 1849, and after the invention of the first carbon filament lamp in 1879, theatre lighting was introduced at the International Electricity Exhibition in Munich in 1881. Four years later, in 1885, the first electric stage lighting made its début at the Residenztheater in Munich. Even then, lighting specialists thought it was important to control the electric light, which had also been possible with gaslight. The oldest way of regulating electric light was the salt pot. The flow of electricity was regulated by the degree of immersion of electrodes in a salt solution. Their position was controlled by cables, wheels and rods, so that several plates could be moved together in groups. The German electrical industry made its first stage control unit in 1888. The voltage was changed by rheostats. The carbon filament lamp was replaced for theatrical purposes by the more robust tungsten lamp in 1905.

## DESIGN AND CONCEPTS

Several theatre artists influenced theatrical lighting and staging around the turn of the century. Edward Gordon Craig, Adolphe Appia and Mariano Fortuny felt that the usual design with backdrop and flats had become outmoded. Electric lighting meant that progressive staging concepts could be developed to supersede this.

In 1901, London experienced a thought-provoking opera production by EDWARD GORDON CRAIG, which broke

384 Stage control unit with water resistors. Equipment like this was used until 1960

new ground for stage design and was classified as 'post-realistic'. Craig banished clutter from the stage, removed the painted flats and the usual borders and restored the stage to what it was intended to be: a playing area. Light was no longer painted but cast. The traditional backcloth was replaced with a broad strip of fabric which was deep blue at the bottom and shaded into violet towards the top. Seen through the relatively low proscenium arch, this gave an impression of infinite distance.

The most important element of Craig's staging was the lighting. The instruments were not placed in usual positions such as footlights or lights in the wings but were concentrated in the upper part of the stage space, anticipating the modern proscenium lighting bridge. This lighting arrangement was not readily adopted by other theatres, however. Craig operated all his spotlights and reflector systems from an electrical control board. His device for directing light on to the stage via coloured reflector surfaces in particular was a new way of seeing and experiencing lighting.

Craig talked about the scene, rather than the stage and the set. He used mainly rostra, columns and steps in his productions and abandoned the traditional painted backcloths. Light had a completely new part to play, becoming a creative force, one which was challenging for Craig. His light compositions became creative elements in their own right, and he used concentrated, highly expressive lighting, supported by effects such as fog, to create realistic and directional light which had been previously unknown. His fundamental changes to sets and lighting afforded him many opportunities for putting his new ideas into practice. He harmonized the creative power of light with the music in his opera productions and started to create a universal work of art using rhythm, colour and light.

ADOLPHE APPIA was also trying to reorganize space at about the same time as Craig. Appia realized that the stage itself was a three-dimensional area in which space could be sensibly allocated. Working with the composer and musicologist Emile Jacques-Dalcroze, he analysed the interdependence of music-time-movement and space. He came up with the idea of rhythmical stage architecture, designing sets for Jacques-Dalcroze with clear, geometrical structures and shaping his playing area with rostra, steps and cubes. Once Appia had removed the backdrop, flats,

385 Two-preset lighting console unit with wire resistors, c. 1880

wings and curtains he discovered that the stage really only needed the right light, which for him was in an inseparable union with space.

Appia distinguished between simple, diffused illumination and dramatically accentuated light. He based his lighting designs on brightness and the direction of the light (shadow value). Articulating these two different kinds of light admitted an atmospheric breathing. He explained that 'light is the most important three-dimensional medium on stage. Without its unifying power we see only what objects are and not what they express.'

In his search for the universal work of art Appia arrived via experimental educational theory at the English concept of the garden city. Here, housing estates were built with parks and commercial enterprises, embracing a natural way of life, architecture, residential and physical culture in the immediate vicinity of large cities. The most important German garden city was Hellerau, near Dresden. Appia hung the ballroom

of the theatre there with transparent linen, behind which an estimated 3,000 to 7,000 coloured incandescent lamps were mounted in rows. In this way he created homogeneous, indirect light for presenting his rhythmic stage architecture in combination with rhythmic gymnastics.

The invention of artificial light made it possible for Appia to implement his ideas about the dramaturgy of lighting. His work had a very powerful influence on later staging developments at the Bayreuth Festival. Wagner's operas particularly appealed to Appia, and he wrote his own production notes for many of them. He saw Wagner's work as liberating the stage artist because Appia believed music to be the consummate art, towards which all other forms of expression strive.

The German director MAX REINHARDT revolutionized and improved the standard of theatre technology around the turn of the century. He implemented his ideas about a 'different theatre' with a small group of actors in

The Development of Stage Lighting

386 Adolphe Appia
'The Valkyries' Rock',
from *Die Walküre*, Act 3,
design dating from 1892

Appia created his production
notes for the *Ring of the
Nibelungen* tetralogy in 1892,
and put his scenic visions
as illustrations on paper.
Symbolic and impressionistic
features can be seen in this first
creative phase: natural elements, reduced to essentials
and represented by shading
make up a three-dimensional,
accessible stage space

387 Adolphe Appia:
'The Alleyway',
from the series of
*Espaces rythmiques*
(Rhythmical Spaces),
design dating from
1909/10

In his Cubist phase, Appia –
influenced by Emile Jacques-
Dalcroze's rhythmical gymnastics –
designed scenic spaces that
were not intended for a particular
story but rather to enable performers
to translate music into movement
appropriately. In this case the
three-dimensional spatial structure
is largely made up of architectural
elements with surface boundaries
such as steps, slopes and cuboid
stone blocks

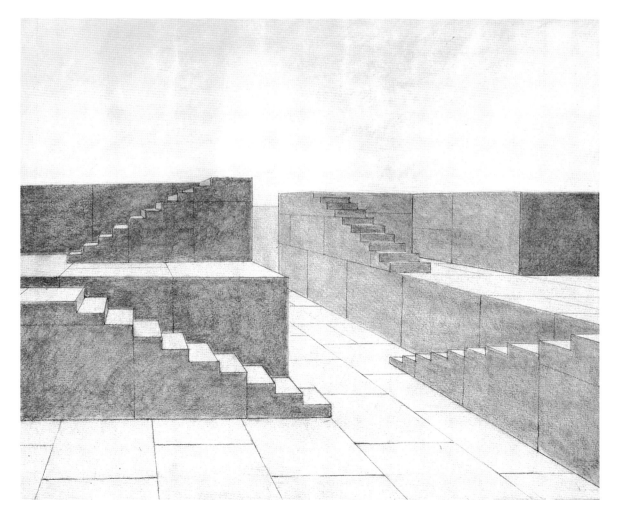

388 Bordoni lighting system, consisting of three stage control units.
From the left: Stage control units 4 x 40, 4 x 28, 5 x 12 control levers. Each unit has a central drive for manual or motor operation

389 Siemens stage alternating current control system, Bordoni type. The control trolleys are connected to the control levers by wire cables

the Berlin 'Schall und Rauch Theater' (Theatre without Meaning) in 1901, where he used lighting design as an integrating medium in his productions. In subsequent years Reinhardt built practically everything that was possible (e. g. revolves and lifts) into his venues and improved the lighting equipment. In 1905, as someone who had studied Appia's discoveries, he took a lively interest in the painter and theatre artist Mariano Fortuny but adopted only part of his fundamental inventions.

In 1911 Reinhardt realized his idea of a giant theatre in London. There he installed even more sophisticated, newly developed stage and lighting systems, the latter of which was so big that 56 electricians and 82 machinists had to be employed to run it. When he introduced his theatre in the United States for the first time in 1923, the electrical equipment at New York's Century Theater was not sufficient, so he added 12 portable units to the existing lighting console and devised a colour plan for lighting the sets and costumes. The New York press was lost in admiration for 'Max Reinhardt stage lighting', and people were visibly astonished that he used the colours blue, green and purple and not amber, white and red to which

Americans were accustomed. Even at that time his staging concepts contained a detailed plot and run times. The number of cues was surprisingly numerous. For *A Midsummer Night's Dream*, for example, he insisted on 107 different lighting states

MARIANO FORTUNY had a number of new ideas about stage lighting. He worked on the basis of nature, direct sunlight and diffuse light zones. He made the right decision in preferring the dangerous and more difficult to handle carbon arc light to incandescent light, which he felt was too red. He used arc lamps to illuminate strips of material in red, yellow and blue; the strips were sewn together in bands and could be moved by rollers according to the colour impression required. He used black velvet to regulate the intensity of light emitted indirectly in this way. A mechanical cover shutter was fitted in front of the arc lamp for a complete blackout. He later perfected his system with additional colour slides that could be placed in front of the arc light as needed. As well as this remarkable lighting invention, he also used cloud machines, which made his imaginary domed horizon all the more successful. The first theatre in which Fortuny was able to set up his complete lighting system was the Deutsche Oper in Berlin, which was built in 1912.

ADOLF LINNEBACH, the former technical director of the Munich Opera

House, invented a projector that was important for stage lighting in the early years of the century. This was the simplest possible device, reduced to the most basic principles, consisting of a lamp, the projected area and a projection plate that was pushed between them. Neither lenses nor a reflector

390 Single levers with intensity stops, connected to a central drive shaft. The large handwheels on the left could be used to move the levers as a group

were needed to create an image, as the lamp filament already provided the necessary focal point. This was an easy way of making wide-angled black-and-white projections, on cycloramas, for example.

The sharpness of the outlines was determined by the ratio of distances from the lamp to the plate and from the plate to the projected area. If the plate was close to the lamp, the projected outlines were indistinct, but this proved to be advantageous in certain cases. To achieve a sharper focus it was important to have the plate parallel with the projected area, which again meant that bent or curved plates had to be used for projection on to uneven or curved surfaces.

The outbreak of the First World War meant that nothing was invented for the theatre for a long period, and after 1918 the Fortuny system had lost its appeal because the indirect light entailed major light losses. Developments thereafter were rapid and numerous. This was when the incandescent lamp came into its own in the theatre. Diffuse lighting was replaced by cyclorama lanterns, and this was followed by rapid developments in spotlight technology. Many of the simpler models still look exactly as they did when they were first invented.

The founding of the Bauhaus in 1919 brought together many experts, and Expressionist theatre was popular and influential. Innovations affecting stage sets and lighting followed each other in quick succession. Bauhaus members sent out strong progresive impulses all over the world. Among the many prominent artists were Schlemmer, Meyerhold, Piscator, Moholy-Nagy and Kandinsky. The painter VASILY KANDINSKY, who was a member of the Bauhaus

from 1922 to 1933, was also interested in stage design and even designed an opera at a Berlin theatre.

OSKAR SCHLEMMER and LÁSZLÓ MOHOLY-NAGY in particular influenced theatre design and stage lighting with their Expressionist concepts. Schlemmer was in charge of the Bauhaus theatre workshop from 1923 to 1929 and primarily interested in using facial masks to enhance expression, dance movements and human beings within the surrounding space. Moholy-Nagy invented what he called the 'lighting prop of the electric stage' in 1930. This light machine presented, as the most important factors, movement, light reflections and shadow effects in a linked sequence. Moholy-Nagy also designed stage sets for Erwin Piscator in Berlin that were avant-garde in style and based on the concept of 'total theatre'.

## TECHNOLOGY

### Control systems

Stage lighting control systems considerably improved in the thirties, and two different systems were competing in Germany. The Bordoni and Salani control systems were both variable ratio transformers with collector trolleys. This technique offered the advantage of returning to cable technology and mobile trolleys. The difference between the two systems was that in the Bordoni method, the control trolley with contact resistances ran directly on the transformer coils, while in the Salani system a sliding contact trolley moved on a linear commutator slide track, whose individual segments were connected by protective resistors to the individual transformer coils. Carbon brushes served as trolley contacts. Both systems were used for a long time, and there are theatres today that still work with this kind of lighting equipment.

A lighting control system introduced in 1955 separated the control board and the dimmers for the first time. Intensity was now regulated electrically, not mechanically. Rheostats were used, then transformers, driven by a central electric drive with magnetic clutches. The speed of the drive shafts could be varied using the pedals on the 'light organ'.

The first step in the direction of electronically controlled stage equipment was the introduction of electron tube control. This control technology was developed by scientists as early as 1937, but it was not until the fifties that it was

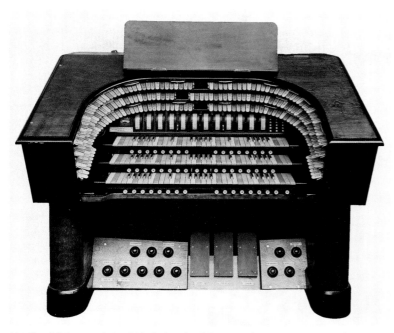

391 First lighting console in which the board and dimmer racks were set up separately, 1950

duly recognized. Phase control became possible by using thyratrons (hot cathode single-way tube rectifiers with anti-parallel connection; ill. 392). This meant that the operating element looked different as well. The control circuits were arranged as twin rows of rheostats and divided into groups. There was an active operating row and a row for presetting the next lighting state. A fader transformer was used to transfer control from the one half of the board to the other.

In 1956 lighting board developers switched their allegiance to the transductor. In this case as well, two inductance coils were linked in an anti-parallel arrangement. The transductor controlled power levels by regulating the magnetic flux. The control and memory system began to develop rapidly. It is almost unimaginable today how lighting technicians had to cope continually with such fundamentally different equipment.

One development followed another at this time. Everything added to the existing standard made it easier to work better and more flexibly. Above all, it gradually became possible for a single technician to operate the lighting console, and the equipment could be much more advantageously placed because it was so much smaller. Finally, lighting states could be recorded electronically, and the memory variants worked relatively smoothly. The memory capacity and operational reliability of the board were especially important, as the memory elements worked in very different ways. Using punched tape and punched cards often involved mechanical difficulties, and it was obvious that drum storage was vulnerable, because its mechanical wear was greater than its electronic advantages.

Various memory systems were available at the time:

• RELAY MEMORIES permitted quick storage and smooth retrieval of states in any given sequence. But the amount of equipment needed increased with the amount of memory

393 Racks for
thyratron tubes, 1955

392 Thyratron control unit with presets and fader wheels, 1955

394 Dimmer rack section with thyratron tubes for two circuits

396 BBC Datalux lighting console, 1968

395 Lighting console with punched card input and backup system, c. 1960

used, so that these devices became uneconomical after only very little information was stored. Relay memories also needed a relatively large amount of space, which was difficult to find.

• PUNCHED TAPE MEMORIES took up less space and had unlimited memory because they could process an unlimited number of tapes. A few seconds were needed to save or retrieve a lighting state. It was not possible to change the retrieval sequence of the states; the settings were predetermined on the tapes in a particular order. It was difficult to find a particular setting on the tape, as the whole tape had to be worked through. Damaged tapes could not be used and were thus worthless because the stored settings could not be read directly.

• PUNCHED CARD MACHINES also took up very little room and could store as many settings as necessary. About five seconds were needed to punch a card, and about one second for retrieval. The retrieval sequence could be chosen as wished by sorting the stack of cards by hand. A particular

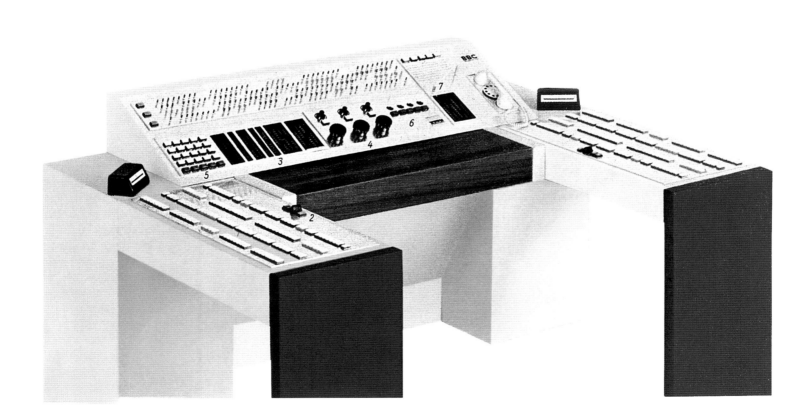

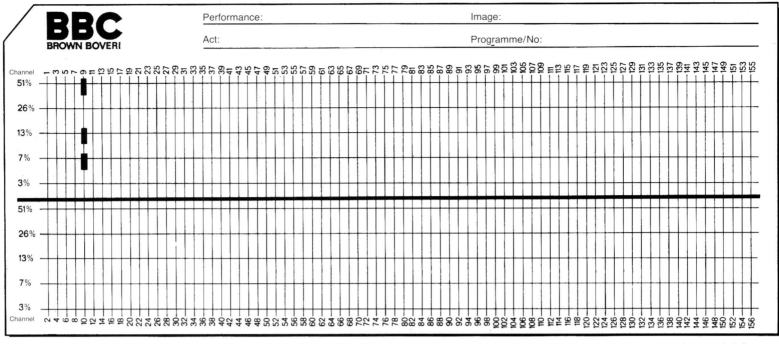

397 Punched card for the Datalux operating unit. The lighting channel numbers are printed at the top. Each lighting level is fixed by five punched holes, whose intensity is shown on the left. This meant that the card could be read without additional aids. One card was needed for each lighting state, e. g. channel 9: 51% + 13% + 7% = 71% intensity

398 Stage transductor dimmer for 2,000 W, c. 1970

399 Thyristor dimmer using plug-in technology for 2,500 W, c. 1975

part of the card was allotted to each lighting circuit, so that it was possible to read off the stored settings directly with the aid of the printed labelling on the card. The disadvantage was that only a limited number of circuits could be stored on one punched card, so two or more cards were needed for extensive control systems, i. e. with a great number of circuits.

- FERRITE CORE MEMORIES worked smoothly for both storage and retrieval. The sequence of settings could be chosen as wished. As there were no moving parts, the memory system needed no servicing. The number of memory units could be chosen within certain limits when buying the equipment. The amount of equipment needed increased with the amount of data to be stored, so that the memory capacity limit was about fifty settings.

- MAGNETIC TAPE RECORDERS had unlimited storage capacity. Each setting could be found within a minute; given this limitation, any sequence could be chosen for retrieval. The equipment included moving parts

that needed maintenance. Damaged magnetic tapes were worthless because the stored settings could no longer be evaluated. Also, the equipment needed an air-conditioned room.

- MAGNETIC DRUM MEMORIES had similar qualities to devices using magnetic tape. However, one great disadvantage was limited storage capacity, as the drum could not be changed by the lighting technician.

- MAGNETIC CARD DEVICES were comparable with punched card equipment. But unlike such equipment, it was not possible to read the stored settings directly or to add handwritten entries.

This listing shows that no memory system was a hundred per cent satisfactory. But if fifty storage locations were enough, ferrite core memories met almost all the requirements and were therefore often chosen as memories for lighting control units.

In 1952 the technical expression 'software' found its way into theatrical jargon. The main thrust in theatrical computer technology came from England. The operating logistics were designed in close co-operation with lighting designers, which made an effective artistic approach possible. The last momentous development was the introduction of the thyristor in about 1960,

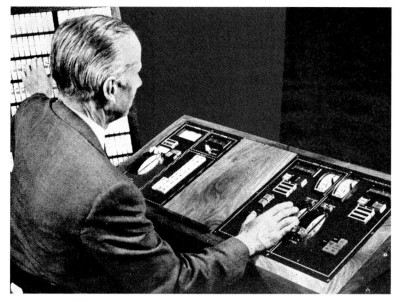

400 Rank Strand Electric, DDM system. On the left is the operating board for 240 channels. Dimmer memory control and numerical selection for sequence fixing are on the left of the operating panel. Playback controls are on the right

401 Plug-in thyristor dimmer for 5,000 W, c. 1980

a semiconductor version of the thyratron tube, for dimming. Up to the present, dimmers are still being regulated by two thyristors in anti-parallel arrangement. The so-called Triac, an electronic component with two thyristors, was used only briefly in stage lighting. Dimmer components are usually built to take 2.5, 5 and 10 kW. The electronic components got smaller and more robust, and new control technology developments came quickly, offering ever greater sophistication.

### Lamps

The first attempts to use gas discharges for lighting were made in the late 19th century. The first luminous tubes were filled with nitrogen, emitted pink light and were used for lighting until 1930. Beginning in 1924 efforts to improve the quality of this tube led in 1935 to the invention of a low pressure fluorescent lamp; that, basically, corresponds to our present technology.

An important development took place in 1932: Night streets were lit by low pressure sodium vapour lamps for the first time. The high pressure mercury vapour lamp followed in 1935. These two discharge lamps, along with

402 Lighting booth with a DDM system. Left: Individual channels
Centre: Operating board
Right: Pinboard matrix for the emergency system
Top: Display panel and special controls

403 Lighting control room for a large system with 640 channels. System: Lightboard, c. 1982

404 Dimmer room for a large system with plug-in dimmer rack in 5,000 and 10,000 W dimmers. The incandescent lamps at the top were intended for the base load on the fluorescent lamp circuits; c. 1980

the low pressure fluorescent lamp, did not make their theatrical début until much later. The fluorescent lamp in particular was used as a flood and also for cyclorama lighting once it could be regulated.

An innovation in discharge lamp research was the xenon lamp, which represented another step forward in producing theatrical daylight. These lamps were first used in projectors in 1951.

General Electric developed the first tungsten-halogen lamp in 1959. OSRAM introduced a new discharge lamp in 1970 to meet television studio needs for brighter, colder light: the Metallogen lamp (HMI®). This caught on quickly all over the world because of its outstanding colour spectrum, colour rendering and high luminous efficiency.

Just as the organ-builder's skill was exploited when developing early progressive lighting systems, modern lighting systems are largely derived from computer technology. This technology offers infinite possibilities, and the most recent systems leave practically nothing to be desired. Of course, there will always be a lighting technician who finds some setting techniques superfluous. But alongside – or better, because of – this technology, there is now great diversity in the ways in which an individual treatment of artistic challenges can be provided.

The Development of Stage Lighting

Arriving at sensible technical solutions and satisfying artistic results requires a sound theoretical knowledge of all the technical and structural features of the venues. When putting artistic ideas into practice, lighting experts should no longer be distracted by having to deal with technical conditions.

Traditional theatres are divided into an acting area and an auditorium. The stage and auditorium can follow several patterns and be in various forms. Some directors depart from this system and shift parts of the stage into the auditorium or put audience seats on the stage. Decisions of this kind are based on production concepts and available technical resources. Every stage has a typical and specific lighting system. And as

every playing area is different, it is impossible to talk about standard lighting equipment. Nevertheless there are key lighting positions that make up the framework on which the logic of the system is based.

## LIGHTING POSITIONS IN THE AUDITORIUM

### Orchestra pit
It is tempting to take advantage of the extremely useful lighting position of the orchestra pit. As this area is often in the form of a mobile platform, it can be used as an additional playing area for non-musical performances. The electrical connections are usually let into the floor.

### Side lights, slots, gullies, proscenium
These terms are used for the vertical spotlight positions at the side of the theatre. They are comparable with the stage tower positions.

### Circle
Auditoria with circle seating (also known as balconies or galleries) often use these for spotlight mounting.

### Auditorium bridge, ceiling bridge
Several lighting bridges of this kind can be built into the ceiling of the auditorium, according to the size and depth of the theatre. As in the case of the proscenium bridge, the lighting technician can reach his working area from auxiliary access points, without needing

405 View of an auditorium

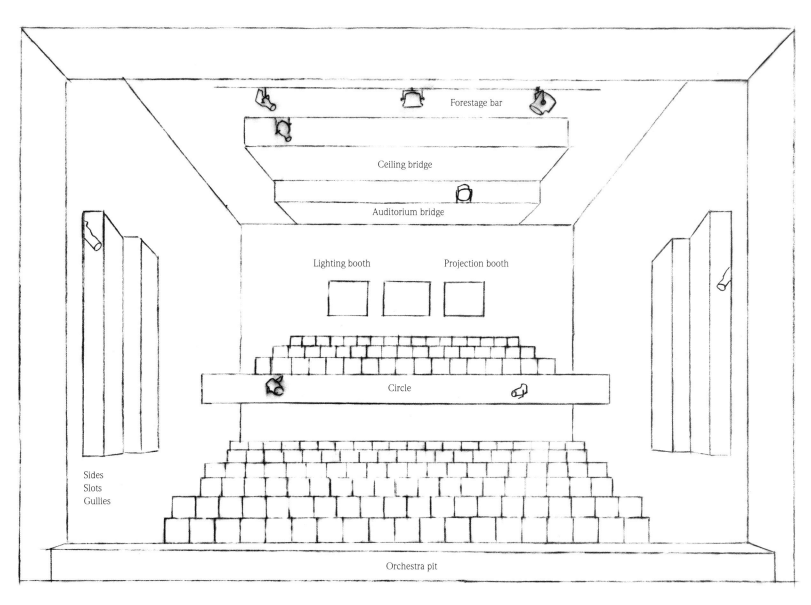

Forestage bar

Ceiling bridge

Auditorium bridge

Lighting booth    Projection booth

Circle

Sides
Slots
Gullies

Orchestra pit

a ladder. These lighting locations should be dimensioned so that profile spots up to 2,500 W can be used in daylight and artificial light.

### Projection booth

This is placed on the rear wall of the auditorium. It is often not very large, but by no means unsuitable as a location for slide, film and video projectors, as well as spotlights.

## ON-STAGE LIGHTING POSITIONS

### Proscenium bridge

The proscenium bridge is a lighting position behind the proscenium arch. It can be movable, to adapt to a variable proscenium height. Two-level or duplex bridge systems are sometimes found in larger theatres. They are almost completely accessible, i.e. the lighting technician can use the bridge as a working platform to adjust the spotlights mounted there. A small number of theatres also have a bridge system that can be lowered to stage level.

### Tower/proscenium booms

This is found on both sides of the proscenium bridge, is accessible at various levels and offers a large number of mainly vertical spotlight positions. Normally the two towers connect the bridge and the side galleries. If the side of the proscenium can be moved, the towers usually move with it.

### Gallery

Galleries are working areas running round the sides and back of the stage. They are very important for general technical purposes as well as for mounting lanterns. Galleries are available on various levels, one above the other and on both sides of the stage, according to the size and shape of the theatre. Some theatres have galleries linked at the back, and a very few stages have motor-driven movable galleries.

### Fly loft, grid

The fly loft and the grid are part of the stage's 'technical roof'. The grid runs across the whole stage area at the highest level, and pulleys and equipment for adjusting the mobile bars or special flying equipment are mounted on it. Underneath this is another level, the fly loft, from which other cables can be fitted. If these two technical areas are separate, as described, it is also convenient to mount lanterns in the fly loft. This is

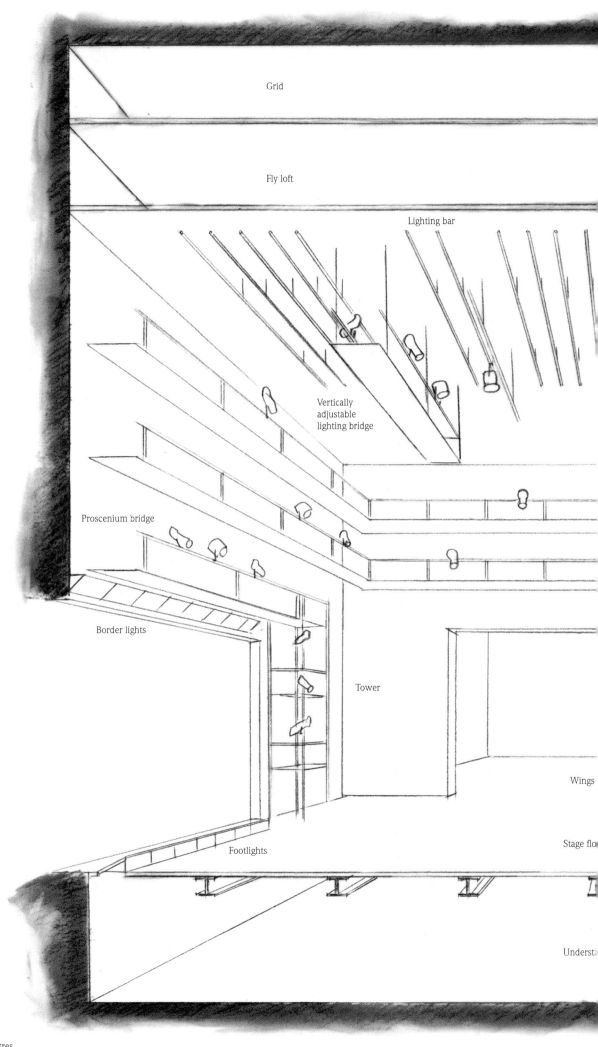

a useful position, as it is enough for light to be directed in ways that are usually not possible. But if they are both on the same level, there is often little room to mount lights, and they are more difficult to operate. Nevertheless, this option should be kept open and potential light blockage by parts of the set avoided.

### Lighting battens/
### lighting bridges/border lights
Border lights are placed between the proscenium bridge and the proscenium arch. If they are used, they are usually a multi-coloured compound system laid out in rows.

Border lights are a fixed system. They have a fixed electrical supply, with cabling in a fabric belt stored in a special cable bag. There are ususally several such installations, depending on the size of the stage.

Larger stages also have mobile lighting bridges as well as the proscenium bridge, and these are part of the fly system. The technicians can step onto them, and they can also be staggered into the upstage area.

### Stage floor/footlights
Connection points for all kinds of spotlights can be available in several positions on the stage itself. Ideally, multi-core plug systems and DMX socket facilities should also be available. The main purpose here is not to define fixed lighting positions, but to create as many connections as possible for mobile lanterns and other lighting equipment. Footlights are also part of the stage position. Like border lights, they are usually a multi-coloured compound system. This system can be folded out from the stage floor electrically, revealed by removing the stage floor or brought into use by simply placing it in position and plugging it in. If the stage has a revolve, this will also have its own connections. Lighting connections linked to such a system are supplied from a central pivot. Power for these connections is supplied from a collector ring system.

### Understage area
Here too, as on the stage itself, there should be enough connections available for lanterns of all kinds. Mobile equipment is then plugged in when it is needed. The understage is usually directly under the stage floor, but there are exceptions, as in the case of double-floored stages, for example.

### Backstage and wings
Lantern connections and special control leads off-stage should also not be forgotten. These areas near the stage are often included for lighting purposes because of the structure of the set.

### Mobile spotlight positions
As there are no limits to the imagination in terms of lighting ideas, it is often necessary to have positions available that are not part of the installed standard system, in addition to all the locations that have been listed. Improvisation can create further possibilities, for example, by installing extra bars and mounting points. But booms fitted out with lanterns often help to get the right lighting to the right place.

### On-stage positions
If an event is taking place at a venue such as a factory hall, concert building or open-air space without its own lighting equipment, the lighting expert has to plot out the necessary positions based on his concept and the surroundings. Here it is important to take into account how the spectators' seating relates to the playing area. Practical, inexpensive lighting stands which are necessary for executing the lighting concept have to be set up.

As well as the traditional positions listed, there should be room for placing equipment wherever it is needed. As every stage set looks different, new locations have to be found for additional equipment such as bars, stands and booms. The bars most frequently used in theatres are sometimes impractical at such venues, but for technical reasons it is often the case that positioning of this kind is essential for certain lighting compositions.

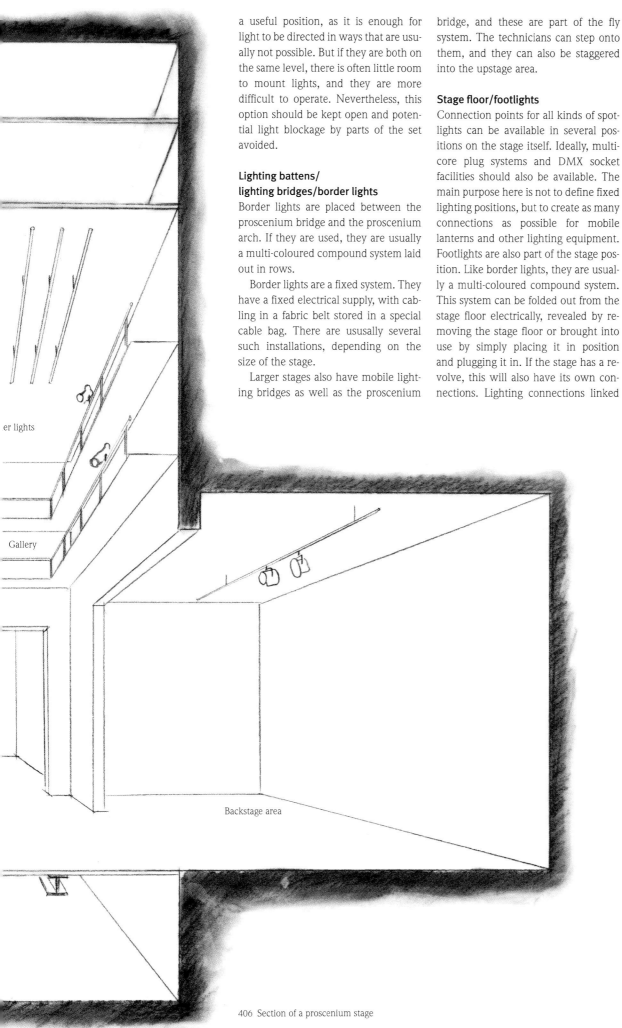

er lights

Gallery

Backstage area

406 Section of a proscenium stage

407 Ill. pp. 166/167
*Schlußchor* (Final Chorus)
Münchner Kammerspiele, 1991

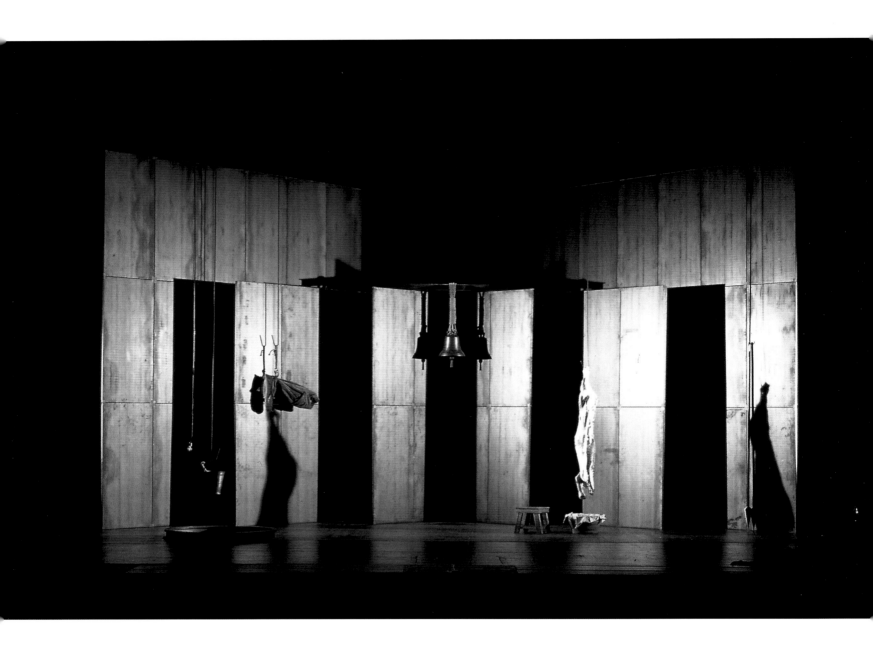

408  Richard Strauss
*Electra*
Director: Dieter Dorn
Set Designer: Yannis Kounellis
Staatsoper Unter den Linden
Berlin, 1994

Six principal angles are available if an object or a space is to be lit. Choosing one angle is seldom enough to create the required effect. The fundamental question is: What is the composition supposed to look like? Beautiful, exciting, uncanny, lacking in contrast, boring? Each angle emphasizes a particular impression and suggests a mood or feeling to the observer.

### LIGHTING ANGLES

The illustrations on pages 170/171 show the effect that differently placed light sources can have on a figure or an object. Whereas a balanced use of all possible angles is homogeneous, it is by

Of course, a number of alternatives are available in the ranges between those illustrated; the eight angles chosen are ideal cases. In practice it is unlikely that a performer will sit quietly within the light. Thus, when deciding on a lighting angle for a person, we have to include a greater area so that the angle chosen covers that person's movements.

The effect the performer is intended to make in the space must also be taken into account. Fixing light for an individual is not enough to structure a space. Consequently, we have to differentiate between lighting the space and lighting the person within it. Both should, of course, be in the right light, but we have seen from previous dis-

space and drawn into the combination of light and shade created by our lighting state. For the spectator, an impression is made above all by space, which not only presents the surroundings clearly but also addresses emotions by carefully selected lighting accents. Space defines and structures the situation in which a story is told. Performers in plays, musicals, operas or ballets reconstruct and convey the message intended by the text, music and movement. Lighting design supports the performers by enhancing the dramatic situation.

no means recommendable as it lacks power and excitement. Light from a particular angle has to fit into a concept in a way that will suit the general atmosphere.

cussions that a person who has been lit does not necessarily exude an atmosphere. A performer can be presented much more excitingly and expressively if he is standing in an atmospheric

409 *Merlin oder Das wüste Land*
(Merlin or The Barren Land)
Münchner Kammerspiele, 1982

410  Lantern positions
for the examples
below and opposite

411  Mixed, composite light

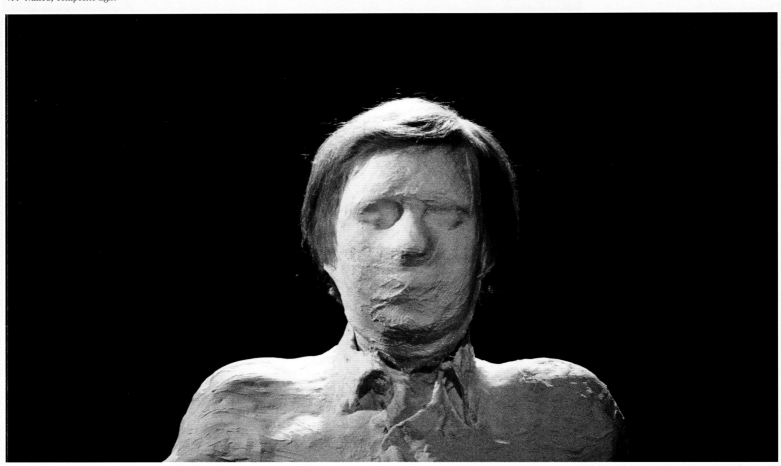

Choosing Lighting Angles

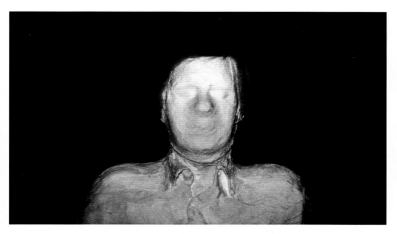

412 Front lighting, 90°, lantern no. 1

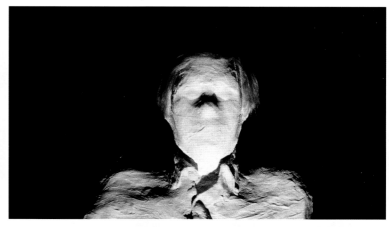

413 Front lighting, 45° from below, lantern no. 2

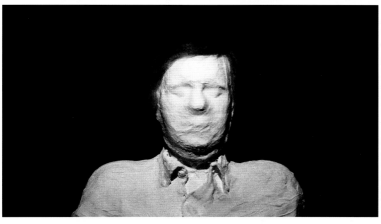

414 Front lighting, 45° from above, lantern no. 3

415 Side lighting from the left, lantern no. 4

416 Side lighting from above, lantern no. 5

417 Back lighting, 90°, lantern no. 6

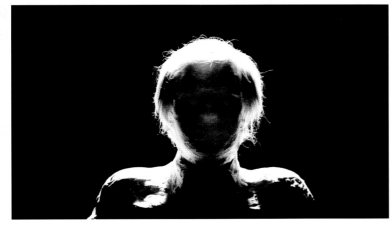

418 Back lighting, 45° from above, lantern no. 7

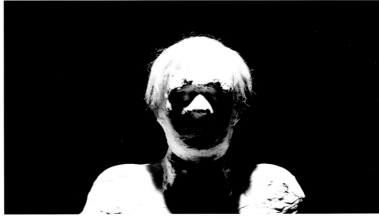

419 Down lighting, lantern no. 8

420  Anton Chekhov
*The Cherry Orchard*
Director: Ernst Wendt
Set Designer: Johannes Schütz
Münchner Kammerspiele, 1982

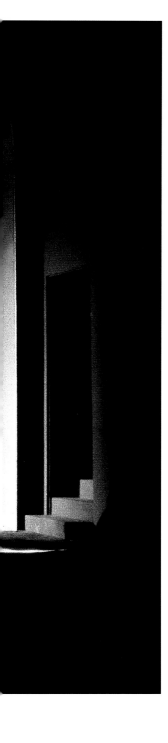

## LIGHTING ANGLES AND LIGHT QUALITIES

The following examples offer only a selection of possible lighting angles. Lantern positions in a space behave similarly to lighting angles for people, though, of course, a single lantern is not sufficient for lighting an entire stage.

### Direct light

Direct light refers to an angle of light that falls directly on the space or the object from the lighting source. Each lantern emits direct light at a certain angle.

### Indirect, reflected light

If the angle is changed or deflected, the light is called indirect or reflected light. Indirect light can be very attractive because it makes the illuminated materials look especially soft and diffuse. Shadows can also be made softer or removed completely in this type of lighting. Reflected light from a vertical source creates an unpleasant effect.

### Lighting from below, footlights

This angle lights the space and the object from below. Lighting from below is difficult to handle because it seems unnatural and creates unrealistic, fantastic moods that are slightly exaggerated.

If a performer is to be lit clearly by footlights, an angle of 45° is useful. This lighting only makes sense from close range, however, as performers near the footlights stand out because of their glowing eyes and shadow-free lines. It is not suitable as the only light source for a space.

When using modern footlights with powerful reflector lamps, the lighting angle should always be chosen so that the light is not cast upon the rear wall of the stage set.

### Front lighting

Here the source is beside or behind the observer and lights the space from the front. There is less contrast between object and space than with any other light. Front lighting is the flattest kind of light as the shadows are wholly or partly behind the object and scarcely visible from the front. The space loses its effective depth. Despite these disadvantages, front lighting cannot be discarded altogether as it makes all the action directly visible. The trick here is to keep the intensity as low as possible, so that space and atmosphere are retained but the outlines that are so important for the viewer remain visible. Strong front lighting is often intended to create a particular dramatic effect. A generously front-lit space suggests clarity and ostentatious superficiality. The angle of incidence is crucial when selecting front lighting. Values from 30 to 45° are the average angles to follow. A shallower angle of incidence is possible, but this creates enormous problems when separating general lighting from the lighting of an object as it is no longer possible to light without shadows.

### Border lighting

Light falls into the space from above and should be used carefully. It creates transitions from front lighting to side lighting and can suggest the atmosphere of an open space if used carefully. Several lanterns are almost always necessary for a particular area. It is important that the cones of light meet without being obstructed or interrupted.

### Back lighting

The light source is behind the object, lights it from the back and casts shadows towards the spectator. This light creates the most convincing spatial depth. It is the most dramatic kind of light and is unbeatable when it comes to atmosphere.

### Side lighting

Light illuminates the space from the side. This is the most frequently used direction for light and is useful for creating a particularly strong sense of space.

## EXPERIMENTAL LIGHTING ARRANGEMENTS

### Colour quality, colour rendering

The quality of any particular light has to be decided along with the choice of angle and direction. It is important to exploit the potential and characteristics of the various light sources. As we know, the colour rendering of the light chosen is crucial. Illustrations 433–435 show the impression given by three very different light qualities.

The colour rendering given by a daylight spot is the most open and sharpest way of achieving clarity. Outlines are distinct, and the contrast between light and dark is great.

Incandescent light, familiar to us all, is the standard type of light. If fluorescent lamps are chosen, people and sets remain flat, pale and without outlines, making it impossible to create a dramatic effect, as there is no contrast between light and dark.

When using spotlights with discharge lamps it is important to take body colour rendering into account (see p. 29). As most discharge lamps (with the exception of sodium vapour types) have a very high proportion of blue in their spectrum, parts of the set, costumes and faces look markedly different in this light. It is extremely harsh and also has a colour quality similar to daylight. This means that body colour rendering in daylight and in incandescent light differ noticeably from each other.

If an early decision is made to use daylight as the dominant light quality, it is essential to point this out during the preparatory period (set construction, costume making and make-up rehearsals). The best results are achieved if the workshops concerned have two different basic types of light: daylight quality working light at 5,000 K and one in the normal spectral range at 3,000 K.

## CHOOSING LIGHT TYPES AND DIRECTION

### General and main lighting

This kind of light is created from strong, focused sources. It determines the direction of incidence of the light, creates a basic structure and fixes the conceptual framework.

### Accents

Accents are used to enliven an object with points of light and highlights, in

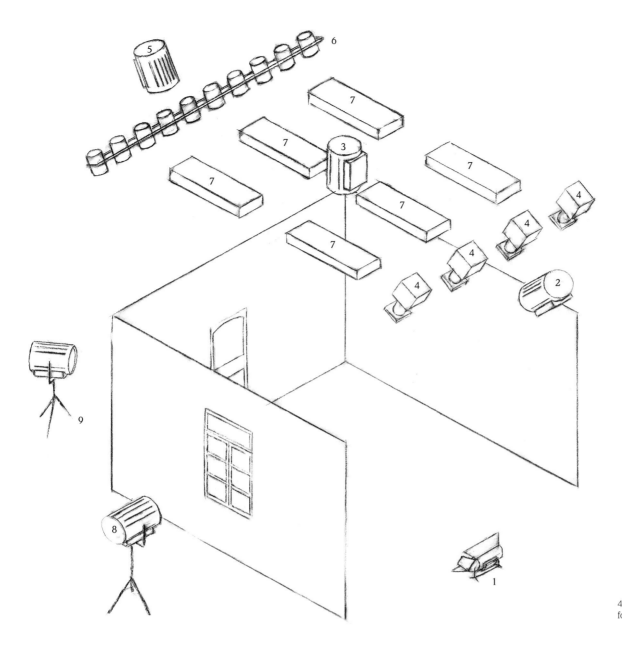

421  Lantern positions
for illustrations 423–432

422  Mixed light
from different
lighting positions

423 Front lighting, approx. 45°
from above, lighting position no. 2

424 Footlight with one lamp,
lighting position no. 1

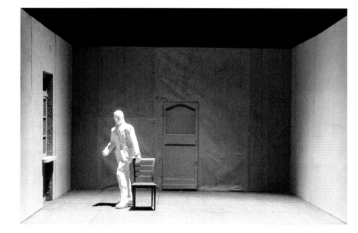

425 Down lighting with a Fresnel
spot, lighting position no. 3

426 Border lighting from several
spotlights with plano-convex lenses,
lighting position no. 4

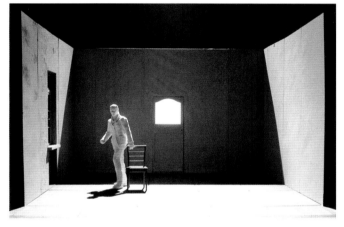

427 Back lighting with a Fresnel
spot, lighting position no. 5

428 Back lighting from several
spotlights with parabolic
reflectors (striplights),
lighting position no. 6

429 Border lighting with
fluorescent lamps,
lighting position no. 7

430 Back lighting and front
lighting used together,
lighting positions nos. 2 and 6

431 Window side lighting
and door backlit from the side
with Fresnel spots,
lighting positions nos. 8 and 9

432 Back lighting from the side
through the door with a Fresnel
spot, lighting position no. 9

433 General lighting
with a daylight spot
for back lighting

434 General lighting
with incandescent striplight
for back lighting

435 General lighting
with fluorescent
border lighting

the case of people, for example, as back lighting on the head and shoulders. Accents emphasize structure and outlines and can create reflections. This kind of light should be used separately for space and objects. Accents are created by sharply focused beams of light, for example, with all kinds of low voltage spotlights.

### Brightening
Brightening is used to make dark zones lighter. It should not throw the general cover off balance but complete the overall effect of the lighting by adding nuances from different directions and

Back lighting almost always creates a bizarre, ghostly effect, especially when used alone.

### Shadows
Shadows can often cause unintended effects in stage lighting. But light can create a lively impression only when there are changes from light to dark. A carefully placed shadow can create a powerful psychological effect. Clarity of outline, choice of lighting source and the distance between the object and the source are all very important factors. If a shadow is being used intentionally, the distance between the light

Establishing incident light as the source in this way can be exciting for a time, but becomes tiring after a while. Brightening and back lighting are used to complement it. The carefully considered use of complementary lighting reinforces spatial clarity without detracting from the realistic impression. Strong incident light always creates reflected light from the floor or wall into the room according to the colour of the reflecting surfaces. But this reflected light is not usually enough to give a general effect of brightness. Careful complementing with additional lighting can support and enhance diffuse lighting zones – in the language of the trade: lighting shadows.

### Bold lighting
The same space can be changed visually by deciding that its limits are symbolic and lighting the whole stage generally. This approach needs very strong front lighting and suggests great clarity.

This sort of lighting is chosen when the image presented is supposed to be blatant, lucid and informative, but without details. It makes a superficial statement about a scene, conveying weak outlines and no atmosphere. If this course is followed, openings such as windows and doors are not used as principal light sources but are evenly and diffusely lit, without any accents.

### Mixed lighting
It is not essential to use only lanterns with incandescent lamps when designing a production, but they do offer the advantage that they can be handled and operated without difficulty.

In the chapter 'Lamps and Light', we established that even the different colour temperatures of incandescent and discharge lamps can make a powerful statement, regardless of the choice of direction. It is not necessary to use only one quality of light or another; an excellent effect can be achieved with a mixture of different colour temperatures. The contrasting behaviour of these two different light sources alone makes a strong and colourful impression. A combination of incandescent and fluorescent lamps complement each other very well, too.

### Colour gels
What white light is, how it is composed, and what warm and cold light sources are have already been established. Now, as well as the fundamental decision about what kind of lamp to choose, there is another important

---

**Floodlighting**
Undirected beams of light without lenses

**Cold light / High proportion of blue**
Uncondensed arc
Short, long or medium-arc discharge lamp

**Warm light / High proportion of red**
Uncondensed beam from an
incandescent tungsten coil

**Spotlight**
Directed beams of light with a lens,
lens system or concentrating reflector

**Cold light / High proportion of blue**
Directed arc from a short, long or
medium-arc discharge lamp

**Warm light / High proportion of red**
Condensed light beam from an
incandescent tungsten coil

---

highlighting areas where audience attention should be focused.

### Background, horizon lighting
This light is used to establish correct brightness levels in the background. It is very important in stage work as it creates spatial depth. Varying the intensity of the light gives the spectator the desired spatial impression. The laws of colour perspective and general perspective must be considered when employing this kind of light.

### Back lighting
This is the best kind of light for creating a particular atmosphere as it is relatively abstract. Back lighting makes the stage and the events taking place on it highly dramatic. It detaches the performer from the surrounding space. By reversing the effect of light and shadow for the spectator, it plunges concrete objects into darkness or light and emphasizes abstract concepts.

source and the illuminated object is of crucial importance. If a shadow is to be the same size as the object casting it, the light sources have to be extremely far away. If the light source is very close to the object, the shadow will not be as sharply defined, but its enlarged size is very dramatic.

There are various kinds of shadow: hard shadows, core shadows and half shadows.

### Realistic lighting
Realistic light is determined by the concept behind the production. If a space contains realistic shapes, it is possible to light it naturally. Thus it makes sense to light through a window or a door to suggest that it is bright outside. The lighting chosen – coming in through a window in our example – explains the statement that is to be made. If we use the natural openings in an inside room, this identifies our light as the main lighting.

436 Blue and yellow used as complementary colours

consideration: the use of colour gels. Filtering light through a colour gel colours the whole beam. Experiments with additive and subtractive colour mixing have indicated how many possibilities there are.

People are always asking for formulas for creating a particular impression or sensation of colour. It is not possible to generalize, but there are some useful guidelines.

Warm colours enhance other warm colours and absorb colder ones. Cold colours enhance other cold colours and absorb warmer ones.

Cold, pure shades of blue in various colour grades are often desired, ideally without a greenish cast. The most suitable blue filters are conversion filters intended to give incandescent light a daylight effect.

Pale violet and pale pink are pleasing and flattering to facial colours but are still relatively neutral. They enhance make-up without changing the light in the space.

With brightly coloured filters, costumes and parts of the set that may be lit can be very effective, but the light is often too bright for the performers – though this could be an approach that is chosen deliberately. Particular colour effects may be incorporated into the dramatic concept, for example. Any kind of light, including light from daylight lamps, can be coloured, but light can only be coloured or have colours filtered out if those colours are present in the light emitted by the lamp.

Ill. 436 shows the use of two complementary colours: Two low-angled side lights are shining on a column. The two beams produce white light at their point of intersection (additive colour mixture).

The various methods of creating images with light are all very similar to each other. We use spotlights to reflect and direct virtual light, in order to fill a scene with atmosphere. This is all based on a great range of systems for projecting light from different positions, in combination with colour filters of varying degrees of intensity. But choosing cold or warm light is important, too, as a combination of both can produce particularly attractive effects. Decisions also have to be made about whether moving light (scanners or automated spots) or visible colour changes (e.g. with scrollers) should also be included in a lighting design.

Having a good combination of lanterns, colour changers, effects devices and filters at one's disposal is expensive and involves problems of its own, as so many conditions have to be taken into account. This is inevitable in professional theatre. But schools, experimental and amateur theatres also want to get decent value for their investment, although they often don't have the right options or information available. Deciding where to begin is something everyone has to do, it is just that the scale will differ in different situations. The fundamental point is that no one wants to light a playing area with only one fixture (except in special cases such as shadow-play, for example). If lighting has to be devised, then a small stock of lighting equipment will be needed, however simple the task to be performed is.

Light for performers and for the set come from various directions, in other words from a combination of different lighting angles and intensities. The essential angles are discussed in the preceding chapter (see p. 173).

The following illustrations show how shadows fall without regard for the actual distance between the source and the object.

## LIGHTING ANGLES

### Front lighting

Front lighting is the simplest, most versatile and most common angle from which to light a space or an object. If light has to be cast over long distances, lenses, Fresnel lenses or profile spots and even spots with parabolic reflectors are available. The last type should only be used for basic light if the distance between the position of the spot and the area to be lit is very great. Fresnel spots are recommended for shorter distances, as their diffused beam can cause a great

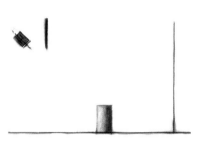

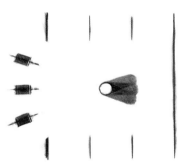

437/438 Front lighting at a 45° angle of incidence

deal of undesirable spill into the auditorium. The best position for these is at an angle between 30 and 45° from above.

Profile spots are especially useful for front of house lighting, as they offer a wide range of adjustments, but they are not recommended for extremely short distances. As profile spots can have changeable focal lengths and can be zoomed, they can be used both front of house and on stage. It would be almost inconceivable to use floods from front of house, however, unless they are positioned very close to the proscenium arch at the point at which the area to be lit starts.

### Front lighting, border lighting

Ill. 439/440 show front or border lighting fixed immediately behind the proscenium. The proscenium bridge makes it possible to link up with front of house lighting. Here there is a much wider range of choices of lanterns, according to whether the lighting is intended to be general or focused on a particular person. It is possible to work with Fresnels, floods in general or moving lights from this position. The proscenium bridge can also be used for slide projectors, follow spots and effects spots of all kinds.

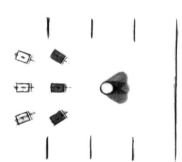

439/440 Proscenium bridge light, light behind the curtain

### Side lighting

Side lighting, whether used horizontally or diagonally from above, creates a great sense of depth. Profile, Fresnel or plano-convex lights are generally used here. Spotlight systems that can light an area from the side can be used at all angles. If they are placed low or at a height of about 3 m they are used in the wings. This makes it possible to light a character without creating light and shadow on the stage floor. But if they are placed higher, on stands, galleries or the bridge, light and shade will fall on the stage floor, too (ill. 441–444).

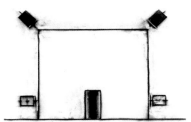

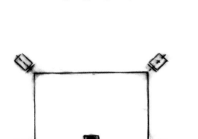

441/442 Side lighting, diagonally from above

443/444 Side lighting from the wings without spilling onto the floor

### Back lighting

Several kinds of fixtures can also be used for back lighting. Fresnels of all sizes make sense here and are practical to use. Profile spots can be used in a limited space provided that no parts of the set obstruct the light. But they are very difficult to focus unless they can be reached from the fly loft or a bridge. Automated spotlight yokes as well as low voltage units, also called Svoboda units, are a great help here when fitting up. Units 2 m long are often placed across the full width of the stage and are at their most effective if directed at the stage diagonally from behind at an angle between 20 and 45°. These traditional back lights can often be tilted automatically.

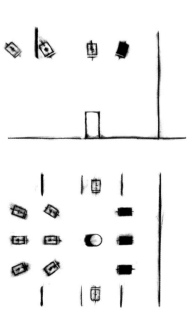

445/446 Back lighting

### Background lighting

Background lighting should always be chosen separately from the rest of the light. Sophisticated effects of depth can be created by different colour and brightness qualities from the main lighting. If the back of the set is made of suitable material, this can also be lit from behind. If larger distances are involved, Fresnels and profile spots can be used. Asymmetrical floods are best for short distances, placed on the floor or suspended from above.

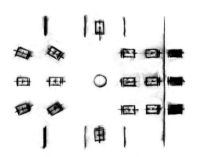

447/448 Transparent background, lit from behind

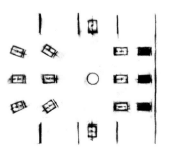

449/450 Background, lit from the front

### Main lighting, directional lighting

In most situations we work on the basis that one main source of light will set the principal direction of the lighting. A decision of this kind is always made for specific dramatic reasons, and is also known as realistic lighting. There is no

451 Directional light with shadow zone

standard position for this. Light sources of this kind can be placed as side lights or back lights and at a range of heights and angles. Powerful fixtures should be used for such sources to make sure that the desired effect is achieved.

## DECIDING ON ANGLES

As with all work, designing light also involves a strategy relating to the personal language of images. The approach should be based on personal sensibilities and free of constraints. All the complexities of colour theory come into play as well as the hardware, such as lamps and lanterns. The use of colour filters is particularly important in the theatre, as we are working first and foremost for the eye, without having to meet the conditions for recording standards, as in film and television. This has enormous advantages, as it means that a great variety of different colour combinations and extreme lighting situations can be integrated into the concept more easily.

The most important qualities of artificial daylight – intensity and colour temperature – are a crucial argument for using this in the theatre as well. Combined with incandescent light it offers a wide range of creative variations which permit much more creatively effective statements than, for example, the exclusive use of incandescent light with subtractive and additive colour mixing. The lighting is ultimately a cumulative product of directorial, choreographic and stage design concepts.

In addition to positioning fixtures, we must also consider the fact that some areas will not be lit with incandescent light, but with discharge units such as metal halide, sodium or fluorescent lamps. In other words, the light sources that we have chosen to use have to be prepared for their specific roles by indicating their precise location, beam size, angle, focal length, colour accessories etc. Thus it is entirely possible to have a main area of day-

452  Coline Serreau
*Hase, Hase* (Rabbit, Rabbit)
Director: Harald Clemen
Set Designer: Martin Kukulies
Münchner Kammerspiele, 1992

light surrounded by an area of incandescent light. In a case of this kind we can use filters to achieve the desired effect. Here a mix is sensible, as the additional light is used only to lighten a zone of shadow that does not have to have the same colour qualities as the main light. It is correct to say that we are 'lighting shadow'.

Both incandescent light and daylight can be effectively combined with fluorescent light. Even the choice of tube colour temperature is the first step towards conformity. Anything that cannot be solved satisfactorily can be achieved by the additional use of colour filters. It is easy to wrap colour filter gels around fluorescent tubes because they operate at such low temperatures.

The sooner decisions are made about factors of this kind, the easier it will be to work with the technicians.

## WHAT IS AVAILABLE?

Almost all German theatres have a complete set of lighting facilities. Let us

further assume that there is a house lighting designer as well. He knows what alternatives he has for responding to suggestions from the director and the set designer. If someone from outside does the lighting design for a production, he will need full and accurate information: first, a ground plan and lateral section of the stage and auditorium, and then information about the number of circuits, possible dimmer loads, lantern models, gel manufacturers, type of console etc.

It is also necessary to find out if any special equipment is available, for example whether it is possible to install special spotlights, mobile lighting stands or to construct devices to provide additional effects.

### Rig positions

Lanterns used to be identified by their position, for example tower L, tower R, proscenium bridge etc. Numbers were allotted to each position: Tower L 1–6, for example, meant six connections on tower L. This method has been replaced by a new coding

| Outside view | Beam paths | Name of device | CIE standard stencil | Stencil symbols |
|---|---|---|---|---|
| | | Flood with symmetrical trough reflector | | |
| | | Parabolic reflector spot | | |
| | | PAR lamp | | |
| | | Spotlight with plano-convex lens | | |
| | | Fresnel | | |
| | | Profile spot with ellipsoidal reflector | | |
| | | Profile spot with condenser optics | | |
| | | Slide projector | | |
| | | Scanner | | |
| | | Automated multifunctional spot (moving light) | | |

Conceptual Lighting Design

453 Lanterns –
beam paths –
symbols used in lighting plots

system, derived from the method of numerical selection used in electronic lighting consoles.

The system involves allotting code numbers to the lighting positions. For example:

1: all circuits in the auditorium
2: tower L, proscenium bridge, tower R
3: galleries L and R
4: flies or grid circuits
5: circuits on stage
6: understage circuits

Numbering starts with one within the individual positions. Starting with the auditorium bridge, the first circuit is no. 101 (the first 1 identifies the location, and the figures 01 define the connection). This reduces confusion and communication problems, as the numbers state where the particular device is or the circuit on the rig that is needed.

Ill. 454 shows a plot drawn up as described. As it is obvious that faultlessly run lighting has a fundamental effect on the quality of the design, it is necessary for as many functions as possible to be controlled from a central point. Thus

454 Circuitry plot

this plot shows all the rig circuits in the theatre, including switchable CEE 400 V/32 or 63 amperes, sockets, individual circuits at 25 and 16 amperes and also fluorescent lamp connections, all of which can be controlled from a central lighting board.

Fluorescent lamp circuits, of course, also need an unregulated, zero-phase supply. To minimize the risk of error, multipolar connections are used that bring all the cables needed for regulation together in a single plug. In the plot, these sockets are marked with ✹, and directly controlled 400 V circuits with ⊗. Flexible multicore circuits that are positioned as required are not marked.

## DESIGN PREPARATION

A sound electrical basis for a lighting system is one of the keys to a designer's work running smoothly. If the system works faultlessly, it gives the designer more scope.

When all the technical problems have been solved, attention should be devoted to the lighting console, which is the 'central nervous system' of every lighting rehearsal and performance. The lighting is tested, developed and

fixed through this central electrical and electronic unit for handling load and control current circuits. It should be checked before starting any work or performance. It is best to have a print-out of the lighting states to provide an accurate, comprehensible and lucid summary of the instructions saved. This should show which circuits are involved in which state. There should also be information about the name of the state, its number, and details of fade-in and fade-out times, wait times and individual times for the circuits involved.

The lighting console should be run by a member of the lighting department who knows his equipment well, can take advantage of all its features and above all knows how to use it in a way that corresponds with the production staff's concepts.

If this key member of the team is to have the best possible conditions for his work, he must be able to speak from the lighting desk in the auditorium to the control booth. This should be set up in such a way that the technician at his desk in the auditorium can talk to his partner in the booth no matter what the volume of the music or speech on stage is. Being able to reach and talk to all the lighting staff involved is also a

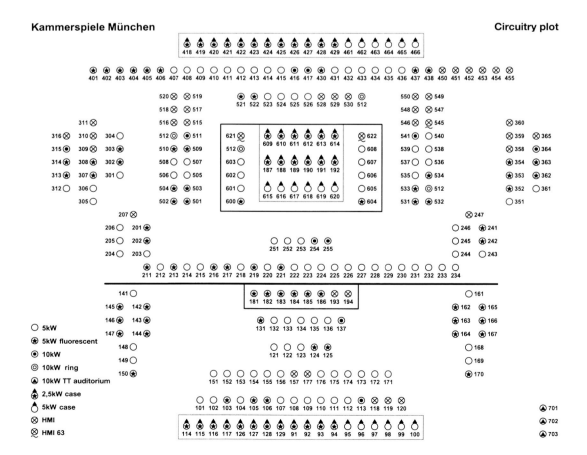

Conceptual Lighting Design

455  Arthur Schnitzler
*Das weite Land* (The Far Country)
Director: Luc Bondy
Set Designer: Erich Wonder
Théâtre des Amandiers
Nanterre, 1984

necessity if work is to proceed smooth-ly. What is the good of having lots of ideas if it is not possible to try them out during the rehearsal process? Thus a communication system is essential, des-pite the costs. Initially most radio head-sets are unpopular, but after a period of getting used to them technicians acknowledge the invaluable aspects of mobile communications systems.

It is up to the user to choose from the available lighting alternatives. The ideas behind direction and design will then suggest a suitable colour tempera-ture for the lighting chosen. As early as 1981 it was absolutely essential for me to have profile spot technology in day-light quality. As the market was not interested in theatrical requirements at the time, we put together the first pro-file spot using daylight technology. Other industrial light sources with dis-charge lamps were also put to use. The optical specifications of a particular spotlight determine its location. Of course there are problem positions

where no particular lantern is suitable. The appropriate correction gels or glass filters, deflectors etc. are then used to complete the desired effect and function.

A major problem is posed by a solid-state lamp working with a discharge lamp. The problem is not the visual effect – this is quite pleasing – but that they are operated differently. When de-vising lighting states the two qualities should behave in just the same way, i.e. a light source can be regulated from 0 to its full intensity, which is simple and a matter of course with incandescent lamps. As a discharge lamp can only be regulated within a certain part of its range, it has to be dimmed mechanical-ly. The more precise a dimming system of this kind is, the more expensive it is, but the interplay of the two light qual-ities is that much better. Excellent re-sults can be achieved with a system for increasing and decreasing the light if a little tactical effort is made. The larger the number of mechanically dimmed

lanterns, the more careful one has to be when using them.

Let us now turn from dealing with technical problems to creating lighting settings. Controlling the light has to be considered as well as the provision of a good range of fixtures and equipment. Regulating resistive loads, driving shut-ters, switching 'direct connections' and flicker-free dimming of fluorescent lamps – these functions require a mod-ern lighting console with appropriately high load levels. DMX controls and the rapid development of sophisticated technology – for example, remote-con-trolled spotlight yokes, colour scrollers, scanners and other automated lantern systems – present creative and innova-tive design variants for productions today.

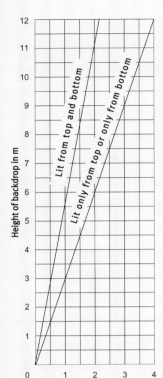

456 Distance of an asymmetrical flood from a lit area

## Slide projection

Practicable lit areas with slide sizes: 18 × 18 cm = 15.5 × 15.5 cm
24 × 24 cm = 21.5 × 21.5 cm

| Optics | | Theatre identification | |
|---|---|---|---|
| Y | Projection material Slide size | b | in cm |
| Y' | Projected image Image size | B | in cm |
| f | Focal length of objective | f | in cm |
| s' | Projection distance Distance from projector to image | e | in cm |
| V | Enlargement ratio | V | |

The following formulas are precise enough for the theatre. Other formulas are listed in the chapter on optics (see pp. 70/71).

To find the image ratio:

$$V = \frac{B}{b}$$

To find the projection distance:

$$e = \frac{f \times B}{b}$$

To find the focal length of the objective:

$$f = \frac{e \times b}{B} \quad \text{or} \quad f = \frac{e}{V + 1} \quad \text{or} \quad f = \frac{e \times b}{B + b}$$

To find the slide size:

$$b = \frac{f \times B}{e}$$

To find the image size:

$$B = \frac{e \times b}{f}$$

## Angle of dispersion

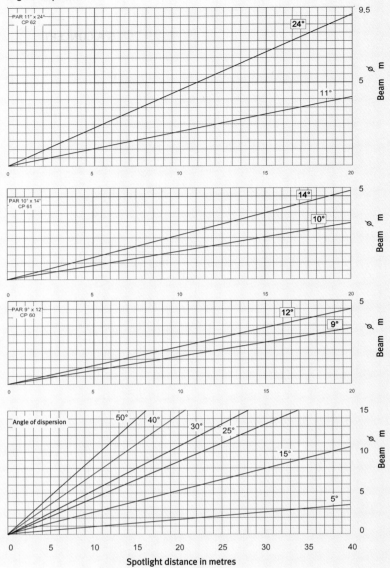

457 Beam angle of PAR spot and dispersion angle of profile spot with lens system

Spotlight distance in metres

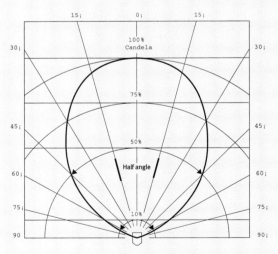

458 For planning purposes: beam angle, half angle, tenth angle. The luminous intensity distribution (candela) of any light projection system is indicated in the form of a spatial beam characteristic. The regularity of the light emitted is given in terms of half and tenth angles. The readings relate to 100% luminous intensity on the optical axis of the source. The half value indicates the point at which the luminous intensity is reduced to half the maximum, and the tenth value a reduction to 10%

## DEVELOPING A CONCEPT

### 1 Light types

- bold lighting (monochrome or regular general lighting), without any outlines or noteworthy shadows (with incandescent or daylight)
- lighting design with directional light, light from a main lighting source, not realistic
- realistic light, recreating a real lighting situation
- mixed lighting, different lighting qualities to enhance the contrast
- colour mixing system, additive or subtractive lighting or colour filter mixing
- accented light, enriched, enlivens structures and outlines
- moving light or moving colour changes

These important design approaches are not mutually exclusive and can be mixed, which further enhances the diversity of lighting compositions.
As my main guideline I take the set design and its qualities and colours, with an aim to complement or emphasize them.

### 2 Available equipment – Choice of fixtures

- floods, general cover, open face
- spotlights with lenses, prism lenses, Fresnel lenses
- profile spots
- fluorescent lighting, neon lighting
- industrial lighting sources, for example sodium light
- low voltage systems
- high voltage systems using PAR
- moving light or moving colours
- large image projector

If an image is to be harmonious then the correct fixtures must illuminate the stage from the correct angles. It is not of primary importance whether this fixture has an incandescent or a daylight discharge lamp. The optical system in the light source is the crucial factor.

### 3 Light contrasts

Light – Dark
These two factors determine the choice of intensity levels of the fixtures.

### 4 Colour quality

- light colour (colour temperature)
- choice of gels or glass filters
- use of colour mixing systems
- use of colour perspective

A subtle but rewarding subject. We determine what the light will look like for the performers or the stage by considering the colour of the light in combination with colour filters as subtractive intervention and in additive combinations using individual spotlights or groups of spotlights.

### 5 Accessories – Effects

- neon light
- sodium light
- sun, moon, stars
- fibre optics
- luminous sheeting (light pads)
- lighting, rain, snow, fire, smoke, fog
- projection, video

## FIRST STEPS IN LIGHTING DESIGN

The designer should not only read the script of the production he is working on, but also literary reference books and theatre or opera companions. For a homogeneous production design, the lighting designer must be accepted as an integral part of the production team, as the design of a space for the stage does not depend only on the physical set, but also on the visual impression created by light. The lighting designer should also explain the technical alternatives and restrictions of the stage to the artistic staff during the planning process. Clearly it is preferable to be

involved in the preparatory and development phases of designing a stage. The approach taken to this preparatory phase depends on whether the theatre is equipped with a full lighting facility or whether a complete lighting rig has to be developed and built from scratch. Often it is necessary to use an existing lighting system and to supplement or change it for the current production. A house designer will be very familiar with the facilities and their potential, in which case he only has to design the production. But this also means that additional fixtures, installations and equipment relating to the specific production have to be planned in such a way that they can be fitted into an existing facility without difficulty.

## DEVELOPING A LIGHTING PLOT

The process of developing a lighting plot, in other words the conventional preliminary work, starts and continues to evolve within the designer's imagination. Then it takes form on the draughting board – on paper.

A new preparation method is virtual representation with a CAD program. Various symbols for fixtures, drawn from international CIE standards (used in Germany) are found in the two following examples. Our British and American colleagues use symbols that look more like the actual piece of equipment. It is possible to use any symbol

that we think suitable, as the key on the drawing shows what is actually meant to be present on stage.

When designing with a CAD program, individuals can adopt their own symbols to represent fixtures and accessories. The symbols chosen should be as similar to the form of the original as possible, making it easier to read the lighting plot. If there is room for more information, the filter numbers, DMX addresses and circuits should also be identified alongside a symbol.

If a lighting concept is being designed for a production that is not to be played in repertory, then it is possible to use more basic equipment relating only to that production.

## Working documents

Whether you are using a draughting board or CAD, you will need the following documents for your planning:

- ground plan of the playing area on a scale of 1:20, 1:50 or 1:100
- section of the playing area and auditorium on same scale as above
- elevation of the playing area
- list of the available lighting equipment
- arrangement of the available rig circuits with details of their capacity
- lighting console model

The rough outline of the set should be entered on the ground plan and section, in order to have a good overview. Then work can begin. A good practical design can be draughted with this information about the specifications of the equipment available.The following is a summary of what is essential:

1. Light types    ⟶
2. Equipment    ⟶
3. Light contrast    ⟶ Draughting
4. Colour quality    ⟶
5. Accessories    ⟶

### Draughting board, CAD or Studio 4:1

Creativity at the draughting board or looking at a virtual stage set on a computer screen need considerable imagination and to some extent a new way of looking at things. This is not for everyone. But there is another preparatory technique available: copying the production on a scale of 1:4. Stage models are usually made on a scale of 1:20, 1:50 or 1:100. A set model on the scale of 1:4 is unusual, but useful for a certain group of people. The set is built in a studio on a scale of 1:4 and lit with appropriate equipment. Lighting consoles and lanterns approximating those to be used in the production can be employed to see whether lighting states and set dimensions will work, and this is not a complicated procedure. This approach keeps the stage free, relaxes the final rehearsal schedule and gives the people involved a sense of security that cannot be achieved with a draughting board or a virtual sequence on a screen.

A studio of this kind has been up and running in Germany for a long time now, and it completely meets the technical requirements: 'Studio 4:1'. The address can be found on page 238 under FOUR TO ONE.

459 Recreating a stage situation in Studio 4:1. Here professional resources are used to simulate complete stage set ups using small spotlights and consoles

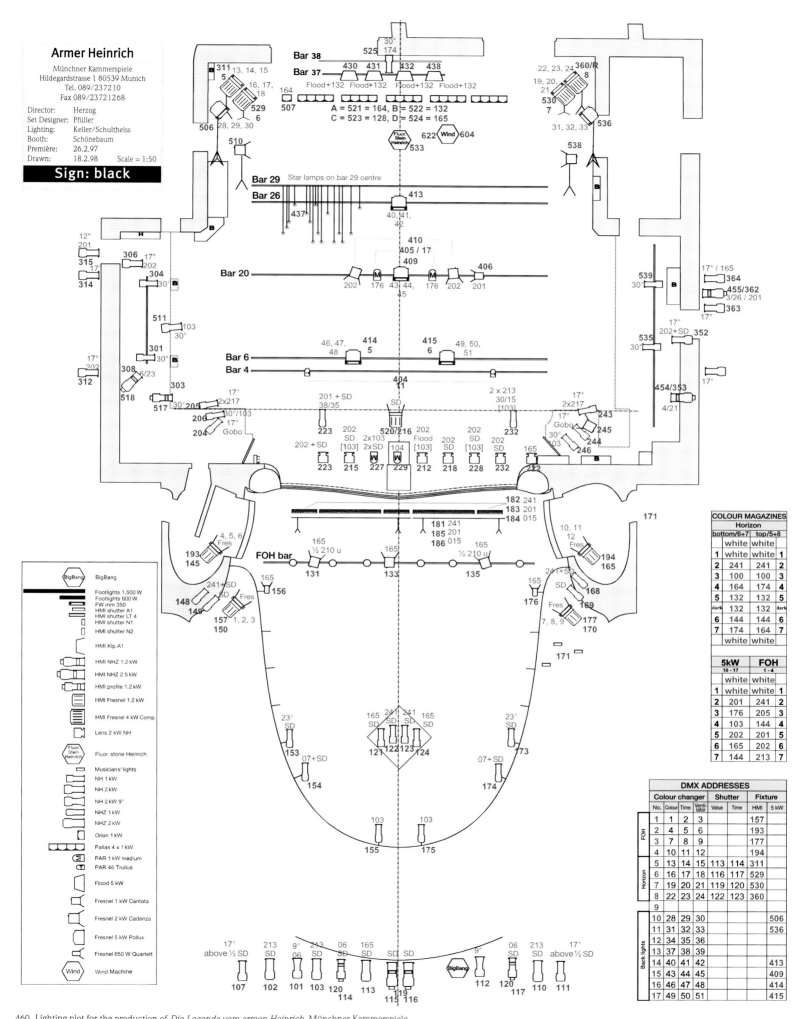

460  Lighting plot for the production of *Die Legende vom armen Heinrich*, Münchner Kammerspiele

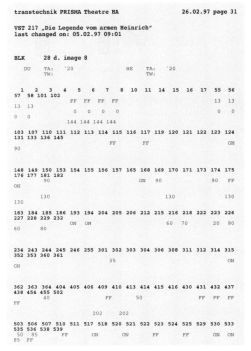

461  Printout of lanterns used in the lighting state

462  Ill. right:
Spotlights involved
in lighting state no. 28

463  Tankred Dorst
*Die Legende vom armen Heinrich*
(The Legend of Poor Heinrich)
Director: Jens-Daniel Herzog
Set Designer: Volker Pfüller
Münchner Kammerspiele, 1997
Lighting state no. 28

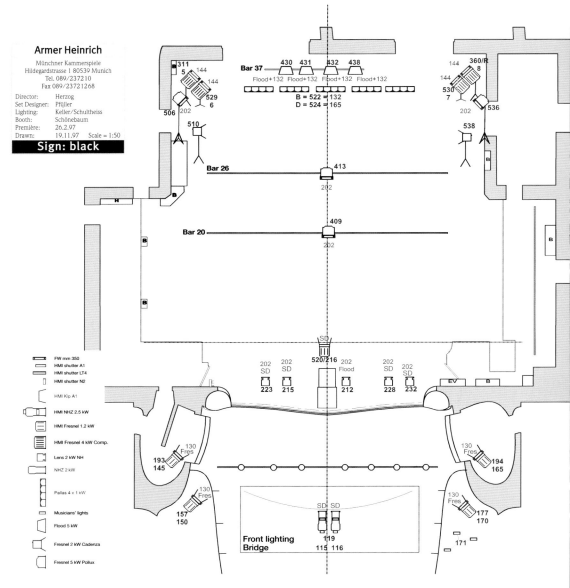

VST 217 „Die Legende vom armen Heinrich"
last changed on: 05.02.97 09:01

BLK    66 d. darkening

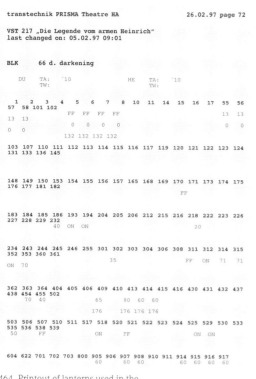

| DU | TA: | ´10 | | HE | TA: | ´10 |
| | TW: | | | | TW: | |

| 1 | 2 | 3 | 4 | 5 | 6 | 7 | 8 | 10 | 11 | 14 | 15 | 16 | 17 | 55 | 56 |
| 57 | 58 | 101 | 102 | | | | | | | | | | | | |
| | | | | FF | FF | FF | FF | | | | | | | 13 | 13 |
| 13 | 13 | | | 0 | 0 | 0 | 0 | | | | | | | 0 | 0 |
| 0 | 0 | | | 132 | 132 | 132 | 132 | | | | | | | | |

103 107 110 111 112 113 114 115 116 117 119 120 121 122 123 124
131 133 136 145

148 149 150 153 154 155 156 157 165 168 169 170 171 173 174 175
176 177 181 182
                                              FF

| 183 | 184 | 185 | 186 | 193 | 194 | 204 | 205 | 206 | 212 | 215 | 216 | 218 | 222 | 223 | 226 |
| 227 | 228 | 229 | 232 | | | | | | | | | | | | |
| | | | 40 | ON | ON | | | | | | 20 | | | | |

| 234 | 243 | 244 | 245 | 246 | 255 | 301 | 302 | 303 | 304 | 306 | 308 | 311 | 312 | 314 | 315 |
| 352 | 353 | 360 | 361 | | | | | | | | | | | | |
| | | | | | 35 | | | | | FF | ON | 71 | 71 | | |
| ON | 70 | | | | | | | | | | | | | | |

| 362 | 363 | 364 | 404 | 405 | 406 | 409 | 410 | 413 | 414 | 415 | 416 | 430 | 431 | 432 | 437 |
| 438 | 454 | 455 | 502 | | | | | | | | | | | | |
| | | 70 | 40 | | | 65 | | 80 | 60 | 60 | | | | | |
| | | | | | | 176 | | 176 | 176 | 176 | | | | | |

| 503 | 506 | 507 | 510 | 511 | 517 | 518 | 520 | 521 | 522 | 523 | 524 | 525 | 529 | 530 | 533 |
| 535 | 536 | 538 | 539 | | | | | | | | | | | | |
| 50 | | FF | | ON | | FF | | | | | ON | ON | | | |

| 604 | 622 | 701 | 702 | 703 | 800 | 905 | 906 | 907 | 908 | 910 | 911 | 914 | 915 | 916 | 917 |
| | | | | | | 60 | | 60 | 60 | | | 60 | 60 | 60 | 60 |

464  Printout of lanterns used in the
lighting state

465  Ill. right:
Lanterns involved in
lighting state no. 66

466  *Die Legende vom armen Heinrich*
Münchner Kammerspiele, 1997
Lighting state no. 66

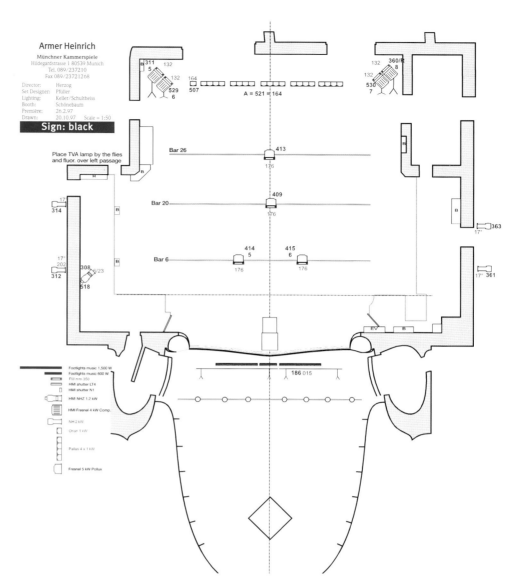

## Armer Heinrich

Münchner Kammerspiele
Hildegardstrasse 1 80539 Munich
Tel. 089/237210
Fax 089/23721268

Director:       Herzog
Set Designer:   Pfüller
Lighting:       Keller/Schultheiss
Booth:          Schönebaum
Premiere:       26.2.97
Drawn:          20.10.97    Scale = 1:50

**Sign: black**

Place TVA lamp by the flies
and fluor. over left passage

Bar 26 — 413
176

Bar 20 — 409
176

Bar 6 — 414  415
       5    6
       176  176

A = 521 = 164

186 015

Footlights music 1,500 W
Footlights music 600 W
FW mm 360
HMI shutter LT4
HMI shutter N1
HMI NHZ 1.2 kW
HMI Fresnel 4 kW Comp.
NH 2 kW
Orion 1 kW
Pallas 4 x 1 kW
Fresnel 5 kW Pollux

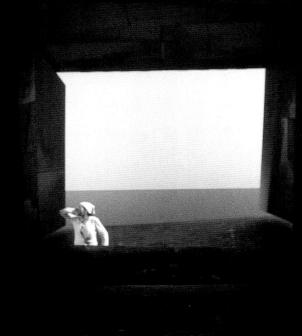

467/468 Ill. left:
*Die Legende vom
armen Heinrich*
Münchner Kammer-
spiele, 1997

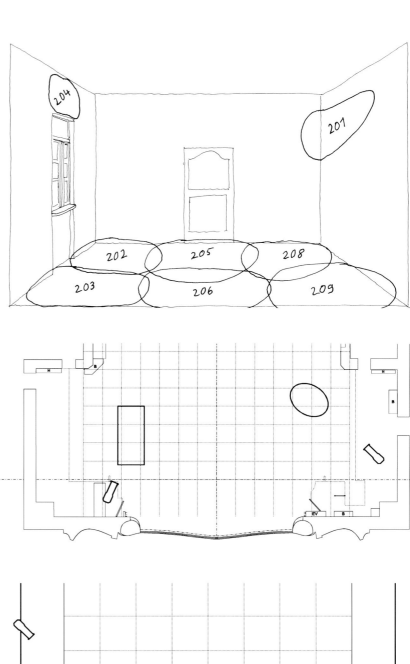

469 Three-dimensional
sketch of the set
with beam positions

470 Using a
grid system
to set lighting

471 Using a
grid system
on the safety curtain
to set lighting

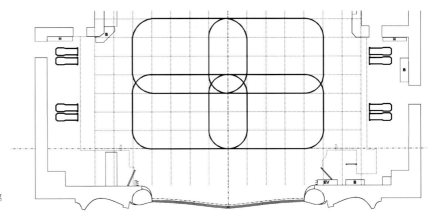

472 Structuring lighting
zones for two-colour lighting

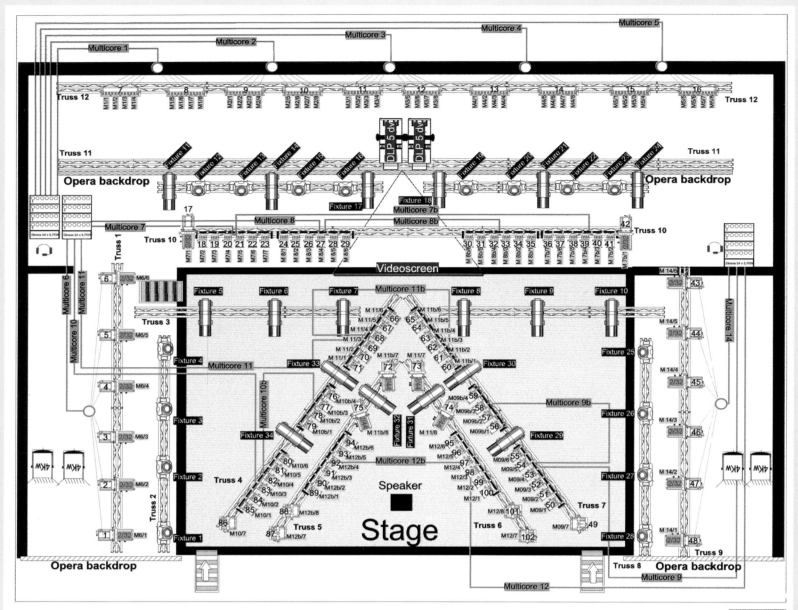

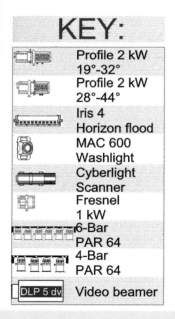

| | |
|---|---|
| Designer: Ralf Wapler | |
| Version: 2 plots as of 19.12.98 | |
| Scale: 1:100 | |
| Sheet: 1 / 4 | |
| Show date: 21.12.98 | |
| www.backstage-online.de | |

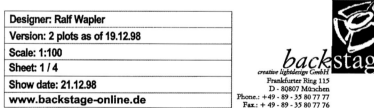

**backstage**
creative lightdesign GmbH
Frankfurter Ring 115
D - 80807 München
Phone.: +49 - 89 - 35 80 77 77
Fax.: + 49 - 89 - 35 80 77 76

This plan is for a multifunctional stage with speaker's podium and video projection. This stage is backed by an opera backdrop lit from behind. The use of cyclorama lighting means that almost any desired colour can be created using additive mixing. Profile spots in the wings and automated washlights for the stage make it possible to light the playing area evenly whitout spilling on to the video screen in the background. Individual spots are used to pinpoint the podium. A moving truss construction is provided for musical shows on this stage. This is fitted with scanners and PAR 64 spots. The PAR 64s in the back truss are highlights in complementary colours to the opera backdrop. Daylight spots light the opera backdrop areas at the sides of the stage.

473 Setting up a mobile lighting rig for touring

## Set-up plan for traverses

| TRAVERSE 4 | Moving Truss | | | | | | | |
|---|---|---|---|---|---|---|---|---|
| HEIGHT 1 | 9.5M | Section | | | | | | |
| HEIGHT 2 | 4.3M | 0.25M | 0.5M | 1.0M | 1.5M | 2.0M | 3.0M | 4.0M |
| LENGTH | 8.00 M | | | | | | | 2 |
| WEIGHT | 500Kg | Steel hangers for bridle (metric) | | | | | | |
| MOTORS | 3 x VBG 70 | 0.25M | 0.5M | 1.0M | 1.5M | 2.0M | 3.0M | 4.0M |
| SUSPENSION POINTS | 6 | | 2 | 2 | | | 2 | |
| NOTE | 3 x Bridle | | | | | | | |

## Motor - allocation

| TRAVERSE 1 | Manufacturer | Load capacity | Controller | Cable name |
|---|---|---|---|---|
| MOTOR 1 | Chainmaster | 500Kg | VBG 70 | Susi 1 |
| MOTOR 2 | Chainmaster | 500Kg | VBG 70 | Susi 2 |
| MOTOR 3 | Chainmaster | 500Kg | VBG 70 | Susi 3 |

## Cable designation, Lighting

| DIMMER | 001 | 002 | 003 | 004 | 005 | 006 | Total |
|---|---|---|---|---|---|---|---|
| Dimmer number | 1 | 2 | 3 | 4 | 5 | 6 | Amps: |
| Desk channel | 173 | 173 | 173 | 181 | 181 | 181 | |
| Fixture number | 80 | 81 | 82+76 | 83+77 | 84+78 | 85+79 | KW: |
| Load in KW | 1 | 1 | 2 | 2 | 2 | 2 | 10 |
| Multicore way | 6 | 5 | 4 | 3 | 2 | 1 | CEE No. |
| Multicore name | M10 | M10 | M10 | M10 | M10 | M10 | D |

| DIMMER | 001 | 002 | 003 | 004 | 005 | 006 | Total |
|---|---|---|---|---|---|---|---|
| Dimmer | 7 | 8 | 9 | 10 | 11 | 12 | Amps: |
| Desk channel | 19 | 20 | 21 | 22 | 23 | 24 | |
| Fixture number | 43 | 44 | 45 | 46 | 47 | 48 | KW: |
| Load in KW | 2 | 2 | 2 | 2 | 2 | 2 | 12 |
| Multicore way | 6 | 5 | 4 | 3 | 2 | 1 | CEE No. |
| Multicore name | M14 | M14 | M14 | M14 | M14 | M14 | D |

Patching lists are used to document all the cabling. This record is necessary so that the multicores arriving at the dimmers can be distributed rapidly and manageably. As on a tour, for example, the cabling always has to be the same, it is very important to be able to follow the individual cable paths at any time.The numbers 001 - 006 correspond to the dimmer outputs. This follows the soft patching allocations in the lighting booth. The fixture number is a means of identifying the individual pieces of equipment with information about the multicore path cabling them to the dimmer.

## State list for lighting booth

| Directors - Cue | Comment | Lighting cue | Event | Scanner cue | Event | Follow spot | Note |
|---|---|---|---|---|---|---|---|
| 23 | Speaker 3 | 75.4 | Speaker brighter | 17 | Accents brighter | none | |
| 24 | Speaker 4 | 76 | Colour change opera | 18 | Colour change | Speaker's entrance | |
| 25 | Scene change | 77 | Worklight | 19 | fadeout | Blackout | Scene change |
| 26 | Dance performance | 78 | 1st dancer | 20 | 1st dancer | 1st dancer | |

## State list for moving lights

### Cue Sheet

| Cue | Comment | Time in | Time out | Follow | Delay | Link | Submaster | Special | Event |
|---|---|---|---|---|---|---|---|---|---|
| 75,4 | Speaker brighter | 25 | 30 | 120 | | | | | |
| 76 | Colour change on opera backdrop | 120 | 120 | | | | | 7 | Fade in some house lighting |

## Set-up – arrangements - focusing

| Day 1 | Arrival, set-up, set lighting |
|---|---|
| 06:00 a.m. | Rigging truck arrives from Hanover |
| 06:00 a.m. | Rigging crew start work Paul, Carli, Glenn, Walter, 4 stagehands |
| 08:00 a.m. | Deadline for rigging motors |
| 08:00 a.m | Rig traverses and fly to operating height |
| 10:00 a.m. | Deadline for rigging |
| 10:15 a.m | Stage truck arrives |
| 10:15 a.m. | Stage crew start work Sepp, Oli, Heinz, Karin, Evi, Sabine, Laki, |
| 11:00 a.m. | Lighting truck arrives |
| 11:00 a.m. | Lighting crew start work Ralf, Lorenz, Rupi, Harry, Rudi, 3 stagehands |
| 11:00 a.m. | Moving light crew start work Tommi, Uwe, Jürgen, Christoph 2 x Stagehand |
| 12:00 p.m. | Deadline for complete set-up |

Crew schedule

## Configuration for moving lights

| MOVING LIGHT ADDRESSES | | | | | | |
|---|---|---|---|---|---|---|
| Fixture no. | Type | From channel | To channel | Channel number | Fixture mode | Desk output | Protocol |
| F1 | MAC 600 | 1 | 12 | 12 | Mode 4 | 1 | DMX |
| F2 | MAC 600 | 13 | 24 | 12 | Mode 4 | 1 | DMX |
| F3 | MAC 600 | 25 | 36 | 12 | Mode 4 | 1 | DMX |
| F5 | Cyberlight SV High End | 1 | 20 | 20 | | 2 | LWR |
| F6 | Cyberlight SV High End | 21 | 40 | 20 | | 2 | LWR |
| F7 | Cyberlight SV High End | 41 | 60 | 20 | | 2 | LWR |
| F8 | Cyberlight SV High End | 61 | 80 | 20 | | 2 | LWR |

## Fitting for scanner gobo wheels

| Fixture no:<br>Patch no: | | Fixture no.<br>Patch no. | | Fixture no.<br>Patch no. | | Fixture no.<br>Patch no. | |
|---|---|---|---|---|---|---|---|
| Fixed Gobo | | Fixed Gobo | | Fixed Gobo | | Fixed Gobo | |
| 1 | OPEN | 1 | OPEN | 1 | OPEN | 1 | OPEN |
| 2 | STARS | 2 | STARS | 2 | STARS | 2 | STARS |
| 3 | DOTS | 3 | DOTS | 3 | DOTS | 3 | DOTS |
| 4 | MOON | 4 | MOON | 4 | MOON | 4 | MOON |
| 5 | CIRCLE | 5 | CIRCLE | 5 | CIRCLE | 5 | CIRCLE |
| 6 | TUNNEL | 6 | TUNNEL | 6 | TUNNEL | 6 | TUNNEL |
| 7 | FOLIAGE | 7 | FOLIAGE | 7 | FOLIAGE | 7 | FOLIAGE |
| 8 | CHINA | 8 | CHINA | 8 | CHINA | 8 | CHINA |
| Rotating gobos | | Rotating gobos | | Rotating gobos | | Rotating gobos | |

74/475  Lighting rig for
*Bridges to Babylon*,
Rolling Stones, 1998

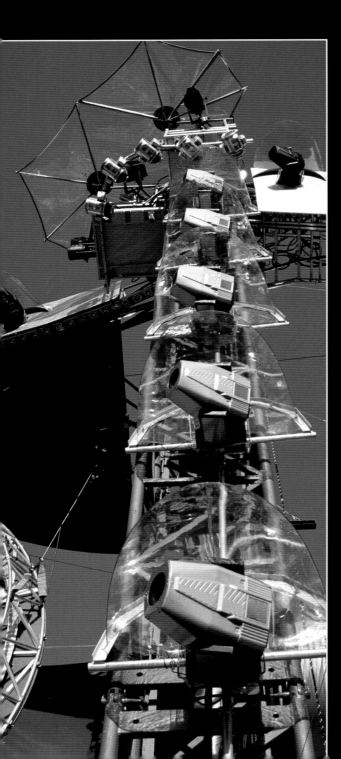

475

474

476/477 Ill. left:
Lighting dolly
with fixtures

478 Ill. right:
Lighting rig
with 4,000 W
daylight spots

479/480 Ill. pp. 198–201:
Rolling Stones
*Bridges to Babylon in Concert*, 1998
Lighting: Patrick Woodroffe

481  *Lucio Silla*
Salzburg Festival, 1993

At last the moment that everyone on the production has been working towards has arrived: The lighting concept is to be realized. Whether this is disappointing or satisfying depends largely on the experience of the people involved and the thoroughness of the preparations. Nothing is ever perfect, but everything that has been prepared and discussed should be right. It is important that the key lights on which the lighting depends are positioned in the right places. The equipment is assembled, adjusted and worked through at the lighting rehearsals.

The lighting designer and his colleagues should have a good working position immediately adjacent to the lighting board. This should consist of a generous working surface, on which it is possible to spread out lighting plots, notes, scripts, and to set up one or more control monitors. It is also especially important to have a voice link-up with all the lighting positions and cue command positions, i.e. with the stage manager and the technicians running the stage machinery and flies. There must also be a link with the operator in the booth. This must be of high quality, so that the designer can be understood even if he is just whispering into the microphone. If people are to be able to react quickly and flexibly to events it is also necessary to set up a radio connection or an intercom system with colleagues, so that a dialogue can be held. Also, it is possible to use a laptop rather than a computer monitor. This means that the lighting designer can intervene in lighting states himself. For major rehearsals it is often also useful to set up the lighting booth facilities right next to the lighting designer, depending on the benefit to be gained versus the amount of effort needed to do this.

There are two fundamentally different working methods for the late rehearsal phase in the theatre. Private and more profit-oriented theatres, pop and rock concerts, variety programmes and shows make sure that the final technical and artistic rehearsals are kept as short as possible, as the venues are hired only for a short time, or too many performances are lost if the show is not playing in repertory. But most German theatres run a repertory programme. Here, the final rehearsals for a new production are held in the morning; for larger new productions it is possible to cancel an evening performance or two. If, however, we are working on a show or a production with very restricted final rehearsals, the preparatory work has to be even more meticulous and comprehensive. This requires very exact lighting plots but also that complete lighting sequences are worked out in advance on paper, which is possible only with precise ideas about the production. The operator in the booth will note every single lighting change according to instrument numbering and intensity settings, which demands extremely concentrated theoretical imagination and also a degree of artistic anticipation. Subsequently these listings will be keyed into the lighting box memory – if such a piece of equipment is available. Today this is not a rare approach and can be compared with keying text into a home computer. If this job is not done at the performance venue, the data are transferred directly to the box or fed in from a disk or CD-ROM. If the lighting is changed during the development process, time should also be available to check the performers' costumes and make-up in the chosen light.

A lighting rehearsal that has been well prepared technically will include a large number of colour filters as well as the stock of lights. We have decided which gels and filters to use in the meantime. If glass filters are still being used it is particularly important that all the filters come from the same manufacturer, so that problems are not created by different colour tolerances in the products of different manufacturers. Here it is advisable to use the manufacturer's official colour coding, and not the out-of-date method of establishing one's own coding, or even the familiar old nick-names like 'Swan Lake blue' or 'Hamlet yellow'. This may all be very poetic, but it is confusing and difficult to use in notes.

When implementing the lighting plan the designer should make sure that the on-stage lanterns are out of the audience's sightlines as much as possible. This is called a cover check. The audience's sightlines can be restricted

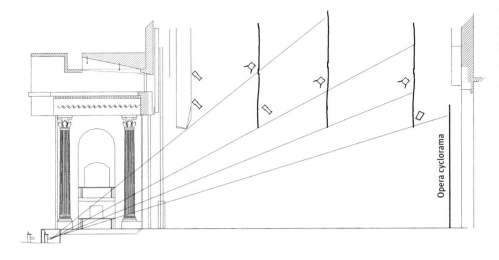

Opera cyclorama

by hanging fabric borders, or by side coverings, called legs. This check does not have to be done on the stage and can be made during planning by comparing the lighting plot with the technical stage plans.

## FOCUSING THE LIGHTING

The lights that are not permanently in position should be hung on the day of the lighting set up before the stage set is built. When the set is in place, the process known as 'focusing' begins; this is the final adjustment of the individual lights.

483  Correctly focused spotlight

484  Incorrectly focused spotlight

Focusing begins with the aforementioned preparations and a darkened stage set. Adjusting the lights so that they are pointing precisely as intended should be carried out as much as possible in groups of lights and in the correct sequence; this means focusing general and directed lighting first, then background and outline lighting, and finally effects lights. A similar sequence should be followed when fitting colour filters. It is obvious that dark colours should be put in place after the lanterns have been positioned, as positioning is easier with a bright, clear light. This sequence of work should be seen as a general guideline, as the various demands are so complex. Some sequence is necessary to avoid the risk of losing a sense of the overall concept when dealing with individual positions. If particularly complicated staging means that the sequence has to be abandoned, then all the lights will be focused together regardless of the role they will play later in the completed design.

The selected, prepared lights are now ready to be focused. A fundamental point to note here is that acting areas are kept separate from decorative lighting. When lighting the acting area the selected lanterns must be focused so that they produce the maximum effect for individual performers. It is no good if the angle of incidence is so low that the centre of the beam falls on the performers' legs. It is also erroneous to think that the ideal location has been found if the performer is in the centre of the light beam. To find the right position, characters stand with their legs at the very front of the circle of light. If this creates a visual problem (shadow, for example) additional lighting can be provided from a lower position or from a bank of footlights for general lighting.

This way of focusing applies not only to front lighting but also to all other lighting directions. If this principle is not followed, the performers do not occupy the scene with presence and clarity. The only way out of this is to reposition the lantern or reposition the performer if this works visually in terms of the stage in general.

Thorough knowledge of the predetermined lighting states is very helpful for focusing. This technical work does not require the presence of the director or designer. Once all the lights are focused and colour changers, multifunctional spots and special effects have been checked to ensure that they are working properly, then the various light sources can begin to come together to create lighting states. It is rather like a jigsaw puzzle; theory is put into practice to form an arrangement of light that then serves as a starting point for working with other members of the production team.

In a sequence of acts and scenes requiring several lighting states, changes only can be made if everybody accepts their consequences. Designers and directors are frequently inclined to assess intermediate settings, and then want to change them. If we are to realize the lighting concept, we should never try to make corrections and changes in agreement with the production staff until after all the lighting arrangements are complete. Various different states come together to produce a lighting sequence and, to make sure that they are homogenous and intelligible, each state is checked and compared visually with its predecessor and its successor.

## WRITTEN RECORDS

It is essential to write down what has been developed and achieved so that we are always in a position to reconstruct the lighting positions, the combination of lanterns and effects involved in a particular lighting cue and the fade-in and fade-out times for it. We have already mentioned sketches for reconstructing lighting positions. The sequence and composition of the lighting states is for the operator the equivalent of describing the positions for the lighting designer. It is somewhat simpler for the man in the booth, as he has a great deal of computer technology at his disposal. He can key cue titles, cue numbers and the times for the transition process into the console. He can also print out the details of each lighting cue

Performance : DER ARME HEINRICH          Date : 19.02.98   Time : 10:52:35   Page : 4

| S | Cue | Type | T down | T up | Special time | Link | Action | Text |
|---|-----|------|--------|------|--------------|------|--------|------|
| | 0.5 | GES | 0 | 0 | | | FADE IN | |
| | 0.6 | FW | | | TVZ 0.0 | | ALL 130 | |
| | 0.7 | F50 | | | TVZ 0.0 | | MACRO: 50 | |
| | 1 | GES | 10 | 10 | | | IMAGE 1 | |
| | 1.1 | FW | | | TVZ 0.0 | | IMAGE 1 | |
| | 2 | GES | 0 | 0 | | | HMI ON | |
| | 3 | GES | 0 | 0 | | | BO%% | |
| | 4 | GES | 08 | 08 | | | 112 ON | |
| | 4.3 | ADD | 05 | 05 | | | 409 ON | |
| | 4.5 | TGES | 10 | 05 | | | 413 + HORIZON | |
| | 5 | ADD | 15 | 15 | | | FOOTLIGHTS | |
| | 6 | TGES | 06 | 06 | | | IMAGE 1 | |
| | 7 | TGES | 15 | 15 | | | TOWER UP | |
| | 7.5 | TGES | 10 | 10 | TVZ 15.0 | | TOWER UP | |
| | 8 | GES | 15 | 15 | | | DKL | |
| | 8.5 | GES | 15 | 15 | | | 315 | |
| | 8.7 | FW | | | TVZ 0.0 | | | |
| | 9 | GES | 0 | 0 | | | FLASH 500A ALONE | |
| | 9.1 | ADD | 0 | 0 | TVZ 0.5 | | FLASH OUT | |
| | 10 | GES | 04 | 04 | TVZ 2.0 | | IMAGE 2 | |
| | 11 | ADD | 08 | 04 | | | FOLLOW SPOT OUT | |
| | 12 | TGES | 05 | 05 | *TVZ 1.0 | | HORIZON | |
| | 13 | ADD | 07 | 07 | TVZ 1.0 | | 413 ON | |
| | 13.5 | ADD | 25 | 25 | TVZ 0.0 | | 145 165 UP | |

as a separate entity. This document shows the relevant circuit and the dimmer setting. For me, this kind of written record is the most important piece of information after a rehearsal. All the information that has been stored is printed out after a lighting rehearsal. Data can then be corrected by hand when reading through these data 'dry', and the new information fed in to the memory the next day or before the next rehearsal. However, if the lighting system is connected to a computer network, changes of this kind can be made from any linked terminal, making things easier for the man in the booth.

If the console does not have this facility, the data have to be written up by hand.

For readers unfamiliar with digital technology it is important to know that a computer-controlled system can react to anything that happens on stage, though it would be mistaken to believe that all this can be done at the touch of a button. Ideally, running the lights at a performance or rehearsal corresponds to what has been planned and stored. But in special situations almost any manipulation can be carried out providing the operator is skilled and familiar with the equipment and the production.

485  Ill. right: Printout of a sequence of lighting states

486  Below left: Possible system for noting spotlight positions

487  Below right: Notes for systematic focusing requiring several parts of the set to be available

| Circuit | Rating Type to Size | Pos.1 Pos.2 | Pos.3 | Color shutter Gobo | Focus |
|---------|---------------------|-------------|-------|--------------------|-------|
| 510 | 2 kW Fres | L BD 1.9 m | | | 3rd alley |
| 511 | 2 kW NH    30° | L BD 2.5 m | 103 | | grotto curtain 2nd alley sharp |
| 517 | 1.2 kW HMI NH   30° | L G1 | | | shut. 303 |
| 518 | 1.2 kW HMI NHZ | L G2 | | | shut. 308 |
| 520 | 1.2 KW HMI Fres | R PB | | | shut. 216 |
| 521 | 5 kW Pallas | L BD | 164 | | horizon below |
| 522 | 5 kW Pallas | L BD | 132 | | horizon below |
| 523 | 5 kW Pallas | L BD | 128 | | horizon below |
| 524 | 5 kW Pallas | L BD | 165 | | horizon below |
| 525 | 1 kW NH   30° | Z 38 | 174 Gobo | | Moon Bar 38 H=3.3m + 50cm to left |
| 529 | 4 kW HMI Compact | L BD | | | horizon below - Rollo 6 |
| 530 | 4 kW HMI Compact | R BD | | | horizon below - Rollo 7 |
| 533 | Fluor. Stone | R BD | | | stone inside |
| 535 | 1 kW NH   30° | Z KR | | | 1st alley sharp |
| 536 | 5 kW Fres | R BD 4.1 m | | | 3rd wall left |
| 538 | 2 kW Fres | R BD 1.9 m | | | 3rd alley |
| 539 | 1 kW NH   30° | Z KR | | | 2nd alley sharp |
| 604 | Wind | R UB | | | wind controller 622 |
| 622 | Wind | R UB | | | wind transformer |
| 700 | Auditorium | V | | | total |
| 701 | Auditorium | V | | | ceiling back |
| 702 | Auditorium | V | | | ceiling front |
| 703 | Auditorium | V | | | below and in boxes |

MÜNCHNER KAMMERSPIELE                                          Lighting Department

"Armer Heinrich"

| Image | Walls from platform | Forestage | Stage | Walls from platform | Image |
|-------|---------------------|-----------|-------|---------------------|-------|
| 10a | 1 | 168 | 205, 243 | 1 | 10a |
| 4 | 1 | 169 | 306, 352 | 2 3 | 14 |
| 10 | 1 | 177/170, 176 | Horizon below: 311/5+360/8 | 2 3 | |
| | | 156, 157/150 | Horizon above: 529/6+530/7 | 2 3 | |
| 4 | 1 | 149 | | | |
| 10a | 1 | 148 | may be 205, 243 finished | | |
| | 1 | 122, 123 | | | |
| 10 | 1 | 121, 124 | | | |
| 13 | 2 3 | 120/114+117 | 518/308 | 2 3 | 13 |
| | 1 2 | 107/111 | | 2 | |
| Image 10: walls, platform and lighting bars | | | | | |
| 10 | 1 2 | 131, 133, 135 L-R | 215, 212, 228 L-R 2nd platform | 2 3 | 10 |
| | 1 2 | 102, 103, 110 L-R | 222, 218, 226 | 2 | 10 |
| | 1 2 | 119/115, 116 L-R | 312, 314 | | 10 |
| | 2 3 | 101 2.+3. platform centre | 364, 363, 361 | | |
| | | | 535, 538, 539 | | |
| | | | 301,304,510 | | |
| | | | 315 | | |
| | 1 2 | 113 1. +. 2. platform with walls | adjust grotto | | |
| | 1 2 | 112 followspot front centre | 204, 244 | 2 | 10 |
| | | | 245 | 2 | 10 |
| | | | Additional bars: | | |
| | | | 413 | | |
| | | | 405, 406, 409, 410 | | |
| | | | 414, 415 | | |
| | | | 404 | | |
| | | | 246, 206 | 1 2 | 9 |
| | | | 227, 229 | 1 2 | 9 |
| | | | 517/303 wall right and alley | 2 | 9 |
| | | | 223, 232, 520/216 | 2 | 8 |
| 8 | 1 | 193/145, 194/165 opposite wall and some platform | 218 2. platform centre | | |
| | | | 226 behind 2nd platform left | | |
| | | | 234 between the walls | 2 | 4 |
| | | | 454/353, 455/362 Zappi + Jule | 2 | 5 |
| Back curtain | | | | | |
| | | 155, 175 | 511 | | 10 |
| | | 181, 182, 183 | 430, 431, 432, 438, 526, 437 | | |
| | | 184, 185, 186 | 506,536 | | |
| | | | 507, 521, 522, 523, 524 | | |
| | | | 525 | | |
| Set at beginning | | | 533, 622, 604 | | |
| | | 153,173  centre sm. curtain | 302, TVA lamp, 503 | | |
| | | 154, 174 whole curtain - gold p | small room right | | |

Die Legende vom armen Heinrich (26.2.97)                    page 1 of 2 / 30.08.98

## WORKING WITH DISCHARGE LAMPS

I have explained above what can be expected from discharge lamps. A description, however, cannot replace practice and experience. Powerful spotlights with discharge lamps can be used as a principal directional light source or for a complete lighting plan. It is possible but extremely difficult to produce subtle, slow lighting changes, as mechanical devices are needed to do this. The result depends on how well the mechanical devices can be regulated and how much spill can be tolerated. If low pressure sodium vapour lamps are being used, the full impact is optimal only if there is no residual light cast on the playing area. The best effects are achieved with these lamps if they are fired under the playing light. Fading the conventional light down once the warm-up period is over ensures a smooth transition.

It is also possible with most discharge lamps to introduce a lighting state with the vaporization process and the colour sequence that this involves. Dimming devices available for industrial purposes can also be adapted for lantern housings, which makes it easier to incorporate them into the lighting. The disadvantage of not being electrically dimmable is outweighed by the advantages when switching off a discharge lamp. Discharge lamps are particularly useful for blackouts; no other kind of lamp can darken the stage so abruptly, and this can be particularly important for dramatic purposes.

## WORKING WITH INTELLIGENT LIGHT AND COLOUR CHANGERS

These new types of lights and colour changers are joining their traditional

488 W.A. Mozart
*The Magic Flute*
Director and set designer:
Herbert Kapplmüller
Landestheater Linz, 1995

predecessors, and they need to be handled in a particular way. Colour changers, scanners and moving lights can only be driven and controlled by DMX signals or a signal determined by the manufacturer. The most recent lighting consoles can process DMX signals, and the commands can be built into the usual lighting sequence. If the available console cannot process such signals, processing can be done with an additional board or via a laptop with special software. It is possible to distribute work between two consoles, but this is often a complicated additional burden for the operator.

## FINAL REHEARSALS

Final lighting rehearsals have to be planned according to the importance of light in the particular production. And of course the final phases of a new production also depend on what the theatre has to offer in general. If there are sufficient staff, it is also helpful to have sufficient time for polishing a lighting design. Most designers will agree that even at this stage a design is never entirely ready, but there comes at point at which one has to stop criticizing one's own work. In this final rehearsal phase the lighting is tested and corrected.

Above all, the various lighting transitions are adapted to the events on stage, colour corrections are carried out and the work of all the other technical departments comes together to form a unified performance – for the première.

There is no generally valid guideline for style within lighting technology. Trends in the various fields of the performing arts are reflected in the design and construction of basic lighting rigs and in lighting methods, and these are, of course, to a large extent dependent on the conceptual ideas of the artists involved.

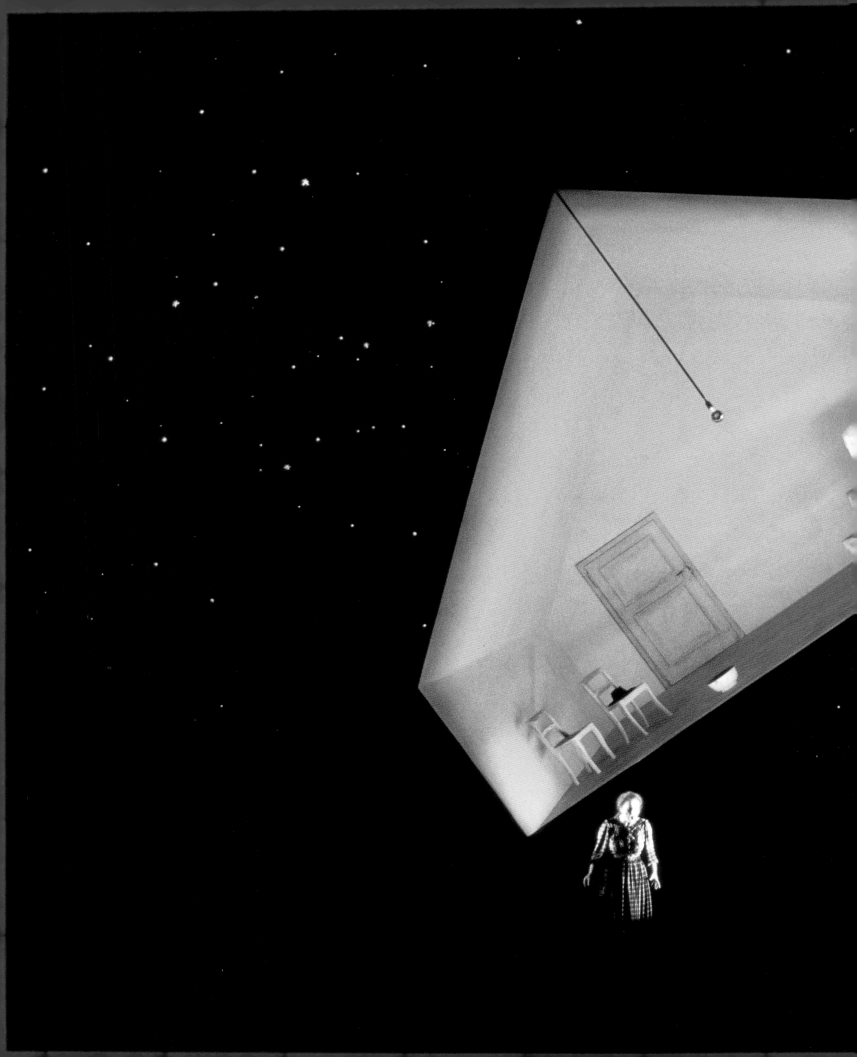

## LIGHTING OPERA

An unpleasant factor when lighting opera is that the indirect light from the music-stands in the orchestra pit illuminates the front section of the stage at all times. Although this is no reason to change the lighting, there are some very specific qualities that justify dealing with opera lighting separately. Most opera houses have very large stages. Building a solid set for this with genuine materials would cause insuperable transport problems. If lighter materials are used for a production, the lighting must not work against this illusionistic element. For this reason the overall intensity and lighting set up have to be managed differently.

A small number of theatres that stage musical productions sometimes use a cyclorama. This is a semicircular canvas extending from the upper part of the stage to the floor. Slides are then projected on to this screen to create a panoramic image, using several very powerful slide projectors to cover the full area. But this kind of stage design restricts the scope of the production considerably and is not necessarily advantageous for the lighting.

Another typical device used in opera or ballet performances is a gauze, or scrim, covering the whole of the proscenium opening, which means that the audience experience the action through a visual filter. This creates a tremendous illusion of depth. At the same time the scrim serves as another projection surface, for fog, or for water and fire effects, for example. However, if a scrim is used there can be no front lighting at all. This demands a relatively precise distribution of light on the stage and a corresponding degree of discipline from the performers, as the light furthest downstage inevitably comes from the side. Follow spots are very often used in opera. This is not necessarily beneficial for the overall visual effect, as a lighting state can be destroyed by an intervention of this kind, and any sense of chiaroscuro is lost. If this is taken into account from the outset, there is the advantage that the set and the space on stage can be lit with particular care without needing to worry

489  Richard Wagner
*The Flying Dutchman*
Director: Dieter Dorn
Set Designer: Jürgen Rose
Lighting: Manfred Voss
Bayreuth Festival, 1990

490 Giuseppe Verdi
*Falstaff*
Director: Jonathan Miller
Set Designer: Herbert Kapplmüller
Staatsoper Unter den Linden
Berlin, 1998

about spatial lighting being disturbed by light needed for the characters.

Two techniques have to be distinguished when using a follow spot. First, one can use a large beam with shutters to cover the performer's whole body. The second variant, when for example only the singer's head is lit, is a more elegant approach, but it needs particular concentration when operating the spotlight. Of course it is also conceivable to light a performer with two or more follow spots. For example, it is visually interesting to use one follow spot as back lighting and two restricted follow spots as front lighting – one for the head and another for the body.

## LIGHTING MUSICALS
## AND OPERETTAS

These two theatrical genres provide a
great deal of scope for technical effects
and colourful, varied light combinations. Here in particular the images
should convey excitement and beauty.
The light zoning system should be used
to meet this demand. As mentioned
above, the colour effectiveness of the
performers' light can be significantly
enhanced by systematically dividing
the playing area into various light and
colour sectors. Additive and complementary colour mixing and careful focusing are tempting choices for such
visually exciting combinations. Satirical
songs with choruses are typical of musicals and operettas, and they are often
supported in their effect by the use of
follow spots. The effect will be enhanced by lighting individual passages
with two or more spotlights, using different colours and angles wherever
possible.

492 Pink Floyd, 1987
Lighting: Mark Brickman

## LIGHTING SHOWS

Here the lighting design can run the gamut of colour and trick effects, and rhythmically changing spotlight combinations. It is almost obligatory to use multifunctional spotlights and colour changers, and all the lighting angles and colour combinations described so far can be used. Everything is possible in show lighting, provided that it is technically feasible and effective. Stirring orgies of light, developed dramatically within themselves, are not only permitted, but *de rigueur*. We should not deceive ourselves, however, as far as concept and approach are concerned. Even the most massive input of light, frequently run from computer-controlled lighting consoles, is composed of a sequence of repeating combinations of light and colour. The resulting extra-ordinary effects are technical processes that can be further perfected, especially by the use of computers, and incorporate elements such as running and flashing lights, stroboscopic effects, laser reflections, scanners, multifunctional spots and the complex use of projections.

491 Jesus Jones, 1993
Lighting: Simon Sidi

493/494  Rolling Stones
*Bridges to Babylon in Concert*, 1998

495  *Apollo*
Ballet by George Balanchine
Bayerische Staatsoper
Munich, 1998

496  *Artifact II*
Ballet by William Forsythe
Lighting: William Forsythe
Bayerische Staatsoper
Munich, 1998

497  Ill. right:
Typical lighting
arrangement for
a stage with wings
and transparent
cyclorama for
background lighting

## LIGHTING BALLET

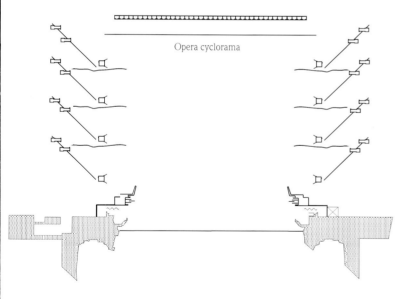

Opera cyclorama

A great deal of space has to be left free for dancers when designing ballets. The classical stage décor consists of legs at the sides with a backcloth. Above, the borders complete the traditional proscenium stage. This arrangement at the sides of the stage creates a space with wings that enables a large number of entrance options and different lantern positions.

In dance theatre priority is given to lighting legs and feet. Lighting from the wings is very useful here, complemented by highlighting at floor level to fill in the lower areas. Diagonally-angled floor-level highlights behind the proscenium are also customary. A proscenium scrim is also often used to make the stage look deeper.

These lighting notes apply to classical ballet. Recent developments in dance theatre allow less restricted lighting concepts, which are subject only to the choreography.

498 *Schlusschor* (Final Chorus)
Münchner Kammerspiele, 1991

## LIGHTING PLAYS

Most plays require lighting without flourishes. They should be lit calmly except when there are special dramatic or directorial changes. Scenes with follow spots seldom occur. There is no system for lighting plays. Perhaps plays allow the greatest degree of freedom for expressive lighting design because there is no constraint of doing justice to a score. The definition and description of location are becoming increasingly important, and this is frequently in- tended to explain the stage area as an interpreted, inner situation within a play. These are dramatically necessary areas that complement the set, and they open up great scope for the light- ing designer.

499  *Merlin oder das wüste Land*
(Merlin or The Barren Land)
Münchner Kammerspiele, 1982

# The Structure of a Lighting Department

Most German theatres operate on a repertory system, which means a different play is performed every day. The structure for a lighting department described here is based on this system. There is also some material on this aspect of theatre organization in the chapter 'General Remarks on Light in the Theatre'.

Developments in artistic lighting for the entertainment and media worlds have had a positive effect on professional lighting. The very fact that operating lighting consoles and electronically controlled equipment needs a different kind of basic knowledge has meant that many aspects of the lighting profession have changed and that there are new training institutions. Despite these developments, many German-speaking theatres still have to work under conditions determined by local authorities. This inevitably leads to restrictions of creative work methods.

The quality of the contribution made by lighting to the success of a production is determined by co-operation between the lighting designer, director and set designer. The lighting designer has to be sensitive to their concepts and intentions, which requires a range of qualifications from colleagues in the lighting department. This is not just a question of professional expertise; motivation is an important factor as well.

But it is not only the employees who can create a good working atmosphere by their readiness to co-operate. The way in which the theatre is run as an institution is important as well, whether it is subsidized by the state or the local authority, managed by a limited company or operates as a private theatre. The commercial form has a major effect on those in charge of the lighting department and on the technical personnel. A newly engaged technician with good qualifications should also be able to work on the artistic side as well, but this is often not the case, at least not in German theatres. The legal requirements theatre management and local authorities have established for qualification as a lighting technician are not as lighting designers and technicians themselves would have them. Efforts to make changes here – e.g. setting up special courses – are a step in the right direction, but the existing conditions still hinder a greater degree of integration. Also, many theatres here now use free-lance lighting designers, which can be very difficult for an in-house head of department, as there is a risk that his efforts could be undermined.

Another problem that should not be underestimated is overloading a department. Given the time pressure to which a whole season is often subjected, staff are usually not in a position to attend to necessary routine matters such as maintenance work and preparations for rehearsals or performances. Also, the technical infrastructure is often deficient. Badly equipped workshops and cheap tools do not guarantee continuous quality. Clear intentions and creative pressure from the theatre management are all that can yield an improvement here.

There is one positive development, however, that will stabilize lighting work greatly. Everyone involved in handling light as a medium should enjoy it, and co-operation between the technical departments, theatre management and the lighting department should not be made any more difficult. On the contrary, it should be taken seriously and imply mutual acceptance, in other words a clear, hierarchical distribution of work with individual responsibility according to the size and specific needs of the stage. This is the secret to high quality performance. It is unacceptable for the majority of German theatres to be heavily subsidized and then offer mediocre work. Unsubsidized theatres will approach their work differently from the outset, as their existence is at stake if they are not successful and popular with the public.

I can only give a broad sketch of the organizational structure here, as it is affected by a number of factors that are tailored to the needs of the institution concerned. Thus the demands posed by the particular building have to be addressed. The repertory programme also helps to determine organizational structure. Smaller theatres are easier and more manageable to organize. Problems occur in state theatres, as here it is often impossible to be flexible.

The technical director is at the head of all the technical departments. He is responsible for every aspect of staging and is the main contact with the artistic staff. At his side are the head of the lighting department and the heads of the all the other technical departments. Staging decisions should be made jointly by the technical director and the lighting designer. It makes things worse if the technical director takes sole responsibility, as this leads to inflexible decisions. The theatre management can show trust and confidence by raising the status of the lighting staff. It is an appropriate use of the organizational, technical and artistic abilities of those involved and makes it unnecessary to bring in additional people.

It is possible to create a post of senior lighting technician as part of the management structure. It is also important that the member of the team who runs the show from the booth is sensitive to all levels of the work. He implements decisions and presents technical information in the form necessary for the computer. This position can be structured so that this individual is responsible for all the lighting operations.

Another decision has to be made about shift work or the unpopular double session (working in the afternoon and the evening). If possible, the same group of people should be available in the final rehearsal phase for new productions, which includes the lighting and dress rehearsals. This inevitably means that one cycle of shifts will have to be omitted.

Even though the lighting department's work is artistic as well as technical, it must be integrated into the overall structure of the technical departments. Lighting can only be practised as an art with equipment that works properly and with staff to operate it. It also makes sense to have a chief electrician within the lighting department. Both the artistic and electrical crew should be set up as a so-called service pool within the theatre, thus guaranteeing flexible staff organization and allocation; the work can be sensibly and effectively distributed. Management staff who do not have to be present all the time can supervise the execution of the concept developed by the team. The technical director and the head of the lighting department can assign work to the service pool.

500 Heinrich von Kleist
*Prinz Friedrich von Homburg*
(Prince Friedrich of Homburg)
Director: Dieter Dorn
Set Designer: Jürgen Rose
Münchner Kammerspiele, 1995

Artificial light is a number of things! A candle burning, a desk lamp switched on or spotlights lighting a show in the theatre – this is all artificial light.

The flood of neon signs, brightly lit shop windows and traffic lights affect our subconscious. We react to different colours as we have been taught. Red means danger, and says one thing in the street: stop! Green means that we can carry on as we wish.

And why is yellow the colour in between green and red at a traffic light? Light and colours control our everyday activities. Generally speaking we are not aware of their power. We react to light and to combinations of colours.

Lighting designers use light and colours to convey brightness and darkness as well. Artificial light in the entertainment world is intended to stimulate and appeal to feelings and emotions. Here the different ways in which we perceive colour make a great deal of difference.

Creating light requires that the lighting designer select lanterns and determine colour combinations, brightness and darkness, and not least the way in which the light is to be experienced: slowly or quickly. And so it is exciting to search the standard colour values for the colour location of artificial light sources – on the one hand with Planck's curve, Judd's scale and the x-y-axes – and on the other hand to play with the various levels at which colours are perceived.

But what is the best way to tackle a lighting exercise like this? The technology available, combined with the various experts' abilities to put an idea into practice, produces a mass of expressive variations. And the basis of this is conveying a lighting concept to all the people involved in a production.

The pictorial language available to a lighting designer is as varied as a painter's brushstrokes. A successful lighting design is comparable to the harmony of a piece of music. It is not wrong to talk about the 'sound of the image', because a lighting state triggers considerable sensual stimulation in the observer. Scientists believe that 25% of our energy resources are used when looking at an image, with 80% nerve involvement. It does not matter here

whether an enormous amount of time and equipment have gone into producing the effect, or whether very simple technical devices have been used. It is not the quantity of light sources and the varying lighting states that establish the quality of an image, but rather the right choices determining them. The interaction of light sources when deciding on angles of incidence, light properties and colour filters are the criteria for assessing quality.

The most common form of theatre is the proscenium stage. Here the audience sits facing the stage opening and watches the action through the 'fourth wall'. The stage set or the spatial design make the inner and outer situations in the performance visible. Thus the available elements of set architecture are limited, because they are always subject to these physical constraints from the start. This handicap also applies to lighting design. Here the intended illusion has to be created to do justice to the task at hand. It is difficult to fit an appropriate quality to an empty space; an object has to be lit. If the space is empty, then all that remains are the floor or the outer limitations. Like all solid bodies, the floor has a body colour, i.e. a colour that is painted on to fabric, wood etc. Thus the incident light illuminates this coloured material. Some of the light that strikes it is absorbed by the material and the rest is reflected. If individual structures are placed in such a space, it is easier to fill the size and depth of the space.

Lighting without shadow effects, creating a contrast between light and darkness, has its own charm. In this case the space will seem like a very even, monochrome light installation. Tension can be achieved here by putting together daylight back lighting and front lighting based on adapted incandescent light. It also helps if the space is bordered by something coloured; then it is easy to create a visually interesting effect by using colour filters. Contrast and tension are always achieved by juxtaposing opposites, most intelligibly with colours, best of all with complementary colours, or between light and dark, or simply by the simultaneous use of daylight and incandescent light. At first glance such images look quite

modest, as it is impossible to see the effort that lies behind them. Using very high intensity artificial daylight makes the lighting more lucid. If the lighting is intended to enhance the drama of the piece, then the shadows produced are stronger, which again heightens the contrast beyond our habitual way of looking at things. However, such decisions about light should always be based on what fits the story and the space in which it is to be performed. Essentially an atmosphere of this kind is created with light for the benefit of the stage and the production, unless a light installation is devised as a work of art in its own right.

Of course it is possible to design lighting with daylight alone. This choice would involve considering the nature of the stage, also including the performers' costumes and the kind of statement the production is to make. Considerable technical effort is needed if the lighting plots also involves fades using mechanical dimming devices, but there are no clear guidelines to determine whether this kind of light is suitable for a particular kind of performance or not.

Today, our visual habits are very much affected by television, and it is difficult to break away from this deep-rooted influence. In the theatre it is not necessary for performers or spaces to be visible down to the last detail. Balancing intensity, colour and lighting angles makes it possible to create extremely subtle lighting states that could not be taken in as overall effects in the cinema or on television. People performing in the interplay of light and shade, as well as lighting angles and colour contrasts are exciting to experience and increase our desire to keep watching. People moving around in a bright space are less exciting and suspenseful to watch, but the task of lighting is simpler and more manageable for the designer. Bright spaces do pose problems, however, as mistakes in the general and character lighting are particularly visible here.

If the designer decides to build and light an artificial space, i.e. a space which is not defined by solid material such as thick fabric, wood or sheet metal, but by something transparent, then the lighting designer has particularly rewarding choices to make for his lighting, although they will not be simple. The material defining the space (such as shirting, a cotton fabric) is lit indirectly from behind. It is possible to avoid or remove shadows cast on the walls by performers when using this kind of lighting. This is useful as shadows on the walls cause problems with perspective, if they are not deliberately chosen to make a dramatic statement. The laws of perspective tell us that, to suggest depth, the parts of the set that are furthest upstage should be darker in terms of both colour and light. Thus lighting characters and lighting the space they are in are two different things.

Essentially what we are doing with all these design possibilities is creating architecture with light. Most of the materials used in the theatre for making sets today are different from those used in the past. At present the theatre of illusion is not the first choice for designing stage sets. If this approach is chosen, however, the stage needs less light, and it is possible to work exclusively with incandescent or fluorescent lamps and projection techniques. Fluorescent lamps are particularly useful as they are available in different colour temperatures. It is also easy to change their colour with filters.

Stage lighting has changed considerably in the last few years. This is due not least to the introduction of daylight technology. As sets and acting areas need ever-increasing amounts of light, spotlight manufacturers have had to enlarge their range. Most automated light sources use daylight technology as well, and so do all effects units and large-image projectors. As a long-standing user and advocate of artificial daylight ratings up to 4,000 K and 6,000 K, I have observed that light architects have been slow to start using this kind of light. They combine low voltage lamps with artificial daylight in every conceivable variation, and this gives them almost limitless possibilities for enhancing built architecture.

Fibre optics technology is also becoming more popular, and daylight lamps have a major part to play here as well. The small arc in the lamps and the outstanding colour rendering are responsible for the varied results in this interesting field. There are many things that can be done other than creating starry skies and frantically writhing colour displays. I am very fond of a well assorted range of discharge and solid-

state lamps and try to use this combination wherever possible. This is mainly because the force and colour of discharge lamps have become important components of lighting design in general. It is important to mention in this context that medical science has established that our sense of well-being is considerably enhanced by artificial daylight with a high degree of illuminance (lux). Of course, this is not about looking at a bright image. It is simply that artificial daylight and its spectrum are not just wonderfully suited to lighting design, but also have a biological effect. A whole variety of new technical developments such as scanners, automated spotlights and scrollers are responsible for very special expressive lighting forms: moving light and moving colour. Major events are inconceivable without these new design variants, but they are often very helpful in theatrical lighting design as well, especially for making forcible dramatic statements. Caution is advisable, however, as this kind of light has a particular weight and can easily become taken for granted.

As there are so many different options available it should not be difficult to put these theories into practice. In fact, it is harder to decide which equipment to choose, and whether it suits the intended concepts for the stage set and the lighting. In most situations realistic lighting has to be designed for a stage set, but occasionally one has to work with lighting combined with a stage set in the form of virtual components such as holograms, spatial demarcation elements intended to take laser lighting, and partial or total image projections. This approach often leads to compromises about spatial design that are deleterious to character lighting, and in most situations these projected spatial illusions, or parts of them, permit only very low levels for characters. Incorporating large-scale projections into lighting design also presents similar problems.

The elements of the idea to be implemented, linked with the director's staging ideas and the designer's view of the scene, indicate the direction the lighting designer should take in developing his contribution. This is always a question of aesthetics as well, without any fixed guidelines. The most important thing is to bear in mind the current range of spotlight technology and then assemble the right equipment for the task at hand. Also, technology devised for staging and lighting are not devel-

oped for a single production. In most situations the essence of an idea can often be used again later, with modified application to suit the current set of circumstances.

Designing realistic lighting means inscribing an appropriate atmosphere on the stage with light. Realism of this kind will always derive from lighting appropriate both to the stage and to the characters who appear on it.

This kind of lighting concept is not mere invention, as we see from natural light and shade, and indoor and outdoor situations all around us every day. On stage we have to allow for a careful distinction between general light (in the space) and light on people. If we were to take the word 'realistic' literally, then all the necessary reflections and gradations of light, areas of shadow and nuances of colour perspective would have to be matched to the performers and the stage set and then correspond with changes in the lighting within a particular scene — an undertaking that would be too much for any available lighting technology! Here the film and television industries have an advantage, because any lighting details that need to be corrected can be dealt with precisely, by relighting during the shooting process.

If equivalent precision is needed in stage lighting, it can be achieved only with a great deal of effort and flexibility, whereby important playing areas are made visibly lighter for a certain period suggested by the action. If the playing area changes again, the supporting light is gently faded back to the general intensity and heightened in the place where attention is now focused.

This approach is inevitable if the set evolved according to the optical rules of spatial and colour perspective. A theatre audience always sees the scene in long shot — in other words the whole image — unlike a film shot, where the viewer's attention can be more closely focused.

A theatrical lighting designer can appreciate the often very clever way in which lighting is handled in a good film scene. This kind of approach can be applied to stage lighting step by step, particularly when a lighting design develops from imagination and craftsmanship. Books on photography, pictorial material about painters and advertising material can be very helpful for visual training of this kind.

## CONTRAST IS EFFECTIVE

Besides the details that are particular to each production, the contrast between colours and shapes creates the dynamic tension that enables us to make lighting an integral part of stage design. The distinction between daylight and artificial light and the effect of colour filters are the tools of the lighting expert's trade. The form of the light should not be random but planned. If a particular form and quality are chosen for the light when we have determined the principal direction from which it will come, this light can have a quite different colour value from the ambient lighting. Light forms always create shadows, and the ambient light of a shadow and the shadow itself can be nuanced in a quite different way from the original colour. The same knowledge that makes it possible to create a particularly careful and inspired lighting design can also be used to create additional, exciting lighting effects, as the interplay between light and shade does not need homogeneous transitions but can have hard edges.

If even, diffuse lighting is wanted, however, the variations in light forms

501  Bernard-Marie Koltès
*Roberto Zucco*
Director: Christian Stückl
Set Designer: Rufus Didwiszus
Münchner Kammerspiele, 1995

are not as diverse and striking. With a concept like this it is not possible to have clear lighting demarcations within a space. A contrast between inside and outside is possible if the two different light sources are visually separate from the stage set.

Colour temperature must always be considered when deciding on light forms. Temperatures should be determined as early as possible, as they affect the overall impression made by the choice of colour filters for incandescent lamps, the materials used for the set and costumes, and the make-up. An early decision made about the quality of the light makes selecting these light sources easy, using our knowledge of the many different planes on which colours are perceived.

## THE PROBLEM OF COLOURS

I find that working with light is a very sensitive and personal matter, though lighting designers often have to suppress such feelings and cannot allow them to influence a production. Nevertheless we ought to address this subject again, because light is not simply white as a medium, but offers all the colours of the spectrum.

VITTORIO STORARO, one of the most famous cameramen in the world, is known for making particular use of colour as an expressive device in his im-

ages. Like anyone who creates images he has developed his own philosophy of the meaning of colours and ascribes the following meanings to them:

| | |
|---|---|
| Black: | the subconscious |
| Red: | the colour of blood |
| Orange: | the colour of emotion |
| Yellow: | the consciousness of human life |
| Green: | knowledge, the cognitive process |
| Blue: | maximum efficiency, intelligence |
| Indigo: | physical strength |
| Violet: | the final stage of human intelligence |
| White: | balance, because all colours are united within it |

The laws of colour are discussed extensively in the chapter 'Handling Light and Colour'. FRANCIS FORD COPPOLA explains that theatre lighting influences film. He used to work in the theatre and used his experience there to persuade Storaro to use a theatrical lighting console in a film they were both working on so that they could play with light. The results of this kind of creative lighting design are particularly attractive in films as well, and reinforce the critical importance of light and colour, and in the case of colour not just from the point of view of chromaticity, but

also in terms of intensity and the speed at which lighting states follow each other.

Also, colour associations should be considered Which colour is loud? Should forms and colours be associated? Do colours correspond with sounds in music? Sergei Prokofiev's musical fairy-tale *Peter and the Wolf* is a good example here. Prokofiev allots an instrument to each of the protagonists – Peter and the animals. But it would also be conceivable to give Peter and the animals colours. When allocating colours to instruments, people and animals, the designer must bear in mind the significance of the colours he chooses. If possible, colours should be allocated

proud animal, for example the majestic flight of a condor or a lumbering bear. A little bird would be given a light, pastel blue and the sound of a flute.

The colour blue shading towards white suggests lightness, airiness, freshness, a relaxed dynamic and fresh starts. As musical instruments, I would give this colour a violin, a flute or a clarinet. This kind of pictorial language can be subject to rigorous analysis by choosing colours in terms of their polarity, looking at complementary colours in particular.

Many factors help to decide whether this kind of colour composition can be incorporated into a sequence of actions at all. But if there is an opportunity to

stage lighting. Creating light does not presuppose light creations. On the contrary, this should be seen as a formula, as the aim of our work. Here it should be particularly clear to the lighting expert that the success of his work depends on designing a production without technical problems, in other words, on his skills as a craftsman, his ability to work methodically and implement his knowledge and experience.

Imagination must be the guiding force for everyone involved in a production. It must inspire us and seduce us to examine our technical and artistic potential. For the lighting designer, this means being able to realize a practicable and lively lighting design.

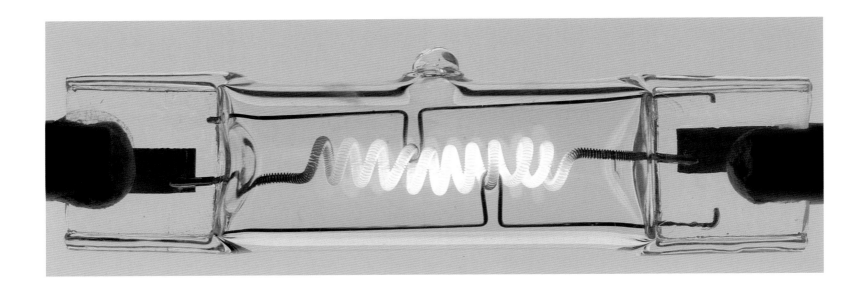

with reference to all planes of perception. This, however, is a very personal choice.

I feel that the colour blue, for example, spans an enormous breadth of meaning. A heavy blue, mixed with red, but not yet swinging towards violet, is contemplative and melancholic. If I were looking for an appropriate instrument for this feeling, I would choose the spacious sound of a church organ, a double bass or a viola. I would envisage the motion of a large, heavy,

use at least some such consideration in a production, the result will be most rewarding for everyone involved.

Any work in the field of the performing arts, especially in the theatre, is always part of an overall effort by all those involved. Thus a lighting design can only be as good as the ultimate effect of the work as a whole. To return to the title of this chapter, 'Creating Light – Light Creations', we should not fall prey to the erroneous belief that this is necessarily a logical sequence for

502 Low voltage tungsten-halogen double ended lamp with quartz bulb and axial coil

# THE NATURE OF LIGHT IN THE THEATRE

by Manfred Wagner

Light is an element of life – and it has been an element of the theatre since 1800 at the latest, when separating the stage from the auditorium increasingly made the fictitious theatrical events stand out from the reality of the audience's world. In fact, this is further evidence of the parallels between art and life, both open systems that can be experienced, associated thematically, but formally subject to other laws and thus remaining divergent in terms of contact with each other.

Theatre light is as virtual as the theatre itself. It never achieves natural quality, indeed is not trying to do that, and thus it creates the necessary distance between itself and nature. Theatre lighting insists that thinking and seeing are connected. It does not allow anyone to get away unless they shut their eyes, which are otherwise entirely at the mercy of what is happening. In other words, there is very little possibility of switching off and thinking about something else. Theatre lighting shows the virtual stage and the people acting on it from a different point of view.

This perceived world is bounded by the curtain as a real symbol of concealment, but the stage is sometimes left open, which almost always produces something of a working atmosphere. Theatre lighting shows colours, spaces, shadows, objects, people and images, in short, the compressed world of the theatre in contrast with the real world, even in the spectators' area, which is physically the same size. In the course of various interpretative approaches chosen according to the production concerned, it recapitulates the philosophical insights into and definitions of light, almost biogenetically. Here, too, as Plato suggested, the sun is the brightest source of light, the messenger of reason, and shadows are the experimental stations of human futility. Here, too, light is sometimes the material quality of a material substance, a kind of distant echo of physical nature, of the kind that thought cannot achieve. Here, too, the Enlightenment offers its *lumen naturale* as the internal, spiritual light of life, which Goethe distinguished as light and suffering in his description of colours.

Theatre-goers experience light as a source or demonstrator of cognition, regardless of whether it does so as a physical indicator or as a metaphysical transformation. And the audience almost always makes the leap with it, transferring light into the realms of optics, or into the into the new discipline that Alexander Gottlieb Baumgarten called aesthetics. Certainly light was demystified when optics became scientific. This happened often enough in the theatre as well, but the theatre did remain the place that carried the symbolic quality of light into the present and can thus be seen as the initial symbol for our world of consumer experience. Sophisticated window-dressing, flickering discos, dramatic silhouettes and experiences that constantly increase in technical calibre while their content is structured ever more simply are ultimately offshoots of this symbolic tradition and are very often created by the theatre's light and space professionals and their pupils.

Lighting technology and all its ever-increasing possibilities have gained in their influence of experience. Again the parallel is made between life (above all urban life) and the world of theatre as open systems. This does not just change the emphasis of what we see, which is increasingly neglected and certainly directed, but also the whole range of perceptions, which are fed on everyday habits and are able to find alternatives only in a change of location.

Theatrical lighting design in the last 200 years has reached a position that places its significance as an interpretative force on a par with that of direction and stage design. A visible expression of this is the fact that the lighting designer is named as a member of the production team and that reviews pay more attention to his work. Neglecting light as a factor and sloppy lighting in repertory theatres have become genuine disruptive factors, like missed lines or cues used to be, or on-stage doors that did not open and shut properly.

It would seem that light has acquired a similar status to managing people and stage design. This status has possibly become less visible in complex stage design in the last twenty years, as stage sets have acquired autonomy as installation-like elements in their own right, making their mark on the whole thrust of the production and directing the audience's attention to interpreting the stage elements and how what the stage provides and what happens on it fits together. But even Gustav Mahler's important stage designer Alfred Roller knew that stage design and light form an indispensable unit. He intervened in the direction to a much greater extent than ever before, but refused to let his own stage designs be exhibited, saying simply that they needed their theatre lighting. Music critics such as Max Graf recognized this phenomenon in their reviews of the famous new production of *Tristan and Isolde* that was premiered on 21 February 1903: 'The nervous colour-Romanticism of the Modern movement now dominates Alfred Roller's new sets for *Tristan*. Light and air make music along with Wagner's orchestra; the basic chords in each act become a glowing light.'

And we can see that this attitude was not a passing phase from an explicit remark made in 1927 by a critic reviewing Erich Wolfgang Korngold's now forgotten opera *Das Wunder der Heliane*: 'In this opera, for example, there are no less than 75 different sets of lighting, it is the opera with the most lighting ever performed in the Opernring.'

This early equation of light and stage, which is probably the principal achievement of the underestimated designer and theatrical reformer Alfred Roller, has so far not affected direction as a factor. But it seems that here, too, there is increasing commitment to highly specialized lighting designers.

There could be several explanations for this: Consumers' awareness of what they see has changed and they have possibly become more demanding, increasingly 'cheaper' stage sets have gained acceptance, and there is a call for more help in interpreting directorial intentions. It is precisely the fashionable lack of literary commitment, which increasingly links original texts by major writers with trivial texts by literary managers, directors or even improvising actors, that needs to be more strongly accented as a corrective to this vagary, and there is no doubt that light can indicate significance here.

This would mean – even though there is a different degree of freedom from production to production – that working with light has to be seen as a formal factor on the same level as personnel management and stage design, so that the content of a production depends on the product of theme (= text) x form (= direction, design, light). Thus, this content could not consist, as is often wrongly asserted by theatre critics, of the exclusion or exclusive dominance of the individual constituents, but would require equal input from each constitutive element to produce a successful performance.

503  William Shakespeare
*Troilus and Cressida*
Director: Dieter Dorn
Set Designer: Jürgen Rose
Münchner Kammerspiele, 1986

For light, this means in particular: material care in terms of the character of the image, emphasizing significant elements, and often changing material aspects to the point of parallels with film (to the extent that this is dramatically necessary). Ultimately, light defines spaces, makes them larger and smaller, lowers and raises them, creates illusions but also real conditions in a virtual world. Light is the advocate of the elements of water, sky, fire and earth, but also of those psychological moods that have an elemental effect on events. This spiritual transformation of psychological states into matter, regardless of whether it is oriented towards individuals or the masses, must be effective in terms of communication, and use all the special qualities of what is specific and unique on the stage as a bridge to everything that is specific and unique in the audience. This dichotomy probably explains why models attempted by the artists of the ecstatic theatre failed to appeal to audiences and therefore remained pictorial essays rather than theatrical experiments.

Theatre light today needs reflection of two quite different constants: historical painting as a series of test stations for handling light, of a kind that the 20th century no longer provides, and precise observation of the everyday qualities that light uses to shape the trivial. Theatre must still tell stories about people, in other words offer specific elements of what is special, yet it must also set itself apart from the banality which is linked in the world of consumerism with the exclusive incentive to buy – partly by using theatrical devices. Added to this is a quite different two-dimensional visual experience, which shines light from the inside outwards as does television, and, as in film, projects the illusion of three dimensions on to flat two-dimensionality.

Theatre can still survive: because most of the time it works with the words of poets, puts real people in three-dimensional situations and focuses concentration in a way that draws its meaning from light. If the formal constituents are no longer correct, or themes are frivolously trivialized, we can be fairly confident that the content will disappear as a differentiation of the outer world around us – perhaps not for everyone, but for many who are still fascinated by the unique interplay of direction, set design, costumes, music, text and light. Neglecting one of these factors means putting the system at risk.

Dr. Manfred Wagner teaches cultural history and the history of the humanities at the University of Applied Art in Vienna

There are two points that I would like to mention in summary:

First, just as all light needs a surface and object if it is to be perceived and at the same time make reality perceptible, so lighting design needs the stage, the performers, the concept behind the production, the lighting crew with their spotlights – in short, the concerted effort of the entire company. Lighting design, even if it is described in all its nuances and variants in this book, should not be seen in isolation or treated as an end in itself. Light alone cannot fill an evening. But lighting design is an essential, independent element among all the factors involved in a stage performance.

The second point is about technical and artistic developments. It is as true now as it has ever been that the most recent technical innovations and the artistic project at hand are seen as the most efficient and most important. But we must not forget, particularly with reference to the rapidity of technical developments, that in the best case we are producing a summary of a particular stage of development and insight. This also applies to the present book, and we shall be only too pleased to see the results of the work described here overtaken by new material based on future innovations.

The quality of the technical facilities available is not always the decisive factor in terms of success. Success can always be achieved if a task is approached ambitiously by every individual involved, even if only a fraction of the enormous range of lanterns and accessories on the market is available for a particular production.

**THANKS**

to all the friends,
colleagues,
companies
and institutions
who have contributed
to the success
of this publication,
and especially to
Dr. Wolf-Dieter Bobst
and Wilhelm Sterff

504 *Reigen*
Théâtre de la Monnaie
Brussels, 1993

**... and off you go!**

**Aberration** A defect in the ideal image caused by imperfections in the optical system.

**Absorption** A body colour reflects its own colour and absorbs the rest of the light shining on it. Colour filters are permeable to the body colour but absorb other colours.

**Achromatic colours** Colours without chromatic value: black, grey and white.

**Additive colour mixing** Mixing different coloured light from at least two sources (see also p. 32).

**Aircraft landing light** → PAR-64 lamp with an aperture of 2°, used on airfields and also for stage effects.

**Analogue dimmer** Lighting control device in which the voltage setting (and thus the brightness of the lamp) is arrived at by an analogue value (= a value that can be anywhere on a scale between zero and a maximum). A range between 0 and 10 V is usually used for this purpose.

**Anode** Positive → *electrode* in a → *discharge lamp* running on direct current. The anode has a smaller surface area than the → *cathode*.

**ANSI** Abbreviation for the American National Standards Institute.

**Aperture angle** The angle at which light is emitted from a spotlight or lens (see also pp. 69, 106ff.).

**Aplanatic lens** Lens without chromatic deviation or aperture errors.

**Apostilb** A unit of → *luminance* for bodies that do not emit light themselves.

**Arc discharge** Discharge between two → *electrodes*.

**Arc rest** Name for a rest period in an arc discharge in → *discharge lamps* (spark gap), e.g. HMI, MSR, CSI and → *xenon lamps*.

**Arcing** Undesirable electrical discharge through the air in an electrical device. It is caused by → *excess voltage* or a fault in the device. The device or its surroundings can be damaged or destroyed according to the type of arcing (fire danger). In contrast with this, a fault inside a component of the device takes place through insulation. The causes and effects, however, are the same.

**Argon** Inert gas used to fill bulbs. Also used as a 'starter gas' in most → *metal halide lamps*.

**ARRI-SUN** Very powerful spotlight series with a daylight lamp in a → *parabolic reflector* with high → *luminance*. They can be focused by using lens attachments, 575 to 12,000 W (see also p. 108).

**Aspherical reflector** Used in the theatre particularly in fluted, → *parabolic* and → *ellipsoidal reflectors* (see also pp. 67ff.).

**Back lighting** See pp. 173, 177.

**Back projection** Process in which a slide or → *gobo* is projected from behind a transparent surface, usually from the back of the stage in the theatre.

**Background light** See p. 177.

**Ballast** Many electrical devices (e.g. → *fluorescent lamps*, → *HMI* discharge lamps) have certain characteristics that make it impossible to connect them directly to the mains or other source (e.g. battery). A ballast is used in such cases to adapt the device to the supply source.

**Balloon light** Artificial and daylight sources built into a balloon. The balloons measure from 1.5 to 5 m and are filled with helium. They can be moored up to 50 m above a site, tethered on cables. The balloon emits light on all sides and has a reflector at the top. It is also possible to have lettering on the

envelope, or to choose a special colour. At present the power ranges from 1,000 to 32,000 W, in incandescent and → *daylight* forms.

**Barn-doors** Two or four folding metal shutters mounted on a frame and fitted to a Fresnel or plano-convex spotlight via an accessory slot at the front of the lantern.

**Basic technical lighting terms**
→ *Luminous flux*: lumen/symbol: φ
→ *Luminous intensity*: candela/symbol: I
→ *Illuminance*: lux/symbol: E
→ *Luminance*: cd/m²
→ *Luminous efficiency*: lm/W

**Biconcave** Form of optical lens (negative lens → *concave*), with two surfaces curving inwards (see also p. 69)

**Biconvex** Form of optical lens (positive lens → *convex*), with two surfaces curving outwards (see also p. 69).

**Biplane** → *Coil* arrangement in a projector lamp. The coils are slightly displaced laterally, and fixed on two planes one behind the other. This achieves greater → *luminance*. These projector lamps are less sensitive to vibration than → *monoplane* projector lamps. Two-pin caps: e.g. G 38/GX 9.5 (see also p. 78).

**Black-wrap** Black aluminium foil, usually used to cut out → *spill*.

**Blackout shutter** Mechanical device to create a complete blackout in an iris diaphragm in → *profile spots* and follow spots. As an iris diaphragm often does not close completely, the final blackout is achieved with a metal disc that closes over the centre of the iris.

**Booster** Enhances signals for → *DMX 512* circuits, for example. Also used for the electrical isolation of circuit segments.

**Border lighting** See p. 173.

**Borosilicate glass** This type of glass, also used for cooking utensils, is highly resistant to chemicals and extreme temperature differences. It is used for → *reflectors* and front covers in → *PAR lamps*. The glass has very low coefficients of expansion and is therefore also used for flashbulbs.

**Brilliance** The luminous quality of a colour, which depends on the surface qualities of the object.

**Cable caps** Lampholder in which the mechanical holder is separate from the electrical connection (see also p. 95).

**Cable shoe** Copper section constructed to take a cable on one side and either a fixing hole or a clamping point on the other.

**CAD program** Computer Assisted Design program – for preparing drawings, lighting plans, mechanical and architectural structures. It requires a high resolution graphics monitor, graphic input device such as a mouse or touch-pad and a suitably powerful computer.

**Camera obscura** Lat.: dark chamber. Primitive form of the photographic camera. A pinhole device, in which an image of the object in front of the camera is reproduced upside down and reduced in size. Aristotle (384 to 322 BC) was the first to observe this phenomenon. First publication 1544 (see also p. 135).

**Candela** Unit of → *luminous intensity*, symbol: cd (see also p. 75).

**Cap cement** Special cement used to make an airtight connection between the lamp cap and the lamp glass. The cement has to be of particularly high quality because of the different coefficients of expansion in these two materials.

**Cap temperature** The cap should not be used to regulate the temperature of a lamp. The cap will acquire a bluish coloration if overheated. Overheating of the cap is transmitted to the → *coil* or the → *electrodes*, which can result in premature failure of the light source.

**Carbon arc** Light arc between two carbon rods.

**Carbon arc spotlight** These spotlights, which are operated with carbon rods, were used largely in the film industry. → *Metallogen lamps* replaced them on the market.

**Carbon filament lamp** → *Incandescent lamp* with clear glass in which the → *coil* is a compressed carbon filament that burns in a vacuum. The carbon filament lamp was developed by Thomas Alva Edison in 1879 and used as an artificial light source until 1905. The light emitted has a higher proportion of red than light from a → *tungsten-halogen* lamp.

**Cathode** Negative → *electrode* in a → *discharge lamp* powered by direct current. The surface of the cathode is larger than that of the → *anode*.

**Cat's eye** Shutter used in stage projections with → *discharge lamps*. Intensity is changed by closing the shutter.

**Chaser** Moving light effect in which individual circuits or lighting states run automatically in a cyclical or random sequence. The speed of the sequence can usually be regulated or can be synchronized with an external musical signal.

**Chimera** Conical spotlight attachment with diffuser.

**Chromatic aberration** Error in optical lenses in the form of coloured edges.

**Chromatic type** Chromatic type determines the relationship of a saturated colour to black and white.

**CIE** Abbreviation for Commission Internationale de l'Eclairage (International Lighting Commission).

**CIE system** System set up by the Commission Internationale de l'Eclairage to explain all colour phenomena.

**Coil** Coiled wire filament in → *incandescent lamps*. There are → *monoplane* and → *biplane* coils for lamps in spotlight technology. Monoplane coils lie on one plane, biplane coils on two, with the second plane displaced in terms of the other by the thickness of the material (see also pp. 76, 78, 94).

**Cold colours** Blue with all the intermediate shades to violet.

**Cold reflector** A reflector layer that is applied directly to a reflector or to a spherical reflector behind the lamp. These allow → *infra-red radiation* to pass and reflect only the light with shorter wavelengths. Such coating can reduce the heat load in the reflected light by up to 75%.

**Colour** Physical definition: light with wavelengths in the visible field between approx. 400 to 700 nm (see also pp. 26ff.).

**Colour cast** Change of a colour as a result of inadequate colour reproduction. This is particularly obvious in media such as television or film.

**Colour co-ordinates** Tint, saturation, intensity.

**Colour degree** Identifies the extent of colour. The higher it is, the more intense the colour.

**Colour errors in lenses** Refraction of light by lenses causes colour errors, i.e. long-wave blue light is more strongly refracted than short-wave red. The higher the quality of a lens or optical system, the less significant are these colour errors.

**Colour field**  Definition of colours according to hue, saturation and brightness (see also p. 28).

**Colour filter**  Gel or glass sheet that changes the colour of the original light. The gel or glass absorbs the light that does not pass through; → *dichroic filters* allow certain colours to pass and reflect the rest according to the coating.

**Colour locus**  The colour locus of a light source relates to Planck's curve and Judd's scale and to the x and y co-ordinates (see also pp. 28, 77).

**Colour mixing**  When mixing light of different colours a distinction is made between → *additive*, → *subtractive* and → *integrated* colour mixing.

**Colour perspective**  Influence of colours in relation to the effect of depth in an image. Dark and → *cold* colours determine depth, light and → *warm* colours determine the foreground.

**Colour rendering**  Colour rendering always relates to the kind of light in which a colour is assessed. All materials have a body colour, their own coloration. For example, a blue material is seen as blue because the blue body colour reflects only the blue elements of the light from the source used. Differently coloured rays are absorbed by the blue material.

**Colour rendering index**  A colour's rendering qualities are determined by a colour rendering index ($R_a$; see also p. 29).

**Colour scroller**  A colour-changing device that carries the colours on rolls. They are stuck together then spooled like a roll of film. A stuck-on marker indicates the beginning and end of the colour to a photoelectric beam (see also pp. 116ff.).

**Colour sequence**  Saturation sequence of a colour from a chosen starting value towards a different colour or towards black and white.

**Colour spectrum**  All the colours that are visible (see also p. 25).

**Colour temperature**  is measured in → *Kelvin*. To determine the colour temperature of a light source, the colour of the light it is emitting is compared with light coming from a matcher device. The matcher absorbs any alien radiation that hits it and is called a 'black body' or 'full radiator'. It is heated until it is the same colour as the light source.

**Colour wheel**  Wheel with circular apertures of different colours that is placed in front of a spotlight or put in the colour magazine. Forerunner of the → *colour scroller*.

**Complementary colours**  Pairs of colours that give black or white when mixed (see also pp. 34, 39).

**Concave**  A lens whose surfaces curve inwards.

**Condenser**  Lens combination in a slide projector.

**Constant colour temperature**  Incandescent and arc lamps are sold with a starting colour temperature. The colour temperature decreases as the lamp gets older, in the case of → *Metallogen lamps* by approx. 1 K (→ *Kelvin*) per hour.

**Conversion filter**  Gel that adapts artificial daylight to incandescent light or incandescent light to artificial daylight. Conversion filters are also available as → *dichroic*, absorption-free filters. These hardly heat up at all as they reflect the unwanted rays.

**Converter**
– Optics: negative lens element in an objective
– Electrical engineering: converts currents and voltages.

**Convex**  A lens whose surfaces curve outwards.

**Cord dimmer**  Slider control (→ *dimmer*), built into a flexible cable.

**Cyclorama**  Projection screen most usually found in large opera houses. It extends from the stage floor to the flies and runs on a rail system in a semicircle around the whole of the rear stage. It can be rolled up for storage and is parked behind a proscenium tower. It is particularly interesting when used with large-format slides.

**Daylight**  In the theatre, artificial light that is similar to natural light at a level of 6,000 K (→ *Kelvin*).

**Daylight lamp**  Discharge source with a colour temperature of over 5,000 K (→ *Kelvin*).

**Dichroic filters**  have an optical coating that admits only a certain colour and reflects the other (see also p. 101).

**Diffusion filter**  Tulle fabric placed in front of a light source to diffuse the light, available in half and quarter thicknesses. It is used in the theatre in the form of a frost filter, also in various thicknesses. The filter that is most frequently used is the → *scrim diffuser*, which hardly affects the consistency of the light.

**Digital dimmer**  Lighting control device in which the ignition point of the lantern is calculated by a digital system (dimmer processor). There are usually various special functions available, such as characteristic curve switching for various lamp types or switching through the full sinusoidal voltage at a given control threshold. The signal can be broken down into a maximum of 12 bits, which means 4,096 steps between 0 and 100%. Control is usually digital as well, e.g. using → *DMX 512* or → *Ethernet*.

**Dimmer**  Device for altering the brightness of electrical light sources. A distinction is made between analogue and → *digital dimmers,* and also between thyristor, → *Triac* and transistor dimmers, depending on the nature of the lamp.

**Dimmer curve**  As the brightness of the customary light sources does not increase on a linear basis with the supply voltage, a correction is necessary to maintain linear control (i.e. the brightness of the lamp increases evenly with the increase in control voltage). This correction curve is known as the dimmer curve. For light sources that cannot be adjusted or adjusted only with difficulty (e.g. → *HMI* lamps) the dimmer is used full on or not at all.

**Direct light**  See p. 173.

**Discharge lamp**  Light is produced by a spark between two → *electrodes;* e.g. → *HMI®*, MSR®, → *xenon, fluorescent* and → *neon* lamps (see also p. 79).

**DMX 512**  (DMX = Digital Multiplexing) → *USITT* internationally recognized standard for digital transmission of signals to dimmers and control devices, based on standard EIA RS-485. Up to 512 dimmer commands are transmitted instantaneously via a shielded, twin-core cable. The resolution per circuit is 8 bits, which means that 256 brightness levels are possible. DMX 512 is also the standard for controlling → *colour scrollers* and → *moving lights*, where the signals are used to control spotlight positions, colours etc. The precise protocol that has been in general use since 1990 is DMX 512/1990. An extension of this is in preparation, and will be called DMX-512/2000 (see also p. 125).

**DNA**  Abbreviation for Digital Network Architecture – a kind of hierarchical network architecture proposed by Digital Equipment (DEC) for computer systems based on existing standards.

**Dots + Fingers**  Set for shadow games with different shapes and coverings.

**Double ended connection**  Fitting system for → *incandescent* or arc lamps in which the mechanical support and the power supply are spatially separated, e.g. for tungsten-halogen tubes or → *discharge lamps* with a high power requirement (see also p. 94f.).

**Efficiency**  The ratio of useful power to input power. If one measures the input into an electrical device and the useful output power (in the case of a lamp the input power and the light produced), one discovers that the useful output is almost always considerably less than the input power. Efficiency fluctuates between 0 and 1, and is often expressed as a percentage.

**Electrical potential**  Difference in electrical tension between two points in space.

**Electrode**  Electrically conductive part, usually made of metal, which transfers electric current into another conductive medium. In direct current lamps the positive electrode is known as the anode, and the negative electrode as the cathode. In alternating current lamps, such as HMI lamps, the electrodes are the same thickness.

**Electroluminescence**  Light created by an electrical discharge (→ *Luminescence*).

**Elementary colours/ground colours**  Key colours for the appropriate specialist field.
– PRIMARY COLOURS: Colours perceived by the cones of the eye: Violet blue – Green – Orange red
– ADDITIVE ELEMENTARY COLOURS: Red – Green – Blue
– SUBTRACTIVE ELEMENTARY COLOURS: Cyan – Magenta – Yellow

**Ellipsoidal reflector spot**  Name for a → *profile spot*. The beam is carried to the second focal point by an ellipsoidal aluminium reflector.

**Emitter**  The part of a transistor that functions as the electron source.

**Ethernet**  Widely available local network, originally developed by Xerox in 1976 to link mini-computers in the Palo Alto Research Center and based on the American IEEE 802.3 standard for collision networks. Ethernet uses bus topology and an access system that allows simultaneous access to several computers with the aid of carrier signals. Network nodes are linked by coaxial cables, twisted pair wires or glass fibres. The original Ethernet standard support basis-band transmission was at a speed of 10 megabytes (10 million bytes) per second. In the expanded Fast-Ethernet the rate is even 100 megabytes per second. Ethernet is used by most manufacturers for communication between lighting and partially also to attach dimmer systems and peripheral devices.

**Excess voltage**  Voltage that exceeds the prescribed working voltage of a device for a short or long period. The normal functioning of the device can be impaired or it can even be destroyed according to the extent, nature and duration of the excess voltage.

**Excess voltage protection**  Fine protection for power points, medium protection for subsections, coarse protection for main sections.

**Fibre optics**  Fibre optic devices are optical systems for transmitting light, images and electronic signals in news technology. An optical fibre is a thin, pliable thread of fragile optical glass with a very small diameter, sheathed in protective material. Light conveyed in this way makes it possible to move 'cold light'. Small lenses to regulate the light are placed at the end of the fibre. Central light sources are used for multiple systems. In such cases the optical fibres come together close to the light source. A distinction is made between end and side light (see also pp. 117 ff.).

**Flashbulb**  Flash discharges from flashlamps last between 0.5 and 2 ms. There are over 50 different types of lamp. A quartz or Pyrex glass tube with → *tungsten* → *electrodes* is ionized at 50 to 100,000 V by a priming wire. Flashbulbs are available up to 5,000 W.

**Flex-Fill**  Flexible, round, folding reflector or diffuser in white, gold or silver.

**Flickering**  Flickering can occur in an electric arc discharge using alternating current as a result of supply frequency. The lamp ignites and goes out 100 to 120 times per second. This effect is scarcely perceptible to the human eye, but very disturbing in association with film or video shots. Electronic ballasts can be used to minimize this problem.

**Flood**  Simplest version of a spotlight, usually a fluted reflector combined with a → *tungsten-halogen lamp*.

**Fluorescence**  Light phenomenon named after the mineral fluorite, which can be observed in various materials according to incident light. As in the case of → *phosphorescence*, crystal phosphors carry the radiation. The luminous coating, when irradiated with → *ultraviolet* light, emits low intensity coloured light corresponding to the consistency of the crystal phosphors. If there is no such radiation, the materials will not glow.

**Fluorescent lamp**  → *Mercury discharge lamp, low pressure*.

**Focal length**  The distance from a refracting or reflecting medium to the → *focal point* (see also p. 67).

**Focal length, change of**  A → *profile spot* has a lens with an angle of aperture appropriate to the arrangement of lenses (long or short focal length). The angle of aperture can be altered by changing the objective. A zoom system is more convenient and versatile, as it means that focal lengths can be changed continuously within a set of given parameters.

**Focal point**  Point on the optical axis where incident beams parallel to the optical axis intersect after refraction or reflection (see also p. 67).

**Focusing**  Setting lanterns for a rig. The process includes setting the direction of the light and the size, shape, focus and colour of the light emitted.

**Foil seal**  → *Molybdenum bands* cemented into an arc lamp cap. They make an electrical connection between the cap and the electrodes.

**Footlights**  Lights positioned at the front of the stage, usually a row of → *incandescent lamps*, → *reflector lamps* or → *fluorescent lamps*, often using 3 or 4 colours (see also p. 165).

**Fresnel lens**  Glass or plastic lens named after the French engineer and physicist Augustin Jean Fresnel, consisting of a large number of steps giving a corrugated effect, each one with a → *concave* surface of the same curvature as a normally shaped → *convex* lens.

**Fresnel spot**  Spotlight with a → *Fresnel lens*. The angle of the beam produced is changed by moving the light source closer to or away from the lens. The light emitted is directed and soft-edged (see also p. 69).

**Gas discharge lamp**  → *Discharge lamp*.

**Glass colour filters**  Coloured glass. Glass filters close to hot light sources are cut into strips and fused into a unit. Glass filters can be placed closer to a light source than plastic filters as they can survive higher temperatures.

**Glass fibre**  General term for glass in fibre form with diameters between 0.1 mm and a few thousandths of a mm. A distinction is made between insulating glass fibres and textile glass fibres.

– INSULATING GLASS FIBRES: are used to insulate against heat, cold and sound. The individual fibres are matted together in manufacture.

– TEXTILE GLASS FIBRES: melted glass fibres, usually with a circular cross-section, made into a fabric and used for heat insulation. In lighting this fabric is used to block spilled light. Non-flammable glass fibre fabrics are also used in stage design for decorative purposes.

– OPTICAL GLASS FIBRES: glass fibres of thickness of 5 to 200 μm – usually 50 μm for lighting – which are bundled to transmit light (see also p. 118).

**Gobo**  Disc made of heat-proof thin sheet metal or thick aluminium foil inserted into the projection slot of a → *profile spot* for negative projection. Light can be emitted in any shape. Colour gobos are used in scanners or → *moving lights*.

**Gobo arm**  Extension arm with two points for fixing masking material or metal shutters.

**Gobo head**  Multifunctional coupler to hold support extensions or negative projections.

**Grey glass**  Glass filter for looking at a bright light source.

**Half angle**  Distribution of light intensity in a projection system or a lamp (see also p. 186).

**Halogens**  General term for the elements fluorine, chlorine, bromine, iodine and astatine. Highly reactive non-metals that combine with metals to form salts (halides).

**Heat radiation**  Light is energy and releases heat, outside the visible field also by longwave → *infra-red radiation*.

**High pressure lamps**  Small volume lamps with short discharge distances and high → *luminance*, e.g. → *Metallogen lamps* and → *xenon lamps*.

**High pressure sodium vapour lamps**  These produce a broader colour spectrum than → *low pressure sodium vapour lamps* (see also p. 84).

**High voltage**  Voltage above 1,000 V.

**High voltage fluorescent tubes**  → *Neon tubes*.

**HMI® lamp**  Name of a metal halide lamp made by OSRAM (see also p. 86).

**Holography**  Process using laser light to create a three-dimensional image, a hologram. The image is created on a glass or plastic plate coated with light-sensitive emulsion. A mirror system deflects the laser beam in two different directions. The object beam is directed at the object to be depicted and is reflected from there to the coated plate; the reference beam is aimed directly at the plate. The interference pattern of these two beams creates the hologram. The exposed plate is developed similarly to a photograph. A light source is needed to make a hologram visible, e.g. incandescent light that illuminates the hologram at the same angle at which the reference beam hit the plate when the exposure was made.

**Hot ignition**  Reignition of a → *discharge lamp* that can be switched off after it has warmed up and then switched on again while still hot. The worst period for the arc is after 10 to 90 seconds. Unfortunately the lamps do not always reignite. The ignition voltage can be up to ten times the running voltage.

**HTP / LTP circuits**

– HTP (Highest Takes Precedence). This principle is usually used in dimmer system control. If the lighting consists of several cross-fade systems, submaster groups, effects etc., the highest total value is established for each circuit.

– LTP (Latest Takes Precedence). This principle is usually used for controlling colour changers and → *moving lights*.

**Hub**  Active star distributor for bidirectional signals, e.g. → *Ethernet* or RS-485 (see also pp. 147 f.), often called a repeater. The attached supply segments are independent of each other electrically, so that a short circuit in one segment, for example, does not prevent the other segments from communicating with each other. The hub is often used to co-ordinate various transfer media such as fibre optics and coaxial cables.

**Ignition devices**  Some electrical devices such as → *fluorescent lamps* and → *HMI* discharge lamps do not react to normal mains current. They can only be fired by creating a short-term ignition state. Fluorescent lamps, for example have starters, and HMI discharge lamps use a high voltage pulse.

**Ignition voltage**  Some electrical devices such as *HMI* discharge lamps need a voltage considerably higher than that provided by the mains in order to ignite. The voltage needed for them to function is called the ignition voltage. This is usually provided by a special → *ignition device*.

**Illuminance**  The illumination of a given area at a given level, measured in lux (lx). 1 lux is 1 lumen per m² (see also p. 75).

**Incandescent lamp**  Light source with a → *tungsten* filament (see also pp. 75 ff.).

**Indirect light**  See p. 173.

**Infra-red radiation**  Invisible radiation with a wavelength over 780 nm. Subdivisions:
– IR-A = 780 nm – 1.4 μm with 31.2% in daylight
– IR-B = 1,4 – 3 μm with 12.7% in daylight
– IR-C = 3 μm – 1 mm without daylight

**Integrated colour mixing**  Mixture of painted colours using all 8 elementary colours (see also p. 34).

**Kelvin**  Unit of light temperature. 0 K = −273°C, 0°C = 273 K.

**Lamp**  → *Incandescent lamp*. In lamps for general use the circular filament is suspended in the bulb. In a projector lamp the burner system is arranged in a filament complex to ensure that a precisely defined starting point of focus is available, in combination with an optical system.

**Lamp glass**  The key role of glass in an electric lamp is to form a transparent casing for the light source (e.g. → *tungsten* coil) that is also impermeable to gas at higher temperatures.

– SOFT GLASS softens at a low temperature and expands evenly. It is used to make lamps for everyday use.

– HARD GLASS is highly resistant thermally and chemically and has a linear coefficient of expansion. It was used for theatrical lamps before the introduction of quartz glass.

– QUARTZ GLASS softens at 1,730°C. This high thermal resistance means that the lamp glass can be placed closer to the → *coil* or discharge spark. It is needed for an effective tungsten-halogen cycle and for making smaller lamps.

**Lamp position**  Projector lamps with a filament or an arc that are placed on an optical axis have a prescribed angle of inclination, horizontally and vertically. This information can be found in the manufacturer's instructions.

**Laser**  Abbreviation for Light Amplification by Stimulated Emission of Radiation. Primary light source, emitting monochrome, sharply focused, polarized light. The most common types are ruby, helium-neon, krypton-ion and argon-ion lasers. Light waves are made coherent by a process within the base material. A reflector system bounces the directed waves back and forth several million times. This multiple reflection makes the avalanche of light form a 'static wave'. The monochrome colour depends on the choice of base material.

**LED**  Light Emitting Diode. Small light in the form of a semiconductor diode that emits red, yellow or monochrome light, used as an indicator or warning light. The latest technology has made white LEDs available.

**Lens**  Glass element used in optical systems to refract incident or emergent light. In lighting it is used at the end of a spotlight or in combination within a spotlight or spotlight objective.

**Lens spotlight**  Simple spotlight with focusing options and a lens. Focusing is achieved by moving the light source near to or further away from the lens. Lenses: plano-convex, Fresnel, prismatic (see p. 106).

**Light arc**  Discharge between two → *electrodes* or between → *anode* and → *cathode*.

**Light box**  Box made of polystyrene sheets measuring 2 x 2 or 1 x 2 m. It has a white reflective surface if it is to provide indirect light. The light source shines into the box. The rear wall is covered with a diffuser to provide direct light. The light source shines though the diffuser.

**Light Centre Length**  (abbreviation: LCL). The Light Centre Length gives the distance between the light source and a certain point in the lamp cap.

**Light colour**  See p. 29f.

**Light pad / Luminous sheeting**  See p. 119.

**Light type**
- MAIN LIGHTING / GENERAL COVER: Accentuated, conceptual arrangement of images. In the theatre or in painting, the handling of light is always an important design device, both in terms of direction (incidence) and as a monochrome, brightness-related representation.
- BRIGHTENING: Soft light used to brighten a design inconspicuously, without changing the overall impression.
- FILL LIGHT: If the outer extremities of a lit area are dim or optically limited in any way, it may be that the area has to be complemented or brightened in a particular direction when being integrated into the lighting as a whole.
- REALISTIC LIGHT: Imitating a realistic lighting situation by distributing the light faithfully to detail.
- MIXED LIGHT: Mixed light sources with different colour temperatures.
- ACCENTS / HIGHLIGHTS: Concentrated light to make people or objects seem more three-dimensional.
- DIFFUSE LIGHT: Very soft light, and often filtered.
- REFLECTED LIGHT: Can be used to light awkward areas on stage by careful placing of the reflective surface.
- MONOCHROME LIGHT: Light with a concentrated line spectrum, in the theatre in the → *low pressure sodium vapour lamp* (see also p. 83).

**Lighting booth**  Place in which all the lighting control devices are located, including the lighting console; today: operating site for computer controlled lighting consoles.

**Lighting console**  Unit for co-ordinating lighting, usually computer controlled.

**Lighting designer**  The lighting designer works as the artistic member of a production team. He must have thorough technical training so that he can implement a variety of artistic ideas.

**Lighting plot**  Plan of the arrangement of lanterns for a production. It is drawn either with lantern stencils or by computer.

**Limelight**  Limelight was used on the stage after the introduction of gas lighting from about 1837. A flame burning a mixture of town gas and hydrogen was used to raise a small cylinder to white heat. The light emitted was very white and harsh.

**Linnebach projector**  Simplest version of a projector, named after its inventor. A mask with a silhouette outline is placed at an appropriate distance from a light source. The outlines are projected in or out of focus according to the distance (see also p. 157).

**Low pressure sodium vapour lamps**  Sodium vapour lamps in which the sodium vapour is energized by discharge. As normal technical glass is destroyed by sodium vapour at high operating temperatures, special barium borate glass was developed, but as this is difficult to handle, a double layer glass was used for this lamp. The light emitted is monochrome (see also p. 83).

**Low voltage**  Supply voltages of 50 to 1,000 V (conductor-conductor) for alternating current and from 120 to 1,500 V (conductor-conductor) for direct current.

**Low voltage lamps**  Incandescent lamps with supply voltages up to 48 V.

**Lumen**  Unit of → *luminous flux,* symbol: F (see also p. 75).

**Luminance**  → *Luminous efficiency.*

**Luminescence**  Light radiation that is not temperature radiation. → *Fluorescence* and → *phosphorescence* are luminescent phenomena. Light produced by electrical discharge in solid materials (e.g. a → *light pad*) is called → *electroluminescence.*

**Luminous efficiency**  Effective transformation of power into light. Unit: lm/W.

**Luminous flux**  Light output of a light source for light emitted on all sides. Unit: lumen (lm), symbol: F.

**Luminous intensity**  Measure for the emission of light in a particular direction. Measurement: candela (cd)/symbol: I (see also p. 75)

**Luminous paint**  Paint that is chemically treated to produce light (→ *Luminescence*).

**Lux**  Unit of → *illuminance,* symbol: lx.

**Lycopodium**  Fine powder made from oily club-moss spores used for flash effects in the theatre since the 17th century. The powder can also be fired electrically and burns up very quickly. No heat is developed in the process.

**Mag Max®**  Colour changer with colour cassette system. The chosen colours are stuck together on a roll, which is placed in a detachable cassette, which in its turn fits into a fixed container built into the spotlight. This means that the colour cassettes can be changed very quickly (see also p. 116).

**Magic lantern**  Seventeenth-century projector, consisting of a light source, → *concave* reflector, slide, two → *biconvex* lenses and an objective (see also p. 135).

**Main lighting**  → *Light type.*

**Mercury discharge lamp, high pressure**  → *Discharge lamp* in which the radiation is created in a tube made of highly UV-permeable → *quartz glass.* The discharge vessel is gas-proof, and built into an outer bulb coated with luminous material, so that the UV radiation can be changed into visible light.

**Mercury discharge lamp, low pressure / Fluorescent lamp**  → *Discharge lamps* in which mercury is stimulated to discharge in a tube made of soda-potassium-silicate glass. The ultraviolet radiation produced is transformed into visible radiation by the layer of

luminescent material on the inside of the glass tube. The → *luminous efficiency* is three times that of an → *incandescent lamp,* the service life five times (see also p. 80).

**Merger**  'Mixer' for one or more DMX 512 signals needed for simultaneous control of a dimmer processor from several consoles. The signals are usually assembled on the → *HTP* principle. Special measures are needed when using mergers to control colour changers and → *moving lights* intended to work on the → *LTP* principle: the merger can either be reprogrammed to work on the LTP system, or the LTP circuits can be controlled from one console only.

**Metal halide lamp**  Further development of the → *mercury discharge lamp.* This lamp can reach a → *luminous efficiency* of 95 lm/W with the further addition of halogen compounds (see also p. 85 ff.).

**Metal vapour lamp**  → *Metal halide lamp.*

**Metallogen lamp**  High pressure vapour lamp (→ *high pressure lamps*) with a colour temperature of up to 6,000 K (→ *Kelvin*).

**Molybdenum**  Heavy metal with a melting-point of 2,617°C. Long life molybdenum seals are used in → *tungsten-halogen lamps,* and can survive a maximum temperature of 300°C.

**Molybdenum band**  Conductive foil 20 to 40 µm thick, squashed into a softened bulb tube, e.g. in → *Metallogen lamps.*

**Monochrome**  Monochrome light: light with only one wavelength; e.g. in → *low pressure sodium vapour lamps.*

**Monoplane**  → *Coil* arrangement in a projector lamp. The coils are fastened to their holders on a single plane (see also p. 78).

**Moving light**  'Intelligent' light, such as computer controlled, automated spotlights and scanners.

**Neon**  Filler gas for gas discharge lamps (→ *discharge lamps*) and fluorescent tubes.

**Neon tubes**  High voltage fluorescent tubes in which neon and other inert gases are brought to discharge. Voltages up to 6 kV, various tube diameters and various lengths with → *electrode* arrangements and various colours are available (see also pp. 92 ff.).

**Network**  System for linking computers or computerized equipment so that there is mutual access to all the resources in the network. The purpose of a network is to facilitate the most rapid and effective exchange of information. The technology most used for networking computers is the → *Ethernet.*

**Optical axis**  Central axis in an optical system, e.g. light source-shutter-centre of lens.

**Optical radiation**  Optical rays are outside the visible spectrum → *ultraviolet* rays below 380 nm, → *infra-red* rays above 700 nm. They are further divided into:
- ULTRAVIOLET RAYS (UV)

| | |
|---|---|
| UV-C | 100 – 280 nm |
| UV-B | 280 – 315 nm |
| UV-A | 315 – 380 nm |

- INFRA-RED RAYS (IR)

| | |
|---|---|
| IR-A | 780 nm – 1.4 µm |
| IR-B | 1.4 µm – 3 µm |
| IR-C | 3 µm – 1mm |

**Overheating**  Metal or glass parts can change colour if overheated. With lamps, it is generally true that the material used to cement the glass to the metal cap suffers most from overheating. There are also stability problems in the case of → *tungsten* and → *molybdenum* material.

**PAR lamp**  Abbreviation for Parabolic Aluminized Reflector. Lamp with an incandescent or discharge unit combined with the reflector. The construction of this lamp unit means that the distance from the light source to the reflector is always precise. The aperture angle is achieved by using different glass surfaces or filters. These are very important, popular lamps and are robust and inexpensive. They are available in various specifications. The beam they produce is ellipsoidal (see also pp. 78, 88).

**Parabolic reflector** Aluminium or, more frequently, glass reflectors for reflecting or collecting beams. In terms of spotlight technology the emitted light point should be as small as possible. The reflected light runs parallel with the optical axis (see also p. 68).

**Parabolic spot** → *Low voltage* spot with a → *parabolic reflector.*

**Patching** Allocation of control circuits to spotlight or dimmer circuits in a lighting console. This allocation is carried out at the console or involves the dimmer processors and can usually be configured freely (see also p. 126).

**Phosphorescence** A → *luminescence* phenomenon. Phosphorescent light is created if waves of a certain length (254 and 365 nm) in the invisible → *ultraviolet* spectrum hit crystalline phosphorous. The radiation stimulates the phosphorus, which glows green, yellow-red or blue according to its consistency. Phosphorus that continues to glow after the radiation ceases is phosphorescent.

**Pin cap** Lamp cap with two pins usually used when the precise position of the filament is important (see also p. 95).

**Plano-convex lens** Lens with one straight and one → *convex* surface (see also pp. 69 ff., 106).

**Polarization** In optics: predominance of one level of vibration in light. A normal ray of light vibrates in all directions, so polarization is needed to restrict this. If unpolarized light hits a reflective surface, the surface creates a 'reflection'. Reflection can be avoided by adjusting the angle of incidence and correcting the rays as necessary. Filtering out one plane causes approx. 50% light loss. Further filtering can also affect the other plane of vibration, to the point of total light loss.

**Primary colours** Colours needed for → *additive colour mixing.* Orange red, green, violet blue.

**Prism** A piece of glass with a triangular cross-section that splits incident light into the → *spectral colours.*

**Prismatic lens** Lightly structured → *plano-convex lens* that throws a spotlight beam slightly out of focus.

**Profile spot** High quality stage spotlight with incandescent or → *discharge lamp* (see also p. 109).

**Pulse motor** Motor whose shaft, unlike that of a normal motor, can only turn in fixed steps. The length of the steps is determined by the structure of the motor concerned. Special pulse generators are needed to control the motors. The fixed length of the steps makes it possible to position a drive (e.g. spotlight yoke) precisely by counting the control impulses. If the pulse sequence is fast enough, the movement of the motor increasingly resembles continuous revolution because of its mechanical inertia.

**Quartz glass** Glass used to make → *tungsten-halogen* and arc lamps, with a melting-point of 1,710°C.

**Rare earths** Various metals vaporized under pressure in → *discharge lamps* to produce light.

**Reflector** Device for changing the direction of beams. In spotlight optics:

– ASSYMMETRICAL ROTATION REFLECTOR: Round reflector in which the light source is placed on the rotation axis.

– SYMMETRICAL REFLECTOR: → *Trough reflector* in which the light source, usually in the form of a segmented → *coil*, is placed horizontally and emits the light symmetrically.

– ASSYMMETRICAL REFLECTOR: Trough reflector in which the light source is placed horizontally and emits the light asymmetrically.

**Reflector lamp** Lamp in which the front section is silvered, so that the emitted light is reflected back and directed in the right direction by a mirror/reflector, e.g. → *parabolic spot*, beam light.

**Refraction index** An optical medium refracts more or less according to its material qualities (see also p. 67).

**Refraction of beams** Beams of light striking a transparent optical medium are refracted. The degree of refraction is determined by the thickness of the medium. → *Refraction index.*

**RS-232** Standard serial interface for digital data transfer (point-to-point connection) created by the EIA (Electronics Industry Association). Can be used for connections up to approx. 15 m long and data rates up to 20 kbaud.

**Scatter** Light is scattered if it is multiply refracted or reflected through the same or similar materials.

**Scrim diffuser** (SD) Gentle → *diffusion filter* made of glass or plastic. The beam becomes slightly fuzzy, and the edge of the light cone is thus softened.

**Sealed beam lamps** Closed → *reflector lamps* in which reflector, discharge unit or → *coil* and cover glass form a complete unit. The most up-to-date form is the → *PAR lamp* (see also pp. 78, 88).

**Selective reflection** Light is usually reflected in its own colour. Light beams that hit mainly metal tend to reflect the metal's own colour.

**Servomotor** Auxiliary motor for adjusting a drive to a precisely defined value. The motor is usually built into a closed control loop that brings the drive to the desired value, or holds it there, by constantly comparing the desired value with the actual value. Pulse motors are often used as servomotors.

**Shadow** Used expressively in painting and lighting design, in both of which the angle of incidence of the light can be controlled. The Chinese shadow theatre, in which two-dimensional figures on sticks are moved between a translucent screen and a light source, is recorded as early as 5000 BC.

**Shutter** In dimming technology, mechanical device for dimming → *discharge lamps* that cannot be brought down to a blackout (see also pp. 112 f., 116).

**Single ended connection** Solid-state and arc lamps with only one mechanical connection to their holder. The parts carrying the current are insulated from each other in the cap.

**SMPTE code** Standard time code of the Society of Motion Picture and Television Engineers (SMPTE), originally devised in the professional video field to synchronize tape machines, but now also used to synchronize sequences in lighting consoles and multimedia applications. The code is usually transmitted as a video, audio or MIDI signal.

**Soft keys** Variable function keys. The function depends on the current usage and is indicated either on the screen or on directly allocated displays.

**Soft light** Indirect light, e.g. 200–5,000 W incandescent light or 200–4,000 W daylight in an asymmetrical → *reflector* (→ *light type*, diffuse light).

**Soft source** Flood or spot with a simple housing and fluted reflector, with symmetrical or asymmetrical light reflection. A quartz-halogen lamp is the usual light source.

**Source four** Profile spotlight series with light injection-moulded housing and a high power → *tungsten-halogen lamp* with special cap. This optimization makes it possible to achieve the same useful light output from a 575 W lamp as from a 1,000 W lamp. (see also p. 109).

**Spectral colours** Unmixed pure colours produced by spectral splitting of light.

**Spectral lamp** → *Discharge lamp* that emits only a certain spectrum line, e.g. → *low pressure sodium vapour lamp.*

**Spherical reflector** Reflector with a spherical surface (see also p. 67).

**Spill** Undesirable light from a lantern, coming form ventilation slits in the housing, for example.

**Spot, spotlight** Focused beam of light or the device used to produce it.

**Subtractive colour mixing** Mixing different colours with one light source (see also p. 33).

**Sulphur lamp** New type of → *discharge lamp* that emits daylight-type light without → *electrodes.* The discharge vessel is filled → with powdered sulphur and argon and is stimulated to flow by microwaves in approx. 20 seconds. These lamps have a useful life of approx. 60,000 hours and the magnetron, which produces the microwaves, will run for approx. 15,000 hours (see also p. 91).

**Svoboda unit** Combination of nine parabolic reflectors with 250 W/24 V low voltage lamps and round metallized reflectors, named after its inventor, Josef Svoboda. They are switched in series and thus need only a 230 V supply (see also p. 107 f.).

**Thulium** Chemical element, metal with a melting point of 1,545°C. It is a → *rare earth* and is used in → *discharge lamps.*

**Thyristor** Semiconductor for switching powerful electric currents. → *Triac.*

**Triac and thyristor** – Controllable semiconductor switch. It can be switched on by a pulse at the control → *electrode* and remains on until the current sinks to a very low level (turn-off level). In the TRIAC the polarity of the current is not important, and thus the unit is very well suited for use with alternating current.

– In contrast with this, the THYRISTOR, which works very similarly, can only be used with current flowing in one direction, as it blocks the other direction. For this reason a dimmer needs two counter-switched thyristors, but only one triac. However, the thyristor is much less sensitive to short-term overloads (e.g. when plugging a cold lamp into a fully loaded dimmer), so that it is preferable for use in dimmers.

**Trough reflector** See p. 68.

**Tube light** Moving light, principle of → *fibre optics* or liquid optics (see also pp. 108, 118).

**Tungsten** Metal used to make incandescent → *coils.* Its melting point is 3,410°C (see also pp. 75 ff.).

**Tungsten-halogen lamp** → *Incandescent lamp* with high → *luminous efficiency* and long life. The bulb is made of → *quartz glass.* A very precisely measured quantity of a → *halogen* is added to the inert gas filling, formerly iodine (iodine lamp), now usually bromine. The filament is made of → *tungsten.* The tungsten atoms vaporize at about 3,000°C and combine with the halogen (tungsten bromide), which remains gaseous. This compound breaks down because of the high temperature; the tungsten precipitates

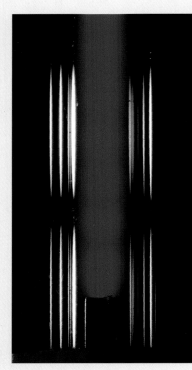

505 Discharge lamp with neon gas filler as a brake light for automobiles

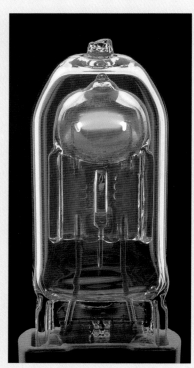

506 HQI/T 150 W Powerstar single ended discharge lamp

on the → *coil*. This process means that the bulb is not blackened as it gets older.

**Ultraviolet** Invisible radiation adjacent to violet in the spectrum.

**Ultraviolet glass** Black glass that allows only → *ultraviolet radiation* to pass. It is used to stimulate fluorescent materials → *fluorescence*).

**Ultraviolet radiation**
– Ultraviolet rays of a wavelength below 380 nm. Ultraviolet rays can change light in certain cases. Materials such as calcite, fluospar, willemite and wernerite absorb these rays and change them into visible light.
– The following wavelengths are also identified within ultraviolet radiation:
– UV-C    100–280 nm
– UV-B    280–315 nm
– UV-A    315–400 nm

**USITT** Abbreviation for United States Institute for Theater Technology, Inc.

**UV** → *Ultraviolet*.

**VARI\*LITE** Intelligent spotlight (see also p. 113f.).

**VGA** Abbreviation for Video Graphics Array launched on the market by IBM in the late 1980s.

**VGA monitor** Device for viewing the colour presentation of computer data permitted by the VGA standard defined by IBM for PCs. Most VGA monitors have electron beam tubes, but there are also liquid crystal displays (more expensive and less bright), e.g in notebook computers and flat screens.

**Warm colours** Colours in the red–orange–yellow area.

**Wedge filter** Mechanical dimmer shutter for daylight projectors consisting of one or two sheets of glass which move in front of the light source in a sequence of grey to black.

**Working light** Light on stage during technical work, thus independent of the stage lighting rig.

**Xenon** Inert gas, used mainly for lighting purposes.

**Xenon lamp** Direct current short arc → *discharge lamp* with a spectrum similar to daylight (see also p. 91).

507 Bernard-Marie Koltès
*Roberto Zucco*
Director: Christian Stückl
Set Designer: Rufus Didwiszus
Münchner Kammerspiele, 1995

# Contact Addresses

508 Single ended Metallogen lamp in the ignition phase

**backstage**
creative lightdesign GmbH
Frankfurter Ring 115
D-80807 Munich, Germany
Internet: http://www.backstage-online.de
e-mail: Info@backstage.t-online.de

**ESTA**
Entertainment Services & Technology Association
875 Sixth Avenue, Suite 2302
New York, NY 10001, USA
Internet: http://www.esta.org
Lori Rubenstein, Executive Director
e-mail: lrubinstein@esta.org

**FOUR TO ONE: scale design**
Institut für Licht und Bühnensimulation GmbH
Hans-Böckler-Straße 163
D-50354 Hürth, Germany
Internet: http://www.4-to-1.com
e-mail: four-to-one@okay.net

**Prof. Herbert Kapplmüller**
Universität Mozarteum
Abteilung Bühnengestaltung
Mirabellplatz 1
A-5020 Salzburg, Austria
Internet: http://www.moz.ac.at
e-mail: herbert.kapplmüller@moz.ac.at

**Kleege Industries**
3487 Noell Street
San Diego, CA 92110, USA
Telephone: (619) 299-5991, 800-995-5822
Fax: (619) 299-5997

**LEE Filters**
2237 North Hollywood Way
Burbank, CA 91505
Telephone: (818) 238-1220, 800-576-5055
Fax: (818) 244-1228

**Lighting Dimensions**
32 West 18th Street
New York, NY 10011, USA
Telephone: (212) 229-2965
Fax: (212) 229-2084
Internet: http://www.etecnyc.net
e-mail: etecinfo@intertec.com

**OSRAM**
Hellabrunner Strasse 1
D-81543 Munich, Germany
Telephone: (089) 62 13-0
Fax: (089) 62 13 20 20
Internet: http://osram.de
e-mail: webmaster@osram.de

**OSRAM SYLVANIA Inc.**
100 Endicoff St.
Danvers, MA 01923
Telephone: (978) 777 19 00
Fax: (978) 777 12 47
OSRAM_USA@osram.de

**Production Arts**
630 9th Avenue, Suite 1412
New York, NY 10036, USA
Telephone: (212) 489-0312
Fax: (212) 245-3723
Internet: http://www.prodart.com
e-mail: pal-info@prodart.com

**ROSCO/Entertainment Technology**
2181 NW Front Avenue
Portland, OR 97209, USA
Telephone: (503) 222-9944, (800) 223-9477
Fax: (503) 227-1562
Internet: http://www.rosco-et.com
e-mail: sales@rosco-et.com

**Rosco Laboratories**
52 Harbor View Avenue
Stamford, CT 06902, USA
Telephone: (203) 708-8900, (800) 767-2669
Fax: (203) 708-8915
Internet: http://www.rosco.com
e-mail: info@rosco.com

**Strand Lighting**
18111 South Santa Fe Ave.
Rancho Dominguez, CA 90221, USA
Telephone: (310) 637-7500, (800) 733-0564
Fax: (310) 632-5519
Internet: http://www.strandlight.com
e-mail: sales@strandlight.com

Strand Lighting New York
151 West 25th Street, Suite 2F
New York, NY 10001, USA
Telephone: (212) 242-1042
Fax: (212) 242-1837

Strand Lighting Canada
2430 Lucknow Dr., Unit #15
Mississauga, ON LSS 1V3, Canada
Telephone: (905) 677-7130
Fax: (905) 677-6859
Internet: http://www.strand.ca
e-mail: strand@strand.ca

**United States Institute for Theatre Technology, Inc. (USITT)**
6443 Ridings Road
Syracuse, NY 13206, USA
Telephone: (315) 463-6463, (800) 93USITT
Fax: (315) 463-6525
Internet: http://www.culturenet.ca/usitt
e-mail: usittno@pppmail.appliedtheory.com

**VARI*LITE**
20-22 Fairway Drive
Greenford, Middlesex
UB6 8PW, Great Britain
Telephone: (0181) 575-6666
Fax: (0181) 575-0424
e-mail: info@london.vlps.com

**Prof. Dr. Manfred Wagner**
Universität für angewandte Kunst in Wien
Lehrkanzlei für Kultur- und Geistesgeschichte
Oskar-Kokoschka-Platz 2
A-1010 Vienna, Austria
Internet: http://www.uni-ak.ac.at
e-mail: manfred.wagner@uni.ak.ac.at

# Selected Bibliography

Albers, Josef. Interaction of Color. Yale University Press, New Haven 1987.
Bellman, Willard F. Lighting of the Stage: Art and Practice. Harper & Row, New York 1967.
Bentham, Frederick. The Art of Stage Lighting. Pitman House, London 1980.
Bentham, Frederick. The Art of Stage Lighting. Theatre Art Books, New York 1976.
Birren, Faber. Principles of Color: A Review of Past Traditions and Modern Theories of Color Harmony. Schiffer Publishing 1987.
Boulanger, Norman C. and Warren C. Lounsbury. Theatre Lighting from A to Z. University of Washington Press, Seattle 1992.
Brusatin, Manlio. A History of Color. Shambhala Publications 1991.
Burton, Jane and Kim Taylor. The Nature and Science of Color. Gareth Stevens 1998.
Cunningham, Glen. Stage Lighting Revealed: A Design and Execution Handbook. Belterway Books, Cincinnati 1993.
Essig, Linda. Lighting and the Design Idea. Harcourt Brace College Publishers, Fort Worth 1997.
Falk, David S. et al. Seeing the Light: Optics in Nature, Photography, Color Vision and Holography. John Wiley & Sons 1985.
Fitt, Brian and Joe Thornley. Lighting Technology: A Guide for the Entertainment Industry. Focal Press, Boston 1997.
Fraser, Neil. Lighting and Sound: A Phaidon Theatre Manual. Phaidon, Oxford 1995.
Frieling, Heinrich. Farben im Raum. Callwey Verlag, Munich 1979.
Frieling, Heinrich. Gesetz der Farbe. Verlag Muster-Schmidt, Göttingen 1968.
Gassner, John. Producing the Play. The Dryden Press, New York 1944.
Gillette, Michael J. Designing with Light: An Introduction to Stage Lighting. Mayfield Publishing Company, Palo Alto 1997.
Goethe, Johann Wolfgang von. Theory of Colours. MIT Press, Cambridge 1970.
Graves, R.B. Lighting the Shakespearean Stage, 1567-1642. Southern Illinois University Press 1999.
Hays, David and Peter Brook. Stage Lighting for Directors and Actors and the Rest of Us. Limelight Editions 1998.
Heimendahl, Eckart. Licht und Farbe. Walter de Gruyter & Co., Berlin 1961.
Howard, Michael. Art as Spiritual Activity: Rudolf Steiner's Contribution to the Visual Arts. Anthroposophic Press 1998.
Huntly, Carter. Theatre of Max Reinhardt. Ayer Co. Publishers 1914.
Huxley, Aldous. The Doors of Perception and Heaven and Hell. Harper Collins, New York 1990.
Ionazzi, Daniel A. The Stagecraft Handbook. Belterway, Cincinnati 1996.
Jobert, Barthelmy. Delacroix. Princeton University Press 1998.
Joseph, Stephen. New Theatre Forms. Sir Isaac Pitmann & Sons, London 1968.
Küppers, Harald. Das Grundgesetz der Farbenlehre. DuMont, Cologne 1981.
Küppers, Harald. Farben Atlas. DuMont, Cologne 1981.
Küppers, Harald. Farbe. Callwey Verlag, Munich 1977.
Lefèvre, Amaury. Degas. Fernan Hazan Editeur, Paris 1981.
Moody, James L. Concert Lighting: Techniques, Art, and Business. Focal Press, Boston 1998.
Morgan, Nigel H. Stage Lighting for Theatre Designers. Herbert Press, London 1995.
Owen, Bobbi. Lighting Design on Broadway. Greenwood Publishing Group 1991.
Palmer, Richard H. The Lighting Art: The Aesthetics of Stage Lighting Design. Prentice Hall College Division, Englewood Cliffs 1993.
Parker, W. Oren. Scene Design and Stage Lighting. Holt, Rhinehart and Winston, Fort Worth 1990.
Parramon, José Maria. Color Theory. Watson-Guptill Publications 1989.
Pilbrow, Richard and Harold Prince. Stage Lighting Design: The Art, the Craft, the Life. Design Press 1997.

Pilbrow, Richard. *Stage Lighting Design.*
By Design Press, New York 1997.

Rees, Terence. *Theatre Lighting in the Age of Gas.* Society for Theatre Research, London 1978.

Reid, Francis. *Discovering Stage Lighting.* Focal Press, Boston 1999.

Reid, Francis. *Designing for the Theatre.* Routledge, London 1996.

Reid, Francis. *The Stage Lighting Handbook.* A & C Black, London/New York 1996.

Reid, Francis. *The ABC of Stage Technology.* Heinemann, Westport 1995.

Reid, Francis. *Lighting the Stage: A Lighting Designer's Experience.* Focal Press, Oxford/Boston 1995.

Reid, Francis. *The ABC of Stage Lighting.* London/New York 1992.

Rinpoche, Sogyal, Andrew Harvey and Patrick Gaffney (eds.). *The Tibetan Book of Living and Dying.* Harper San Francisco 1994.

Rubin, Joel E. and Leland H. Watson. *Theatrical Lighting Practice.* Theatre Arts Book, New York 1954.

Sambhava, Padma and Robert A. Thurman. *The Tibetan Book of the Dead.* Bantam Doubleday Dell Pub. 1994.

Sandstrom, Ulf. *Stage Lighting Controls.* Focal Press, Boston 1997.

Schopenhauer, Arthur and E.F.J. Payne (ed.). *On Vision and Color.* Berg Pub. 1994.

Sellman, Hunton Dade. *Essentials of Stage Lighting.* Prentice Hall, Englewood Cliffs 1982.

Shelley, Steven Louis. *A Practical Guide to Stage Lighting.* Focal Press, Boston 1999.

Steiner, Rudolf. *Beleuchtungs- und Kostümangaben für die Laut-Eurythmie.* Rudolf Steiner Verlag, Dornach 1975.

Steiner, Rudolf. *Beleuchtungs- und Kostümangaben für die Ton-Eurythmie.* Rudolf Steiner Verlag, Dornach 1975.

Steiner, Rudolf. *Eurythmie, die Offenbarung der sprechenden Seele.* Rudolf Steiner Verlag, Dornach 1980.

Stoddard, Richard. *Stage Scenery, Machinery, and Lighting: A Guide to Information Sources.* Gale Research, Detroit 1977.

Sweet, Harvey. *Handbook of Scenery, Properties, and Lighting: Lighting.* Allyn & Bacon 1995.

Walker, Morton. *The Power of Color.* Avery Pub. Group 1991.

Walters, Graham. *Stage Lighting Step-by-Step: The Complete Guide to Setting the Stage with Light to Get Dramatic Results.* Belterway Publications, Cincinnati 1997.

Warfel, William B. *The New Handbook of Stage Lighting Graphics.* Drama Publishers, New York 1990.

Warfel, William B. *Color Science for Lighting the Stage.* Yale University Press, New Haven 1981.

Warfel, William B. *Handbook of Stage Lighting Graphics.* Drama Book, New York 1974.

Watson, Lee. *Lighting Design Handbook.* McGraw-Hill, New York 1990.

Wehlburg, Albert F.C. *Theatre Lighting: An Illustrated Glossary.* Drama Book Specialists, New York 1975.

Williamson, Samuel J. *Light and Color in Nature and Art.* John Wiley & Sons 1983.

509  Low voltage tungsten-halogen reflector lamp with curved and facetted reflector

## Photo Credits

Numbers given refer to illustrations unless otherwise noted.

ADB, Mühlheim am Main 249, 257, 272, 374
AKG Photo, Berlin 85
Altmann Lichttechnik, Stuttgart 247
Arnold & Richter, Munich 228, 237–239, 241, 243, 244
Artothek (Blauel/Gnamm), Peissenberg 83
Bönzli, Markus, Zurich page 4; nos. 40–52, 62, 63, 112, 113, 290, 305, 306, 311–317, 358, 359, 401, 404, 409, 411–420, 422–435
Caleidoscope, Stuttgart 285–287
Columbus Museum of Art, Ohio: Museum Purchase, Howald Fund 87
Deutsches Museum, Munich 330
Dia Center for the Arts, New York 4
Fischer, Jürgen, Munich 338, 340, 341, 343, 345, 411–419, 422–435
Fisher, Marc, London 474
Focus, Hamburg (Peter Menzel) 5
Hardware-Xenon, Cologne 366
Herrmann, Oliver, Berlin 455
Hoffmann/Junker, *Laterna Magica*, Berlin 1982 321, 322
Hösl, Wilfried, Munich back cover: dancers centre; nos. 495, 496
Jacobs, Johann, Brussels 333
Kapplmüller, Herbert, Munich 92–111
Kaunat, Angelo, Munich 114–116, 311
Keller, Max, Munich back cover: background photo and bottom left; nos.142–144, 158, 171, 308
LBM-Berching 275
Lee, Levis, VARI*LITE, Texas back cover: top left; page 5: centre right; nos. 491, 492
Lichttechnik, Munich 274
Lightpower, Paderborn 248, 250–252, 269–270, 381
Louvre, photo: RMN – Hervé Lewandowski 82
Maranzano, Attilio, Siena back cover: left centre (screens and stool); no. 408
Estate of Henri Michaux. Courtesy Verlag Fred Jahn 88
Moses, Stefan, Feldwies 325
Münchner Kammerspiele 179–181, 222–224, 276, 294–295, 368, 369, 453, 454, 456, 457, 460–462, 464, 465, 469–472, 482, 485–487, 497
Nähr, Moritz. Courtesy of the Wittgenstein Archive, Cambridge 91
National Gallery, London 81
National Gallery of Art, Washington, DC, photo: Dean Beasom 84
Nauschütz, Moritz, Munich front cover; front flap; page 1; frontispiece; pages 5 and 6: both

far left and left centre; nos. 1, 3, 21–25, 39, 64, 65, 67–80, 109–111, 145, 146, 225, 278, 280–282, 309, 310, 318, 367, 407, 452, 463, 466–468, 481, 488, 490, 498, 500, 501, 503, 504, 507
O2, Munich 27, 28, 32–34, 155, 157, 166, 168, 174, 175, 184, 186–188, 192, 194, 202, 204, 205, 208, 209, 212, 216–221, 458
Osram, Munich 159–165, 169, 170, 197, 198, 200, 2001
Pani, Ludwig, Vienna 360–365
Rauch, Wilhelm, Bayreuth back flap: left; no. 489
Reiche & Vogel, Berlin 236, 240, 327–329, 332, 334–336
Schilling, Dagmar, Stuttgart back cover: carbon arc top right; page 7; nos. 6, 117, 147, 148, 154, 190, 199, 203, 210, 211, 213–215, 502, 505–506, 508, 509
Schönebaum, Urs, Munich 2, 53, 176, 178, 182, 183, 185, 189, 191, 193, 195, 196, 206, 207, 229–231, 235, 242, 245, 246, 254, 255, 258–264, 273, 283, 284, 288, 289, 291, 293, 296–299, 301–303, 307, 372, 375, 382, 476–478
Schweizerische Theatersammlung, Berne 286, 287
Scrimgeour, Diana, London page 6: far right; nos. 475, 479, 480, 493, 494
Siemens, Erlangen 384, 385, 388–390, 398, 399
Soundlight, Hanover 371
Sprafke, Uwe, Bergisch Gladbach 459
Staatliche Museen zu Berlin – Preussischer Kulturbesitz, Kunstbibliothek 15
Sternberg, Oda, Munich 66
Strand Lighting, Berlin 234, 253, 383, 391, 396, 400, 402, 403
Strong International, Omaha, USA 256
Transtechnik, Holzkirchen 370, 373, 376, 377
VARI*LITE, Cologne back flap: right; page 5: far right; nos. 265–268, 378–380
Wapler, Ralf, Munich 473
Weiss, Johannes, Munich back cover: prism refraction centre; page 6: right centre; nos. 7, 8, 26, 29–31, 35–38, 54, 55, 59, 118–141, 149–153, 156, 172, 173, 177, 226, 227, 232, 233, 304, 337–357, 405, 406, 410, 421, 436, 437–451, 483, 484
Winter, Dieter, Gröbenzell 292
Xtra-light, Heilbronn 277, 279


Original source for 'Colour Character' on pages 40/41:
© 1996, Erich Küthe/Axel Venn, *Marketing mit Farben*, DUMONT Buchverlag Cologne

# Index

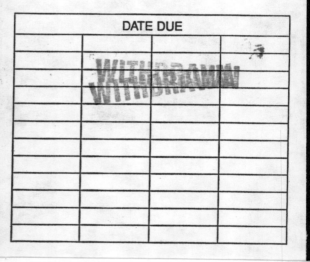